THEY
DIDN'T
SEE US
COMING

Also by Lisa Levenstein

A Movement Without Marches: African American Women and the Politics of Poverty in Postwar Philadelphia (2009)

THEY DIDN'T SEE US COMING

THE HIDDEN HISTORY OF FEMINISM IN THE NINETIES

LISA LEVENSTEIN

BASIC BOOKS

New York

Basic Books
Hachette Book Group
1290 Avenue of the Americas, New York, NY 10104
www.basicbooks.com

Printed in the United States of America

First Edition: July 2020

Published by Basic Books, an imprint of Perseus Books, LLC, a subsidiary of Hachette Book Group, Inc. The Basic Books name and logo is a trademark of the Hachette Book Group.

The Hachette Speakers Bureau provides a wide range of authors for speaking events. To find out more, go to www.hachettespeakersbureau.com or call (866) 376-6591.

The publisher is not responsible for websites (or their content) that are not owned by the publisher.

Print book interior design by Amy Quinn

Library of Congress Cataloging-in-Publication Data
Names: Levenstein, Lisa, author.
Title: They didn't see us coming : the hidden history of feminism in the nineties / Lisa Levenstein.
Description: First edition. | New York, NY : Basic Books, [2020] | Includes bibliographical references and index.
Identifiers: LCCN 2019040903 | ISBN 9780465095285 (hardcover) | ISBN 9780465095292 (ebook)
Subjects: LCSH: Feminism—United States—History—20th century. | Feminism—History—20th century.
Classification: LCC HQ1421 .L48 2020 | DDC 305.420973/0904—dc23
LC record available at https://lccn.loc.gov/2019040903

ISBNs: 978-0-465-09528-5 (hardcover), 978-0-465-09529-2 (ebook)

LSC-C

10 9 8 7 6 5 4 3 2 1

For Anna, Owen, and Jason

CONTENTS

INTRODUCTION

On November 9, 2016, the night after Donald Trump's election as the forty-fifth president of the United States, a retired attorney living in Hawaii created a Facebook event page calling for a march on Washington. Before she went to bed, she had received around forty positive responses. By the time she woke up the next morning, more than ten thousand people had replied. After others began to post similar suggestions, four national organizers took charge and consolidated the effort. This Black, white, Muslim, and Latina leadership team announced a "Women's March on Washington." The massive DC demonstration they helped create, along with "sister marches" held in more than six hundred US cities, drew over 3.3 million people. In a rousing speech delivered from a platform on Independence Avenue, the radical Black activist Angela Davis described the surging crowd representing "the promise of feminism" and called on people from all walks of life "to join the resistance." Television cameras rushed to cover the largest single-day protest in US history.[1]

How did a lone message on social media inspire the eruption of such passion? Some pundits pointed to Donald Trump. Before his election, women had been complacent, the story went. Now, suddenly, they had woken up.[2]

Trump certainly frightened those who valued gender equality and bodily autonomy. But millions did not take to the streets just because of him. What enabled such sudden and massive mobilizing was an unsung movement, one that had faded from the headlines but never ceased to organize and to evolve. The insistence of the marchers on the dignity of all people and their aspirations for a just world had been encouraged by a critical turn in one of the most influential and least understood social movements in history.

The feminism that helped shape the consciousness of millions in 2017 had distinct roots in the 1990s, a period in which the ideas and strategies of US women of color and activists from the Global South garnered increasing attention.[3] Driving their activism was their steadfast belief that every social justice issue was a feminist issue and that the movement should focus on improving the lives of those most oppressed in order to make any meaningful progress. People had made these claims for decades. By the 1990s, growing numbers of activists of all backgrounds shared this worldview and had access to powerful virtual and institutional platforms. Many were embracing the internet as a new tool for communicating and networking. More and more people were turning social change-making into careers, embedding feminist thought and practices into the nation's culture and institutions. They disseminated their ideas through universities as well as churches and remade other transnational social movements into hotbeds of feminist activity. Involvement with these multiracial and global forms of feminism stretched people's minds and nourished their souls.

Paradoxically, as nineties feminism became ever more diverse and ubiquitous, much of the movement became almost wholly invisible to the public.[4] In 1998, the front of *Time* magazine asked, "Is feminism dead?" and its cover story concluded that the movement had become "divorced from matters of public purpose," obsessed with fashion, celebrity, and "mindless sex talk."[5] Many people still expected feminist activism to look like the iconic black-and-white photographs from the 1960s of young white women, wearing sandals and blue jeans, holding consciousness-raising meetings in their living rooms and protesting the Miss America Pageant. Even in the sixties, these images had not captured the full range of feminist activity.[6] But the stereotypes persisted. Very few people in the 1990s understood who most feminists were or what they were doing.

The lack of a single well-known definition of feminism made it particularly difficult to appreciate the movement's scope. Many women of color—and growing numbers of white women—followed the lead of the Black lesbian-feminist Combahee River Collective, which in 1977 had argued that liberating Black women would result in freedom for all people because Black women's liberation required the destruction of all systems of oppression.[7] Activists of all kinds were drawn to visions of international solidarity, with many inspired by the feminist theories about women's poverty and economic justice developed by researchers in the Global South.[8] Others integrated analyses of racism and class inequality into approaches to abortion, gay rights, and violence against women. Historian Premilla Nadasen has called the many different intersecting and simultaneous versions of feminism one of the most generative features of the movement.[9] But because no one definition ever emerged to supplant the popular imagination's outdated version of feminism (that is, of a movement primarily concerned with white women's equality with men), it was hard to succinctly describe what was happening.

It was not just the theories that were multiplying, so were the organizing strategies. Few onlookers recognized the growing numbers of feminists working as paid professionals rather than volunteers. And the media did not expect to find feminists pioneering the use of email and the internet to share their ideas. Nor did most journalists pay much attention to those who were promoting feminist perspectives from within other social movements or to the activists who were using a technique known as popular education to foster conversations about economic inequality. With so many different and unfamiliar forms of activism taking shape, much of the public assumed the movement was waning or fracturing—even as it was flourishing.

Throughout the 1990s, activists fiercely debated who feminism should represent and what strategies it should employ. Such disagreements proliferated not because feminism was losing its way but because so many different people increasingly felt invested in shaping the movement. People read feminist websites and attended women's conferences and workshops seeking communities of activists with similar goals, but they also craved exposure to new ways of thinking, including those that felt unsettling. The veteran Black women's health activist Loretta Ross pointed out that differences of opinion were an essential component of social justice organizing. "A group of people moving in the same direction thinking the same thing is a cult," she observed. "A group of people moving in the same direction thinking different things is a movement."[10]

Activists needed an arsenal of strategies to do battle in a rapidly changing and unfriendly world. By the 1990s, conservative economics was pervasive, particularly the idea that the market was the most effective arbitrator of social and political decisions. Multinational corporations moved well-paying jobs to foreign cheap-labor sites, while Republicans and Democrats supported both a major disinvestment in social services and a drastic scaling back of financial regulations. These policies fostered a yawning gap between the ultrarich and the rest. Between 1978 and 1999, the top 0.1 percent of income earners increased their share of the national income from 2 percent to over 6 percent. The intensification of economic inequality went hand in hand with the rise in mass incarceration: between 1973 and 2004, the prison population grew from 200,000 to over 2 million, with another 4.5 million people on probation and parole.[11] The majority of those swept up in this dragnet were poor people of color, including growing numbers of women.[12]

It was happening in the rest of the world, too. Despite the hopes that bloomed after the destruction of the Berlin Wall in 1989 and the dissolution of the Soviet Union in 1991, the Cold War gave way to a "hot peace," one human rights activist claimed, evidenced by the international rise of right-wing movements.[13] Others warned that nations around the world—from the new countries that emerged out of the USSR collapse, to longstanding social democracies such as New Zealand—were also promoting the idea that well-being was best achieved by maximizing entrepreneurial freedom and promoting unencumbered markets.[14]

This was neoliberalism, a new kind of freedom from governmental interference, and it was everywhere in the nineties; it even seeped into public discussions of feminism. Corporate elites declared the broad-based social movement to be dead, irrelevant—while they celebrated (and even sold) individualism dressed as "girl power" and women's "empowerment." Cultural critic and *Bitch* magazine founder Andi Zeisler has shown how women's magazines claimed that their beauty tips would boost women's confidence and power, while ads for goods ranging from high heels to motorcycles promised similar results. In 2003, the satirical newspaper *The Onion* summed it up: "Women Now Empowered by Everything a Woman Does."[15]

Power was operating in new ways and feminists were on the front lines, wrestling with how to respond. They analyzed how multinational corporations, wealthy donors, and international financial institutions increasingly dictated public policy and saw how the emphasis on efficiency and profits was infiltrating even fields that had traditionally prioritized human development and well-being, such as health care and education.[16] The election of a Democratic president in 1992 did not stem the tide; after the Republicans took control of Congress in 1994, Bill Clinton focused on passing measures that could garner bipartisan support, such as the reduction of deficits and the elimination of the entitlement to welfare support for poor single mothers.[17] Progressive social movements' inability to stop the continued policy assaults on those who had the least drove home the need for broad-based and far-reaching movements that could change public conversations, ones rooted in alliances across activist communities and some-times even across national borders.[18] For this reason, during the 1990s, many feminists prioritized coalition building and culture change, which they increasingly accomplished online and through organizing workshops and conferences. A history-making case in point: in 1995 more than eight thousand people traveled to China from the United States to attend the United Nations (UN) Fourth World Conference on Women in Beijing.

This story begins at that conference, where we meet activists forging relationships and acquiring new knowledge that propelled their organizing. My own interest in this event was piqued in 2010, when I came across an article on the back page of a local paper stating that more than a thousand US women of color had attended. Like most North Americans, I had heard only of a celebrated appearance by Hillary Rodham Clinton, who was First Lady then; I had no idea that over thirty thousand activists from around the world had participated. Wondering what else had happened during the twelve-day affair, I dug up firsthand accounts of the panels and demonstrations that took place at the conference's Non-Governmental Organization (NGO) Forum. Their range and rich content surprised me, so I sought out some of the people who were there.

Captivated by their stories, I followed tantalizing evidence that led me from the conference events to the many versions of US feminist organizing in the 1990s. As I traveled around the country visiting archives and conducting interviews, activists welcomed me into their homes—from a shotgun shack in a working-class California suburb to a modest townhouse in the hills of San Francisco and an elegant condominium in Manhattan. We drank mint tea and ate chocolates as we pored over their scrapbooks and photo albums. One woman followed up on our conversation by combing through the filing cabinets in her office so she could send me the transcripts of the speeches delivered at the first national conference of INCITE!, an organization of women of color opposing interpersonal violence and police brutality. In an archive at an elite university, I found grant proposals and newsletters from a lesbian group that was building coalitions and mobilizing queer people of color in the US South. Over Skype, I spoke with women with disabilities who had spent years organizing feminist leadership conferences with their colleagues overseas. And through Facebook, I connected with a technology specialist who helped invent what today we call "online feminism." Finding these generative forms of activism convinced me that this period I lived through—and had thought I knew—deserved the kind of historical scrutiny heretofore reserved for the women's movements of the 1960s and 1970s.

My archival research and oral history interviews have yielded lessons we can learn from, including rich stories about the human dimensions of movement building. Listening to people talk about their experiences taught me how their family histories and cherished ties with other feminists inspired and sustained their activism. Whether their organizing involved sharing confidences and insights online, or they were meeting face-to-face in conference rooms or on front porches, they were sustained by their personal and intellectual collaborations. As one veteran organizer told me, "People are brought to movements through personal relationships [and] people stay in movements because of personal relationships."[19] Exploring the strength of these connections helps us see our own personal ties anew.

Collectively fighting for one's beliefs can be exhilarating, these activists taught me, but it could also come at a cost. Many sacrificed creature comforts and leisure time in order to accomplish their work. In the face of mounting threats, they persisted, rooting themselves in the rich history of social movements that spanned generations, with long troughs between short peaks in endless oscillation, yet demonstrably wider and deeper catchments over time. Just as that prior history proved a sustaining resource for their troubled times, I offer this piece of the story to those invested in the social movements making change in our world today.

This is a largely forgotten history, an account of some of the people in the nineties who changed the world. Most (but not all) of them self-identified as feminists, refusing to cede that name to the white middle-class women who dominated media coverage of the movement, such as it was.[20] Nationally recognized organizations and groups that have been the subject of other studies, such as campus activists, union members, AIDS activists, immigrant rights activists, and those who worked through popular culture like the Riot Grrrls and Guerrilla Girls, do not receive much attention.[21] Nor do I focus on why some people chose to leave the movement or trace the growing appropriation of feminism by mainstream institutions and corporations.[22] And though the scope is wide, it is not comprehensive; each group that I explore could be the subject of an entire book, and some forms of intersectional activism don't feature as prominently. We need many different accounts of feminist history. My emphasis here is on how theory and activism intersect in our lives and on how people defy incredible odds to come together and create change.[23]

One of the biggest surprises I found in uncovering these stories was the multiple generations of people involved in feminist activism. The subset of youth who commanded public attention for embarking on what they called the "Third Wave" represents only a slice.[24] Those young feminists had grown up benefiting from the victories of earlier generations, and they confidently embraced gender and sexual fluidity, highlighted racial injustices, and made savvy use of new forms of communication and cultural production.[25] Yet I encountered many older activists who were engaged in similar endeavors, sometimes alongside their younger peers. The Southern lesbian organizer Suzanne Pharr told me that claims of persistent generational splits had never resonated with her or her colleagues, who saw themselves as extending rather than departing from earlier iterations of feminism. As a white woman engaged in antiracist activism, Pharr's role models and mentors were Black women in the civil rights movement such as Ella Baker and Evangeline K. Brown.

In turn, the youth activists that Pharr mentored sought to carry forward rather than break away from her legacy, finding it not a burden to be sloughed off but an inheritance to be treasured.[26]

They needed all hands on deck to address the pressing dilemmas of their day, as we do in ours. How should activists address the stark inequities fostered by the rapid growth of neoliberalism and environmental destruction? In an increasingly wired world, to what degree can electronic communications effectively augment or replace face-to-face organizing and mass protests? What does a movement gain and lose when employees of established institutions and nonprofits engage in advocacy alongside volunteers? And how can diffuse movements working on behalf of people who are oppressed build strong local and international coalitions that will create tangible changes in people's lives? Feminists' efforts to answer these questions in the 1990s shifted consciousness and fostered relationships that shaped the future of progressive movement building.

Their innovations took root in places you might not expect.

ONE

A MOVEMENT WITHOUT A CENTER

Susan Sygall stared down the three flights of stone stairs leading to the customs booths at the Beijing airport. As a wheelchair rider since age eighteen and the founder of an organization that ran worldwide exchange programs for people with disabilities, she was familiar with the challenges of international travel. But she had never confronted a situation like this one.

It was August 1995, and Sygall was accompanied by fifty other women with disabilities, all headed to the Fourth World Conference on Women, a United Nations–sponsored event where governmental authorities and representatives of advocacy organizations would grapple with problems facing women around the world and propose solutions. About half of Sygall's group were also in wheelchairs, and many of the rest were blind or deaf. After deplaning, they had made their way through the airport terminal and had arrived at the stairs. Of the two elevators right near the steps, only one was working, but the security guard would not let them use it. He pointed to a line on the ground between the two elevators that stretched all the way down the stairs. If you were inside the line, you were officially in China. If you were outside the line, you weren't. Since the working elevator was inside the line, anyone who had not yet cleared customs could not step inside.

For close to an hour, the security guard responded to the group's appeals by shaking his head and pointing to the stairs. Maintenance workers eventually arrived to carry the women down, but when they hoisted the chairs into the air by the wheels, several women almost tipped out.

Sygall had not spent over a year planning for the Beijing trip to have her group seriously injured in the airport. After dismissing the workers, she and her colleagues came up with a strategy. Those who could walk without assistance teamed up and carried others down the steps. The rest of them got out of their chairs and crawled down.[1]

Like many parties that had traveled to the Beijing conference from the United States, the women with disabilities were not a group typically associated with feminism. From welfare rights activists to environmental justice advocates, most of the US conference participants represented facets of a movement that the public knew very little about.

Even most feminists misunderstood the scope of nineties activism. A 1991 study concluded that, "instead of 'sisterhood,'" the word that summed up the state of US feminism was "isolation."[2] The movement had grown so rapidly that it was impossible to keep track of all of the organizations and initiatives. From 1982 to 1995, the number of national feminist groups nearly doubled, from 75 to 140. Thousands of activists were now working in nonprofits or had carved out feminist niches in professions such as medicine and academia. Growing numbers were turning popular culture into a battleground, critiquing sexist and racist representations in mainstream news and culture while offering new visions of female empowerment through music and media. Specialization could be seen at all levels. Some groups focused on domestic violence, others on lesbian rights, others on labor organizing. The list seemed endless.[3]

Many of these activists had participated in galvanizing experiences, including supporting the struggle against apartheid in South Africa, which served as boot camp for nineties feminists in the same way that the civil rights movement had been formative for many activists in the sixties. In 1992, they had helped elect Bill Clinton to the presidency, along with record numbers of female candidates in what became known as the "Year of the Woman." Large numbers had taken courses offered by the nation's 621 women's and gender studies programs, where they found inspiration in the writings of lesbians and women of color such as Gloria Anzaldúa and bell hooks. After the legal scholar Kimberlé Williams Crenshaw coined the term "intersectionality" in 1989 to describe how Black women's multiple and overlapping identities shaped their experiences of discrimination, many began to describe their organizing against multiple forms of oppression as "intersectional."[4]

The frameworks taught in women's studies classrooms resonated with what was happening outside the academy's Ivory Tower, too. This was the generation that witnessed the police beating of Rodney King and watched the Anita Hill–Clarence Thomas hearings and the O. J. Simpson murder trial unfold on national television. Some learned not to pin their hopes on electoral politics after watching a Democratic president they had helped to elect eliminate the entitlement to welfare support for poor single mothers. Many believed the problem was not just that Bill Clinton was enacting conservative policies that he dubbed the "third way" but also that he seemed to have so few tools at his disposal to effect broad-scale political and social change, even if he wanted to.[5] Clinton expressed support for women's right to control their bodies. But as Operation Rescue turned abortion clinic parking lots into war zones, he could not stop the fallout from Supreme Court decisions such as *Planned Parenthood v. Casey*, which allowed states to impose waiting periods and parental consent policies on a legal medical procedure. Journalist Susan Faludi described the cascade of antifeminist initiatives and sentiments as a "backlash."[6]

What Faludi missed—and what one ambitious organizer named Marie Wilson saw—was that this bleak political climate was fueling diverse forms of feminism. In anticipation of the Beijing conference, Wilson, who was the head of the Ms. Foundation for Women, received a grant for nearly half a million dollars from the Ford Foundation to create and lead a new national feminist network. The Ms. Foundation, a separate entity from the magazine that bears the same name, had been established in 1972 by Gloria Steinem, Patricia Carbine, Letty Cottin Pogrebin, and Marlo Thomas to raise money to distribute to groups working on behalf of women and girls. When Wilson was recruited to lead the foundation in 1984, she was working as the Director of Women's Programs at Drake University, leading initiatives that had drawn national attention for their success in helping women find jobs. She arrived to discover the foundation was "broke" and immediately got to work, increasing the budget from $400,000 to nearly $3 million in 1990.[7]

To some, Wilson seemed like the perfect choice to replace Steinem as the media darling of the movement. In 1992, she had cofounded "Take Our Daughters to Work Day" to encourage girls to strive for professional success. The idea of young women going to work with a family member or friend had drawn immediate acclaim, catapulting Wilson and the Ms. Foundation to fame. After that project took off, Wilson began to look beyond the foundation to the broader feminist project. Sending a delegation to Beijing was part of an ambitious plan to connect the thousands of feminists organizing in different parts of the country.[8]

Wilson's perch at Ms. gave her unique insight into the richness of feminist activity at the local level. Yet she was concerned the movement had grown in too many different and disconnected directions. She feared that it had lost its collective power and believed the solution lay in national leadership.[9] Some looked to the National Organization for Women (NOW), which, with seven hundred local chapters, was what one author called "the McDonald's of the women's movement; recognizable and accessible to millions."[10] NOW remained the media's go-to feminist voice; it conducted high-profile litigation in the courts and lobbied for causes in Washington, DC—but Wilson and many others suspected the organization no longer had its finger on the feminist pulse. With women of color increasingly claiming feminist identities and pressing for change, NOW's reputation as a white organization made it seem out of touch, even as it rushed to enact an agenda that addressed racism and poverty and grappled with the unique concerns of young people. Although NOW attracted growing numbers of dues-paying members by organizing major national marches for reproductive rights, Wilson was convinced that the organization represented the past, not the future.[11]

Some activists identified the Women's Action Coalition (WAC) as the NOW of the nineties. This "all-issue" women's organization emerged from the grassroots in New York City and spread to places like Chicago, San Francisco, and Seattle. Known for its creative, direct actions, WAC used street theater, rallies, postering, and picket lines to draw public attention to issues such as abortion access and the injustices in rape trials. Like NOW's, however, WAC's membership remained largely white. Those committed to fostering a diverse movement believed that it was an ineffective mouthpiece for the country's varied feminist initiatives.[12]

As Wilson's star continued to rise, she saw a real opening for her foundation. Ms. had developed relationships with feminist organizations across the country by awarding them grants. Many of these groups were multiracial and led by women of color, and they worked on issues ranging from women's economic security to reproductive freedom. In addition to providing activists with funding, Ms. frequently organized workshops that offered peer training and networking opportunities. With the foundation's coffers growing, it was carving out new niches for itself and developing a reputation among activists as an important sponsor of grassroots organizing.

When major philanthropic foundations began to express interest in the Beijing conference, Wilson seized the moment. In a series of funding proposals to Ford, she laid out how the Ms. Foundation could become a "lightning rod" of the US women's movement.[13] According to Wilson, the movement was not living up to its potential because there was no structure to help connect and coordinate the different initiatives. Her plan addressed that: Ms. could fill this role by convening a network of women's groups to prepare for the conference and developing a media strategy to help the organizations find a public voice. With Ford's support, several well-connected organizers received grants from Ms. to participate in a "Beijing and Beyond Advisory Committee" intended to help coordinate the activism happening in different parts of the country. The foundation also raised money to recruit and fund a delegation of grassroots activists to travel to China. "Fragmentation . . . hampers all of our efforts," Ms. asserted. Serving as the "organizer of organizers," Ms. planned to use Beijing as a springboard for creating a "comprehensive and permanent" nationwide network that would lead the women's movement into the twenty-first century.[14] Enacting those plans would turn out to be far more challenging than Wilson and her staff envisioned.

Ms. introduced itself as the coordinator of the movement in a major press conference held prior to the conference. The foundation convinced other feminist groups to participate by presenting the press conference as an opportunity to showcase their goals for Beijing and gain greater exposure for their causes. Several of the organizations demanded "that the speakers at the press conference not be the standard line-up of women's movement speakers, that the group be diverse, and that the speakers should be representative—that is, from both grassroots and national organizations." Ms. heeded their call, selecting participants who represented different facets of feminist activism, over half of whom were women of color.[15]

Yet when the press conference aired live on C-SPAN, no one doubted who was in charge. Ms. brought out its biggest celebrity—founder Gloria Steinem—to introduce the event and serve as master of ceremonies. When Steinem stepped aside, Wilson took over to facilitate the Q&A. A handout prepared by Ms. and given to the participants in advance instructed everyone to present a "united front," demonstrating their "strength and solidarity in numbers."[16] What the handout did not say was that Ms. planned to present itself as the leader of the cause.

With the TV cameras rolling, the participants followed the Ms. Foundation's directives. The delegation of grassroots activists invited to Beijing, however, would not fall so easily in line.

Though committed to fostering a racially diverse feminist movement, Marie Wilson, like most other white activists of her day who had led national organizations, often worked in ways that placed women who were not white or middle class on the margins. In 1970 the radical feminist Jo Freeman had condemned the "tyranny of structurelessness" in women's organizing. Feminists' commitment to nonhierarchical leadership, she believed, often prevented them from accomplishing specific goals or remedying the social inequities among them.[17] Many feminists of the 1990s worked in nonprofits or professional institutions with clear hierarchies, and they did not reject the idea that some people would take on formal leadership roles. But how to choose those leaders and distribute power remained key points of contention.

A number of white feminists tried to build more inclusive programs by "reaching out" to women of color. Yet they never contemplated handing over power. "Essentially we designed the meetings, we set the agenda, and then we invited . . . women of color groups to join us," explained Helen Neuborne, who worked at the NOW Legal Defense and Education Fund. "Many of us learned later on that that was really a very inappropriate way to go about building bases with colleagues. . . . Nonetheless, that's pretty much the way it was done."[18]

Such practices had deep roots. By the 1990s, however, success at organizing on their own behalf gave women of color new leverage in these negotiations. Most white organizers knew that any national initiative claiming to represent the feminist movement would draw immediate criticism if it were exclusively or predominately white. As white women scrambled to conduct "outreach," women of color refused to be tokenized. After decades spent advocating for Latina health rights on a shoestring budget, Luz Alvarez Martinez was one of many who began refusing invitations to participate in white-dominated conferences or on boards of directors unless the organizers asked other women of color to join her. A similar revolt was happening among those working to end violence against women.[19]

Ms. Foundation leaders claimed to understand that their new national feminist network would need to give ample voice to grassroots activists, particularly women of color. The staff believed they had a strong track record to draw on. Wilson had come out in some circles as a lesbian, and her vice president was Puerto Rican. The foundation's professional staff was over two-fifths nonwhite and Ms. had established a strong reputation for funding racially diverse groups—nearly 75 percent of its funded projects were run by women of color or a multiracial staff.[20] Planning documents for the foundation's Beijing initiatives emphasized the importance of ensuring that members felt "influence and ownership" over the process.[21] Yet when it came time to choose the activist delegation that would travel to the Beijing conference, Ms. seemed to stray from this pledge. The process was kept under wraps and was controlled by the Ms. staff, who spent hours in meetings deciding who to invite. The foundation was so committed to ensuring the diversity of this group by race, ethnicity, region, age, sexual orientation, disability status, and issue area that staff members created spreadsheets to check off the categories each woman represented—but they didn't ask for much input on decision making.[22]

By the time all the boxes were checked, Ms. had chosen thirty-four activists. These women worked on the full gamut of feminist issues, from child care and welfare to refugees and domestic violence, and they ranged in age from twenty-five to sixty. Women with disabilities and those who were able-bodied, lesbian, straight—they came from large and small organizations operating in every region of the country. Sixty percent of the delegates were women of color, with relatively equal numbers of Latinas, Native Americans, Asian Americans, and African Americans included. Most had participated in projects that had received funding from the Ms. Foundation.[23]

Ms. had put together a group of activists who remain among feminism's most innovative foot soldiers. Their ranks included Pamela Chiang, who had come to the foundation's attention through her organizing at the intersection of the environmental and economic justice movements. Raised in a Chinese immigrant household in San Francisco, with "three generations in an apartment building," she found her calling while attending the University of California, Berkeley, in the late 1980s. There, Chiang helped build the emerging environmental justice movement, which was led by people of color addressing the toxic conditions in the nation's workplaces, neighborhoods, and schools. When Ms. contacted Chiang, she was building a résumé that read like a who's who of immigrant-led environmental and labor organizing in the Southwest.[24]

Ellen Bravo had been involved in feminist activism for decades. Growing up in a Jewish family grappling with the legacy of the Holocaust, she had learned "that in the face of injustice you can't be silent." When an accident put her father, an aluminum siding salesman, out of work for two years, she watched her parents struggle as her mother became the family's sole source of support. In the late 1960s, Bravo gained a deeper understanding of her mother's predicament when she joined a feminist consciousness-raising group.

"This makes so much sense of all these things that have been troubling me in my life," she said. Decades later, the strain of holding a full-time clerical job while caring for two young children compelled her to start advocating for better working conditions for women. In 1982, she founded a Milwaukee chapter of an organization of pink-collar workers called 9to5 and quickly rose through the ranks to become the national executive director. Bravo saw the Ms. delegation to Beijing as an opportunity to "learn from the organizing that women were doing in countries I barely could find on a map," who were far ahead of the United States on work-family issues.[25]

Rinku Sen, an Indian American lesbian with a degree in women's studies who had made racial justice her life's work, was also chosen. She had gravitated to activism after a childhood spent in white towns where race was barely mentioned. Attending Brown University in the mid-1980s was a revelation. The theories she learned in the classroom were complemented by her participation in a "watershed" moment of campus activism. Sen experienced thrilling victories lobbying Brown's administration to establish a Third World Center and joining an anti–sexual assault campaign that resulted in two fraternities leaving campus and the administration agreeing to institute a dusk-to-dawn shuttle service. After graduating, she took a job at the Center for Third World Organizing in Oakland, where she worked with low-income people campaigning for health care and economic justice. She also helped build a Campaign for Community Safety and Police Accountability, which she described as a "precursor to Black Lives Matter." Ms. reached out to Sen at an ideal moment: she was strategizing about how to integrate gender equity into her initiatives. She accepted the invitation, eager to learn from other "race, class, and gender liberation fighters, like me."[26]

Ms. had assembled the players for an all-star team. But before they even took the field in China, tensions began to build.

During the flight to China, many of the activists learned for the first time that Ms. had invited some of the foundation's donors, whose presence aroused suspicion. At the same time, the behavior of some foundation staff members generated resentment. Young staffers were responsible for keeping track of the delegates as they traveled through airports, customs, and baggage claims. "People were tired and fatigued," explained Chiang. Several bristled at being "shepherded along . . . [by] young white gals . . . barking at us, telling us what to do." At a certain point, some of the "women of color became . . . vocal." After being "herded along," they said, "'Come on! Don't treat us like that.'" The dynamic was too familiar. "It didn't feel good."[27]

A night in an expensive hotel room in Beijing did not change the mood. The delegates woke up jetlagged in a foreign country to find that Ms. had planned for them to go straight into a jampacked two-day orientation. The goal was to introduce the activists to the major themes in global feminism and the history of women's lobbying at the UN. At one of the opening sessions, a confrontational question asked by a Black woman burst the dam. Others immediately joined what Wilson described as "a conversation about America and race" that escalated into a heated debate about whether the Ms. Foundation was racist.[28]

Attempts by Ms. Foundation leaders to "get control" and return to their planned conversations on global issues went nowhere. "The orientation pretty much could not move forward," one staff member explained.[29] A group of women of color activists took the reins and canceled the scheduled activities. They drew up an agenda for a very different gathering, one that focused on what people at the time called "identity politics." The schedule included separate caucuses for each racial group and a Quaker-style meeting designed to allow everyone to express their opinions in a respectful atmosphere.

During the activist-controlled sessions, there were tears and a great deal of tension.[30] A few people grew frustrated and left, while some of the other participants lashed out or shut down. Bravo was one of several veteran organizers who had been part of conversations about race and identity in the women's movement for decades and had learned to stay open to new ideas and experiences. She saw the frank discussion of racism as a "positive development," but observed that some of the other white people in the room took it "personally rather than thinking about it in . . . the bigger context."[31]

It is hard not to take things personally when you feel directly targeted. The Ms. communications director recalled how uncomfortable she was hearing things like, "Why were white women in charge of the trip, why were white women deciding everything?" She felt like her own identity was under a microscope. "Here I was: straight, Ivy League educated, Jewish, raised upper middle class," she reflected. "I represent everything that everyone is criticizing." A stickler for details, she had spent months organizing the communications for the trip. Once the delegates arrived at the hotel, she and others had gone into high gear, making sure everyone's luggage was delivered to their rooms, meals were served on time, and the meeting rooms were ready to go. When it was finally time for the orientation to begin, she was totally spent. "I kept saying [to myself], 'You want to be in charge? . . . Fine! Be in charge!' Being in charge sucks."[32]

But who was "in charge"—who had *power*—was the fundamental question. Many believed Ms. had erred in not involving activists in planning the orientation. Having a diverse group of people in the room (or on a spreadsheet) did not guarantee that they all felt included or heard.[33]

Sen positioned herself as bridge builder, seeking to foster greater understanding and communication among different groups. "When I was in college and dealing with white feminists, I could have been kinder," she recalled. She remembered several conversations from her Brown years that resulted in white women breaking down in tears. A decade later in Beijing, Sen tried to listen and model compassion. "I had no interest in tearing down the foundation" or alienating potential white allies, she said. Generating defensiveness "shuts doors." To convince people and institutions to change, "you have to leave the door open."[34]

Several Ms. staff members responded positively. Sara Gould, who would later become president of the foundation, said that she "learned a ton" from the delegates about the mistakes Ms. had made in organizing the orientation.[35]

By the end of the orientation, the participants had aired a range of views and many had come to new understandings. But they had not developed any kind of blueprint for coordinating their future organizing. The only thought that had become crystal clear was that none of them believed the future of US feminism should consist of a national network organized by the Ms. Foundation. Without buy-in from a broad base, the foundation would continue to fund grassroots feminist groups but would never be recognized as the coordinator of the US movement.[36]

The delegates did not unite under the Ms. banner, but nonetheless many began to forge the kinds of ties that Ms. had hoped would develop among them—the friendships and relationships of trust that propel all social movements. During the arguments, caucuses, Quaker circles, and breakfasts, clusters of delegates connected in a variety of ways. They caught each other's eye during emotional or cringe-worthy moments and debriefed in the hallways. People talked over meals and even shared a few doses of Valium to help everyone get some sleep. Over the next ten days, as they set out to join the thousands of others exploring the conference's NGO Forum, these bonds deepened.

TWO

"WE HAD FAR LESS TO TEACH THAN TO LEARN"

Urvashi Vaid didn't know what to expect when the taxi transporting her and a few friends pulled up to a three-story disco in the heart of Beijing. She had shown the driver a flyer that mapped the location of a dance party for the lesbians attending the women's conference that had been circulated at the conference by Chunsheng Wu, a gay Chinese activist. After an extraordinarily difficult week, many of them welcomed the opportunity to blow off some steam. Yet, to their horror, they were met by a "gauntlet" of heavily armed military and police, standing on either side of the path leading to the bar.

With some trepidation, they entered the club. More green-clad police were stationed around the dance floor, some holding cameras. Within an hour, though, over a hundred lesbians had arrived, and the liquor and loud music emboldened them. They could not speak the same language, but they communicated with their bodies, swaying together to a world beat in defiance of the authorities. When a slow, bluesy song came on, a Black woman and a white woman climbed up on the small stage and began intimately dancing as the crowd cheered them on.

It was a profound experience. US participants saw firsthand what it meant for queer people to organize under repressive regimes. Upon leaving the bar, Vaid and several others from the States stayed up late into the night talking with the Chinese organizers and then processing the evening's events with each other. Tapping into the "subversive power of music and dance" together in such a highly charged environment had strengthened their connections, providing one of the most "joyful memories" from the conference.[1]

Many other feminists connected with one another in equally unexpected ways during the ten-day forum. Conference-goers formed lasting bonds as they grappled with unfamiliar ideas and shared personal stories over plates of steaming noodles and dumplings. Asian Americans, moved by being in China, experienced a new sense of solidarity and decided to amp up their organizing at home. Groups of lesbians and women with disabilities bonded over the hostility and marginalization they encountered at the forum and learned to trust each other by waging collective protests and standing up to the police. For many US activists, the concepts people from Asia, Latin America, and Africa taught them revolutionized their thinking. When they returned home, the personal relationships and theories of globalization and social change that they had encountered in China would propel and energize their organizing.

"There is no simple way to describe the NGO Forum," wrote the feminist journalist Jo Freeman. With thirty thousand participants from nearly two hundred countries, the 1995 event was far larger than previous gatherings in Mexico City in 1975, Copenhagen in

The flyer advertising the dance party for lesbians who were attending the NGO Forum. *Courtesy of Chunsheng Wu.*

1980, Nairobi in 1985. The official purpose of NGO forums was to give "civil society"—the representatives of advocacy and activist organizations, rather than of national governments—an opportunity to influence the proceedings of the official meetings. Yet the majority of people who attended did not interact with the UN delegates. They attended the forum to participate in the activist-led panels, plenaries, and workshops, which offered unparalleled opportunities to learn from and forge relationships with people from other places. Beijing's theme was "Look at the World Through Women's Eyes"; it was time for thirty thousand activists to demand just that.[2]

Chinese authorities had initially proposed holding the 1995 NGO Forum in the Beijing Workers' Stadium. They changed their plans a few months prior to the women's convention after Prime Minister Li Pin was heckled about human rights by activists at a UN conference in Copenhagen. Hoping to avoid a similar humiliation in their capital, authorities banished the forum to a hundred-acre area in the town of Huairou, over an hour away from the city. Despite a worldwide feminist protest against moving the event to the isolated and inadequate Huairou facilities, the Chinese government refused to change the location.[3]

Freeman described the Huairou site as resembling a "county fair with theme tents, an exhibition hall, booths and tables. . . . Throw in a dab of flea market. Add a computer room. . . . Sprinkle with bulletin boards and poster walls, many spontaneous ad hoc demonstrations and lots of dancing and singing." Activists conducted these spirited displays even though much of the infrastructure posed problems. The participants arrived to find several of the new buildings that Chinese authorities had promised to build missing walls; none had ramps or elevators. Many of the paths remained unpaved. Rain soaked the grounds during the first few days of the forum and, coupled with the high humidity, turned the site into a muddy, mosquito-infested swamp.[4]

The activists procured umbrellas and rain slickers and refused to be deterred. The "essence of the conference," Freeman observed, was the "thousands of conversations and exchanges of ideas and experiences that took place in small groups, over meals and on the buses." The printed schedule resembled a telephone book, with 199 pages listing thousands of events put on by women from every region of the world on nearly every conceivable topic. At the morning plenaries, which typically featured prominent activists from each continent speaking on a single topic, four thousand women packed into a hall designed to hold fifteen hundred to hear about the most pressing issues of the day: the international rise of conservatism and religious fundamentalism; globalization and the economy; peace and human security. Colorful flyers posted on walls, windows, and telephone poles advertised protests, discussions, and meetings that were being organized. Although construction was no longer happening on the infrastructure, a movement was building around it.[5]

The forum showcased how global and diverse the women's movement had become. Participants came from every part of the world. The major speakers included representatives of indigenous groups as well as university affiliates. Conference-goers communicated in multiple languages and wore everything from colorful saris and sarongs to head scarves and blue jeans.[6] Even the eight thousand activists representing the United States were themselves far more diverse than the ones who had traveled to previous international meetings. The cost of international travel meant that attendance skewed toward those who put energy into raising money or who won grants. African American women had the largest presence of all minority groups—between a thousand and two thousand. Asian Americans, Latinas, and Native Americans numbered in the many hundreds.[7]

Some of the most dynamic interactions took place in the tents that dotted the grounds of the forum. Each continent had its own, and a series of smaller "diversity" tents celebrated identities that cut across regions: lesbians, women with disabilities, older women, indigenous women, youth, peace activists, and grassroots activists. Over the ten days, tents developed their own subcultures. The Latin American and Caribbean tent was one of the most spirited, opening with a festive *encuentro* intended to connect the "women of the Americas" to one another. The activists decorated the walls of the tent with their handprints, built an altar of photos, lit candles, and hung banners from the rafters. Interspersed with strategy sessions were cultural celebrations in which women read poems about feminism in English, Spanish, and Portuguese and danced the Brazilian samba, Mexican folk dances, and Trinidadian calypso.[8]

The contrast with the North American tent could not have been starker. Sterile and empty, and used only sporadically as a meeting place, the tent signaled the very lack of national leadership that had bothered Marie Wilson. It also served as a reminder that among the thousands of US activists at the forum, few felt much affinity to a *national* movement. US governmental officials held Q&A sessions in the tent and a few national groups held meetings there, but none had a significant following at the conference.[9]

Bypassing the North American tent, US activists eagerly sought out people in the other tents who shared their passions. Many US women of color visited the tents of their continents of origin, hoping to make connections with women from Africa, Latin America, and Asia. Most found such interactions disappointing.[10] The problem, one Indian American activist observed, was that women of color could not avoid the suspicion and sometimes outright hostility often directed toward conference-goers from the United States. Many recognized that the history of imperialist behaviors and policies had created understandable distrust, and they took great care to be respectful and humble. Nevertheless, perceptions of people from the United States as "interfering, arrogant, ignorant, insensitive, and imperialist were ascribed to women of color as well as to white women," making it difficult for some to forge real connections in brief encounters.[11] It would take sustained interactions and the sharing of resonant experiences to break down these suspicions and foster trust between women from different parts of the world.

When Asian Americans gravitated to the Asia tent, their most meaningful encounters happened when they bumped into one another. When they recognized another Asian American person, they took advantage of being able to communicate in English and struck up conversations. What began as casual banter often became deeper exchanges, as they found commonalities with people from different Asian backgrounds that they had not recognized at home. For many, it was their first time traveling to an Asian country, and being surrounded by so many Asian people had stirred unexpectedly intense reactions. Some felt like it was the first time they had experienced a sense of belonging and they were enjoying how it felt to be in a majority. Others felt acutely aware of the distance between them and the people there who were from Asia. Many took great pride in seeing Chinese workers act with dignity and efficiency at registration desks, restaurants, bars, and hotels. Far from home but feeling connected in some way to this continent, they gravitated to one another in the Asia tent because nobody else understood what it meant to be an Asian American at the forum.[12]

Lora Jo Foo found her interactions with people who were not Chinese to be the most unsettling. Fluent in Cantonese, she had worked alongside her mother in a sweatshop in San Francisco's Chinatown as a young girl and had over a decade of organizing immigrant garment workers and hotel maids under her belt. She had traveled to China in 1980. During that trip, she had learned that Chinese people could spot an "ABC, American-born Chinese," a mile away. "They just know it by the way we stand, the way we talk, what we wear, how we walk, our facial features," she said. What surprised her about the forum was not that the Chinese saw her as a foreigner but that so few people from other parts of the world understood that she was not native-born. Contending with their assumptions was wearying.[13]

Foo looked forward to commiserating at a workshop for Asian American women advertised in the conference program. Even the organizers were shocked when nearly one hundred people showed up. No one had any idea that there were so many of them walking around Huairou. As they introduced themselves and exchanged information, their shared experiences in China helped bridge gaps of class and country of origin. The conversations were so rich and productive that they decided to hold a second meeting. They posted flyers around the forum and, again, almost a hundred people attended.[14]

The task before them became clear. That they had not known each other before the forum, even though much of their activism was related, felt unconscionable. They realized that of all the US racial-ethnic groups represented at the conference, they were the

Lora Jo Foo (standing) presenting at one of the workshops for Asian American women held at the NGO Forum. These meetings led to the founding of the National Asian Pacific American Women's Forum, the first multi-issue organization of Asian and Pacific Islander American women in the United States. *Courtesy of Lora Jo Foo.*

least organized on the national level. Encountering the strength of women's movements in India, the Philippines, Japan, and other parts of Asia also convinced them of the necessity of creating something of their own. They resolved to form a national organization of Asian American women when they returned home.[15]

When they got back to the United States, several of these women started organizing. After contacting those who had traveled to the conference and those who had not had the opportunity to attend, they founded the National Asian Pacific American Women's Forum, the first multi-issue organization of Asian and Pacific Islander American women in the country. "It was ridiculous that it took us all coming thousands of miles to Beijing to get together as a national gathering of Asian American women," observed Foo. But it did. They were one of several groups who learned that sharing a profound experience away from home could help them identify common cause—and collaborate to advance those causes once they returned.[16]

For many US activists, the most transformative cross-cultural experience they had at the forum was the exposure to entirely new ways of thinking—frameworks and ideas shared by women from Latin America, Asia, and Africa. "The women globally offered us lessons and strategies that we simply did not know in the United States," explained the Black women's health advocate Loretta Ross. "We had everything to gain from becoming a global activist as long as we . . . understood that we had far less to teach than to learn."[17] In hundreds of panels and in every major plenary session, the majority of US activists found themselves completely unprepared to participate in substantive conversations with people from Latin America, Asia, and Africa. It was humbling. The fundamental problem was the US participants' parochial understandings of politics and the economy. Most knew that the United States had lost thousands of manufacturing jobs to factories overseas and many had decried the mounting cutbacks to their nation's social welfare programs. But they did not fully understand how these developments were bound up in seismic economic and political shifts happening worldwide.

In makeshift tents and large lecture halls, activists from Latin America, Asia, and Africa schooled the US feminists. They systematically outlined the effects on women of the spread of global capitalism and described the havoc wreaked by the structural adjustment programs promoted by the International Monetary Fund (IMF) and World Bank—programs that were supported by the US government. Under structural adjustment programs (SAPs), developing countries received loans from the IMF and World Bank on the condition that they implement various free-market economic policies such as privatizing state-owned industries, opening markets to foreign investors, and reducing government spending on social services. It was incredibly eye-opening for the US activists to see how the underlying logic of the policies that they were pushing back against at home echoed what was happening in the Global South. One economic justice organizer described being "blown away" upon learning "the United States was actually enacting welfare reform all over the world" by promoting the policies of the World Bank and IMF. "It really helped politicize me," she said, "in a way that . . . opened the doors to things that now I know but I just had no idea."[18]

It was not only the ideas that astounded the activists from the United States; it was that they were being conveyed by some of the world's most marginalized women. "We'd be sitting there in workshops with . . . women from small countries in Africa who are breaking down structural adjustment programs, SAPs, and what it directly means for them as peasant women," recalled Ms. Foundation delegate and environmental organizer Pamela Chiang.[19] Seeing how people in other places mobilized with few resources under extremely repressive conditions gave many US activists renewed hope for their future. They had come to China knowing very little or nothing about the World Bank, the IMF, and structural adjustment programs. They left convinced that these institutions and policies should and could be confronted at home and abroad.[20]

One of the most important contributions US activists made to the intellectual life of the forum was disproving stereotypes about their own country.[21] In panels and one-on-one conversations, they challenged the common assumption that there was a dichotomy between a prosperous "Global North" and an impoverished "Global South." Many US women of color described themselves as representing the "South within the North," and activists of all kinds explained that their country did not look like the set of a TV soap opera like *Dallas* or *Dynasty* that had made its way abroad.[22] A panel featuring two formerly homeless women organized by the Women of Color Resource Center in Oakland portrayed this message starkly: "We wanted to try to get other people of the world to see how the richest country in the world had people who were really down and out," recalled an activist who worked with the group.[23]

Some US activists' cross-cultural interactions went beyond myth-busting and intellectual exchange to include the forging of personal relationships. This happened most often when they shared intense and consequential experiences with conference attendees from other nations. For women with disabilities, such bonding began the day before the forum opened, when 250 activists from different countries attended an all-day planning meeting run by Susan Sygall's Mobility International USA (MIUSA), a disability rights organization that promotes equal access to international travel. The cavernous meeting room they gathered in was freezing cold and the pounding rain on the tin roof made it very hard for them to hear each other. But activists like Corbett O'Toole felt grateful to be in the midst of so much energy and passion. A white queer woman who had contracted polio as a child, O'Toole had moved to Berkeley after graduating from college in the early 1970s. She delved into the "hotbed" of disability rights organizing happening in the Bay Area and met Sygall at an International Women's Day event in 1974. O'Toole found Sygall's organizing to be holistic, incorporating multiple identities, and has been working at the cross section of feminism and disability rights ever since. Frustrated by the white male disability activists who prioritized accessibility through infrastructure, O'Toole tried to expand the purview of the disability rights movement to include the fight for women's access to services offered by domestic violence shelters and counseling centers. Negotiating with feminists who were able-bodied had often proved discouraging because they frequently resisted her efforts to include women with disabilities in their projects.[24] Seeing so many people from different countries, all united in common cause and engaged in productive dialogue around the issues she cared most about, was new to O'Toole.

The women who met under the tin roof wanted to ensure their voices would be heard at the forum. But first, they needed to find a way to communicate with one another across language barriers— thirty-five different languages were represented at the planning meeting. The workable, albeit cumbersome, solution they developed involved people making statements in the microphone, then pausing after each paragraph to allow audience members to translate into other languages. It made for a very long day in the cold, drafty room. Yet they were exhilarated by the sheer fact that they were part of this unprecedentedly large, truly global gathering of women with disabilities, all collectively discussing the issues that mattered to them.[25] The group strategized about how to promote their perspectives at the NGO Forum. Not only would they attend one another's workshops on disability, but they would also be "infiltrating" the hundreds of panels and plenaries on topics like sexuality and parenting that did not include their voices. They were determined to show how disability was part of every feminist issue, from low-wage work to reproductive health.[26]

Some of the most important exchanges in that cold room involved US activists comparing their situations to those of people who worked in less developed countries. The first thing they learned was that they were behind the curve when it came to forging links with other people in their own nation. Many of the US activists worked with similarly disabled people—the wheelchair riders worked with other chair users, blind women worked with other blind women. They were inspired by the women from other countries who spoke of forging "cross-disability" coalitions that united disparate groups.[27]

US activists also found that they lacked essential supports from their own government that people in countries such as Uganda took for granted. Women from other nations were equally surprised to learn that their US counterparts were "the beggars of the society" and did not have access to services they considered necessities, such as universal health care. Breaking down the myths was "a great equalizer on both sides," O'Toole said. "It really brought people together."[28]

Their bonds deepened when they traveled to Huairou the next day and confronted a new set of challenges. The "accessible" buses

Sygall had arranged to transport them had only a few rows of seats at the front and wide-open spaces in the back with no tie-downs for wheelchairs. "We basically jammed the wheelchairs in and held on for dear life," O'Toole recalled. As the buses made their way down the bumpy roads, some of the wheelchairs tipped over. People were shivering because the bus windows did not close.[29]

Things did not improve when they arrived at the forum. They had successfully advocated for a disability tent, but they arrived to find that its location could not have been more remote. Getting there required traversing puddles, mud, and cracked and slippery pavestones. Wheelchairs and crutches got stuck; people slipped and fell. Once they arrived at the tent, the blind and deaf women who had brought guides and interpreters could venture out, but those who couldn't climb stairs or travel long distances "literally couldn't go anywhere," said O'Toole. They again rejected a solution presented by Chinese authorities, who offered to carry them up the flights of stairs in the buildings without elevators—déjà vu from their arrival at the airport.[30]

As plans were hatched to mount a formal demonstration, a small group that included several wheelchair riders made a great effort to get themselves to one of the panels on disability. But they found it scheduled to take place on the third floor of a building with no elevator. Acting on the spur of the moment, they staged a protest. They got out of their wheelchairs and crawled up the steps and along the paths outside the building.

Television cameras rushed to capture the shocking images of activists with disabilities crawling on the ground while onlookers cheered them on. It was an important consciousness-raising moment for many of the conference attendees, who had already witnessed women with disabilities' difficulties navigating the site. And it fostered solidarity and confidence among the activists, who still take pride in launching the first demonstration at the forum. "The hard parts were useful because they really brought us together," O'Toole later recalled.[31]

When word of the protest got back to the disability tent, it was like a shot of adrenalin for those who were there. They decided to go ahead with their plans for a formal demonstration and staged their own mini-conference inside their tent, with workshops on issues like sexuality and labor rights. One activist shared lessons from Whirlwind Wheelchair, an organization that was addressing the worldwide shortage of wheelchairs by teaching people to assemble them from inexpensive recycled materials such as old bicycle parts. She set up a welding shop in the tent and enlisted other women in building a chair from scratch.

Women with disabilities made their presence known at the NGO Forum. Their panels and demonstrations emphasized their abilities to take charge of their own lives. *Courtesy of Pamela Sparr.*

Meanwhile, women with disabilities extended their hand to other conference-goers. Several of them put up signs encouraging people to come over to the tent. A number of panels demonstrated solidarity by purposely meeting there. One of the most high-profile guests was the US ambassador to the United Nations (and later secretary of state) Madeline Albright, who chose the tent as the place to deliver a speech. Many were also moved by an appearance by former congressperson and outspoken feminist Bella Abzug, who had been trying to hide the fact that she was traveling around the forum in a wheelchair from the press. Abzug spoke from the heart about how the activism of the women gathered in the tent had helped challenge her own stereotypes of people with disabilities.[32]

Experiencing the humiliations and the triumphs together built lasting networks. O'Toole credited the "explosion" of the international movement for women with disabilities in subsequent years to the time women spent together at the forum.[33] Many wanted to capitalize on their momentum and continue to organize collectively after the conference, so MIUSA answered the call by creating its first program focused exclusively on women. In 1997, the organization launched a biannual International Women's Institute on Leadership and Disability (WILD), bringing together thirty-four women with disabilities from around the world for a three-week intensive training program on gender and disability rights organizing. The institute was followed by an international conference on women with disabilities, which brought over six hundred activists to Washington, DC—a direct legacy of what happened at the forum and in that freezing room outside of Beijing. The networks forged in China have "lasted forever," O'Toole explained, opening up "new avenues of thinking and working."[34]

Similarly, lesbian activists from different parts of the world built solidarities by collectively facing challenges and drawing other people's attention to their struggles.[35] The Beijing conference took place at "a very mobilizing moment" for gay people, recalled Julie Dorf, executive director of the San Francisco–based International Gay and Lesbian Human Rights Commission (IGLHRC): "People were dying all around us" from HIV/AIDS. Raised in a close-knit Jewish family in Milwaukee, Dorf became an antiapartheid activist at Wesleyan College in the 1980s and majored in Russian studies. A trip to the former Soviet Union to conduct research for her senior thesis opened new worlds. She discovered underground communities of feminists and dissident writers and artists, including many "extremely closeted LGBT people." After graduation Dorf moved to San Francisco and continued to visit the Soviet Union, acting as a "human courier" for political texts. She smuggled in Adrienne Rich's "Compulsory Heterosexuality" and brought home writings by gay Russian dissidents. In 1990 Dorf turned her side hustle into a career. Working together with US-based groups, she founded IG-LHRC to infuse gay rights into international human rights policies. One of her first international lobbying experiences was the 1993 UN Human Rights Conference in Vienna, where feminists fought to expand human rights frameworks to include violence against women. She seized the opportunity to address the struggles of gay women at the Beijing conference.[36]

In Beijing, Dorf took her cues from lesbians from Thailand, Mexico, and South Africa, who had been lobbying on the international level for much longer.[37] Though they had succeeded in convincing the conference organizers of the need for a lesbian tent—the first of its kind at an NGO Forum—it provided only minimal protection from Chinese authorities' suspicion and harassment. Many conference-goers had heard that the authorities feared the lesbian attendees planned to take off their clothes and run around naked. It sounds far-fetched, but the activists believed cab drivers were issued blankets to throw over the naked women.[38] Dylan Scholinski, a transgender man who attended the conference as Daphne, is not the only one who recalls seeing "stacks of blankets . . . ready to cover us up."[39]

Authorities monitored the lesbian tent with extraordinary intensity. The activists persisted in holding their planned workshops, movie screenings, strategy sessions, and social gatherings, but they could not stop security personnel from rifling through their leaflets, staring at the notice boards, and intimidating people by training their cameras on those who were coming and going from the tent.[40] Anything written in Chinese was immediately confiscated. Many lesbians reported returning to their hotel rooms at night to find that the rooms had been rifled through while they were away.[41] When they complained of being bone tired, Scholinski, who had spent four years involuntarily detained in mental hospitals for "not being appropriately feminine," told them: "This is what surveillance feels like. When you see cameras all around and you know someone is watching you at all moments, it's exhausting."[42]

Still they persevered. The number of women who came to the conference to lobby specifically for gay rights was small, but they had allies everywhere—lesbians who were working in different tents on other issues and straight women sympathetic to their cause. A call announcing a lesbian rights march drew over five hundred women from thirty countries. Linking arms, they marched down Huairou's main thoroughfare chanting, "Lesbian rights are human rights" and "Liberté, Egalité, Homosexualité." The joy and laughter were a perfect tonic.[43]

A few days later, a smaller group of lesbians staged a dramatic protest at the government meeting in Beijing. Sexuality had emerged as a crucial sticking point in the negotiations over the Platform for Action, the document that would be signed by the world's governments at the conclusion of the event. Many countries were refusing to support anything that explicitly mentioned gay rights. To draw attention to their cause, twenty lesbians from the forum attended one of the official plenary sessions, taking over a row of seats in the top gallery of the meeting hall. From this perch, they unfurled a twenty-five-foot banner proclaiming "Lesbian Rights Are Human Rights" and held up multicolored placards emblazoned with similar slogans. UN security guards immediately snatched the placards out of their hands, ripped down the banner, and removed the women from the gallery. When two of them resisted, the guards played into their hands by taking them into custody.[44]

To free their comrades, the group sought help from none other than the widely beloved and media-savvy Bella Abzug, who had recently been shocked to discover that most of her staff at the nonprofit she had cofounded, the Women's Environment and Development Organization (WEDO), were lesbians. Rachel Rosenbloom, a member of Dorf's staff, found Abzug "in her wheelchair with her giant hat." She ran up to her, exclaiming: "The lesbians have gotten arrested! They're holding . . . two women." In a moment that has become part of global feminist lore, Abzug turned her wheelchair around and yelled: "Give me my lipstick!" With lipstick applied, she successfully negotiated the activists' release. "Bella, even in a wheelchair . . . staring down Communist Chinese guards, is a very formidable opponent," explained Jessica Halem, Abzug's assistant at the time. The outcome could not have been better for the lesbians, whose daring escapade had attracted media attention and given a boost to those lobbying on their behalf.[45]

Ultimately, the term *sexual orientation* did not appear in the final version of the Platform for Action as the lesbians and their allies had hoped. But the protest in the top gallery had moved and inspired those organizing the lesbian tent. So did the late-night party at the disco, which they were amazed to have pulled off. They were proud, too, of a speech delivered by Beverley Palesa Ditsie, a delegate from South Africa and the first lesbian to address the UN about gay rights.[46] The Platform for Action didn't mention gay rights explicitly, but these activists had placed sexuality on the agenda of UN negotiations and established a strong presence in the global feminist movement. Many of the cross-cultural connections they developed still exist today. "I met people in that process who I'm still in touch with," recalled Rosenbloom, "friendships and networks that I still draw on."[47]

For the dance party attendee Urvashi Vaid and Ms. Foundation delegate Rinku Sen, one of the highlights of the conference was

A panel at the NGO Forum featuring queer women from different regions of the world, including the US activist Urvashi Vaid (in the center) and the South African Beverly Palesa Ditsie (to Vaid's left). *Photograph by Rachel Rosenbloom.*

befriending a multiracial "crew" of US queer women. The two of them became close with four other lesbians—Linda Villarosa, Frances Kunreuther, Katherine Acey, and Eliza Byard—who joined Sen as part of the Ms. contingent.[48] The group developed an invigorating and nourishing evening ritual, sitting and talking for hours over plates of food in a "little shack of a restaurant." They talked about the racial tensions in feminism and possibilities for new alliances, how institutions could change domestically and internationally, and the intersections of the struggle for queer rights with other movements. Evening after evening, the conversations deepened as they began to take more risks and "think out loud." All of them were—or have since become—influential movement leaders. They continue to draw on the insights and friendships cultivated in that dive restaurant in China.[49]

Networks formed, friendships deepened, and intellectual breakthroughs happened at the NGO Forum with remarkable speed. By sharing resonant experiences abroad and learning from those organizing in other countries, activists developed insights and personal relationships that propelled their work in the United States. New feminist innovations in technology helped keep the spirit alive when they returned.

THREE

THE WORLDWIDE DEBUT OF ONLINE ACTIVISM

Edie Farwell spent eighteen hours a day at the NGO Forum without attending a panel or a plenary, joining the marches or visiting the tents. Yet no one worked as closely with women from different parts of the world or encountered more conference attendees than she did. Farwell had arrived in China several days before the forum opened to coordinate a team of forty women, representing twenty-four different countries. These women would connect the activists at the conference to the wider world: they were responsible for setting up the computer center.[1]

Once the forum opened, thousands of conference-goers trekked across the mud each day and waited patiently for their turn at one of the two hundred machines donated by Apple and Hewlett-Packard. They were greeted by Farwell's all-female team, whose warmth and efficiency demonstrated their mastery of new technology and comfort in using it. When something went wrong with a machine or a server, they fixed the problem. When a visitor had trouble sending a message to a loved one or finding a document from the conference, a member of the team taught her how to do it for herself. Navigating computers at this time was a specialized skill set, and onlookers marveled at such technological prowess. Few of these observers recognized that Farwell's group was part of a wide-ranging network of female technology specialists who were using the Beijing conference to build the infrastructure for what would become online feminism.[2]

The UN event took place at an ideal moment for those looking to harness the tools of the internet to advance global feminism. It was the cusp of the digital revolution, the year when millions of people encountered email and the internet for the first time. Almost everyone who attended the conference in 1995 had heard about people going online to exchange and retrieve information. Some were already proficient with email, but many others had never touched a computer.[3]

The online universe of 1995 did not look like the world we know today. There was no Facebook, Twitter, or Wikipedia. The founders of Google, Sergey Brin and Larry Page, had only just met each other as graduate students at Stanford University. No one had smartphones or access to Wi-Fi services. Sending an email message required first connecting to the internet through a scratchy-sounding modem that plugged into a telephone line, a process that could take minutes. To explore the World Wide Web, people had to pay for a subscription to an internet service provider, such as America Online or CompuServe. And the technology was slow; even for "early enthusiasts," one scholar observed, navigating the internet demanded "as much patience as know-how."[4]

Barbara Ann O'Leary had both qualities. Having grown up in St. Louis during the 1960s, with parents who had been part of the

Catholic Worker Movement, she was a visionary nonconformist, with a passion for communications. From an early age, O'Leary wrote letters to a number of relatives and Girl Scout pen pals. Every day, she would listen for the postal delivery truck and rush out to grab the mail from the letter carrier. Packages from her aunt were a special treat; they often included feminist books and magazines, which helped spark her interest in the women's movement. Captivated by the television coverage of civil rights and antiwar protests, O'Leary supported striking Filipino and Latino farm workers by boycotting grapes. By the time she was a teenager, she was a political junkie, who "watched every single minute of the Nixon impeachment hearings" and "read almost every book about Watergate, including the entire transcripts."[5]

In the 1980s, O'Leary's mother, a grade school librarian, taught basic computing skills to children and learned how to build computers from scratch. Her example taught O'Leary to view computers as tools, no different from ballpoint pens or telephones. "Some kinds of tools interest me more than others," O'Leary said. From a young age, she avoided telephones but loved taking apart mechanical pencils. When personal computers became available, she embraced them. She majored in theater in college and did not take a single class in programming. Yet as she pursued her passion for stage managing and dramatic literature, she was also teaching herself about computers and the internet outside the classroom.[6]

O'Leary saw computers as the successors to the tools that previous generations of feminists had used to circumvent the mainstream media and communicate with one another. During the 1970s, while activists fought to change the sexist practices of corporate news outlets such as the *New York Times* and *Ladies' Home Journal*, they also created their own newspapers and magazines and launched small independent presses. By the 1990s, thousands took advantage of inexpensive photocopying to publish "zines"— pamphlets that looked like scrapbooks, combining elements of personal journals, newsletters, and collages. They traded zines with one another, gave them away, solicited subscriptions, and sold them at independent music stores and bookstores.[7]

Most people have assumed that men crafted and led all of the important initiatives in the male-dominated technology sector, but women were essential to the development of computer programming and the internet.[8] As the digital revolution got under way, an international network of women—who have not received much public recognition—realized that the emerging forms of electronic communications could augment longstanding feminist practices. One international organization, the Association for Progressive Communications (APC), put substantial resources into fostering women's technological leadership. This nonprofit was largely responsible for social movements' early adoption of new communication technologies. Under Edie Farwell, the woman who worked eighteen-hour days at the NGO Forum's computer center, the APC helped global feminism become a leader among all social movements in pursuing online activism.[9]

Farwell served as the APC's executive director for nearly a decade, and through her work, the organization sought to close the gender gap in the use of digital communications and to promote women's leadership in technology. She saw the Beijing conference as an opportunity to devote more resources to empowering women in tech and get more women worldwide connected to the internet. The APC had already had great success introducing activists to computers and the internet at prior UN conferences in the 1990s—but Beijing promised something bigger that could be directed to women worldwide. Two years before the women's conference, the APC established a Women's Programme devoted to "putting Beijing online."[10] Between 1993 and 1995, the largely female staff of the Women's Programme helped organizations in more than thirty countries incorporate digital communications into their preparations for the conference.[11] Thousands of female activists received training in using the new technology to communicate and amplify their voices on the public stage.

While the APC's female staff members focused on training the foot soldiers, O'Leary joined a group of prophetic feminist technology leaders in crafting an online infrastructure. In 1991, having recently graduated from college, she was reading the latest issue of *Ms.* magazine in her New Jersey apartment when she took note of a sidebar. It described the Women's Environment and Development Organization (WEDO), a new group being formed by Bella Abzug, which was planning a conference on global feminism and environmentalism in Miami. O'Leary felt passionately about both causes and had experience organizing around environmental issues in college, so she put together a résumé and got on a train and delivered it to the WEDO office in Manhattan. In January 1992, Abzug called to offer her a position.[12]

When O'Leary arrived at the office on her first day of work, she was shocked to find several cramped rooms filled with documents stuffed into overflowing boxes. There were a few outdated computers that no one touched. Abzug asked O'Leary to find contact information for a woman who had attended their conference, whose name she could not remember. The task required O'Leary to spend several hours digging through boxes of papers "looking for clues." Perturbed by the chaos, and unintimidated by her formidable boss, O'Leary convinced Abzug that the organization could not build an effective global network of feminist environmentalists without acquiring new computers. After helping order and install the new machines, she went to work.[13]

Her first task was the mailing list, which consisted of names typed hastily in rows into a word processing file. O'Leary moved quickly to digitize the information and make it sortable and searchable. She built a database using a program called FoxPro that correlated people's names with the major events they had participated in and their areas of expertise. With this database, an organization working to end domestic violence in Rio de Janeiro could search for groups doing similar work in Brazil, elsewhere in South America, and worldwide. Word of O'Leary's efforts quickly spread within global feminist networks. "People started to come to us for information when they wanted to know who to talk to around the world on different themes and areas of work."[14]

The next item on O'Leary's to-do list was email. Like many other international organizations at the time, WEDO relied on the fax machine to communicate. After watching interns spend hours sending and receiving faxes, O'Leary determined that the system was not practical or sustainable. Faxes were expensive and for people working internationally "challenging timewise," O'Leary said. "Sometimes I'd fax someone and wake them up in the middle of the night." Faxes were also a unidirectional form of communication. Even when the interns faxed the same document simultaneously to multiple recipients, they could not create a conversation among the group.[15]

O'Leary had a hunch that once her officemates experienced the speed and interactivity of email, they would be hooked. The WEDO office had already acquired email addresses through the APC, but the accounts had never been used. After the new computers arrived, O'Leary activated the accounts and acquired email addresses for as many other activists and organizations as she could. She added all of that information to the FoxPro database.[16]

She soon encountered a network of feminist technology specialists who were grappling with many of the issues she faced at WEDO and were finding ways to support one another. A 1994 Women Empowering Communications conference in Bangkok drew more than four hundred communication specialists from over eighty countries to share resources and plan for the future. The same year, O'Leary joined around thirty-five technology activists from North and South America to plot strategy at a weekend retreat held at a ranch outside of Austin, Texas. "We weren't operating in isolation based on nations. We were working together internationally," O'Leary said.[17]

She felt energized by the network's generative conversations about equality and access. "Fairness was always in our minds," she emphasized. She and her new comrades knew that other people's ability to get online depended on their economic circumstances and the technological infrastructure where they lived. Those living in the Global South generally faced the highest barriers—but there were also substantial variations in access across countries and regions of the world. At the retreat in Texas, for example, many participants had trouble getting online, and O'Leary remembered the women from Buenos Aires being startled by this fact. "They didn't realize that online access in the US had any challenges," O'Leary said. "We told them that rural America was more in line with Third World communications conditions than major cities like theirs."[18]

The specialists made it their goal to provide technology for the masses rather than fancy toys for the few. They focused on extending access to more people rather than developing cutting-edge tools. Their mind-set echoed that of APC's, which emphasized its dedication to providing "appropriate" rather than "highest" levels of technology to progressive organizations. At this point in the internet's development, the web and email were not yet seamlessly connected, and email was a text-based communication tool without any of the images and graphics commonly included today. Because accessing the World Wide Web required much more technological infrastructure and personal expenditure than it took to use email, feminists focused on connecting people to email and other text-based tools.[19]

Even those who did not own a computer could benefit from email if they lived in places with strong information networks. Formal communication networks such as FEMNET in Africa and the Women's Feature Service in South Asia were well established. Other networks were more informal, made up of colleagues and friends. Because of these networks, in many parts of Africa, Latin America, and Asia, if one person set up an APC email account, a large group of people without accounts could gain access to information. Typically, when an important message came in through email, the point person would send the relevant information to a set of primary contacts. The recipients would distribute the information by fax to an even broader network of people, whose distribution tools included mimeographs, regular mail, hand-carried letters, radio, and word of mouth.[20] It was essentially a version of a phone tree that integrated the digital world with every available type of communication.

As email rapidly replaced the fax as the main correspondence tool used by feminists, colleagues in other countries had to school US activists in how to use it in ways that met their needs. Farwell said that for people in the United States, email etiquette had initially seemed straightforward: "I send you an email, you hit 'Reply,' you type back, and we go back and forth." The fact that the messages got longer and longer, because the previous message was included in each reply, seemed not to matter. In fact, it was often convenient to be able to look back on earlier exchanges when conversations stretched on. Yet at this stage of the digital revolution, some online service providers charged per kilobyte of information sent or received and several of Farwell's African and Asian colleagues worked in places with high usage costs. "We have to pay by data bit coming through," they told her. "Only email what you need me to see. Don't just hit 'Reply' and carry on." It soon became standard practice among the people in Farwell's and O'Leary's networks to delete the text from a previous email before sending a reply.[21]

To share information with colleagues who did not yet have access to the World Wide Web, O'Leary used a nimble tool known as a Gopher, which organized text files hierarchically and could be accessed through dialup modems. She built a Gopher for WEDO and used it to post about matters of import, like the drafting of the Beijing Platform for Action, and to share documents that would have otherwise gathered dust on an office shelf. Because the Gopher protocol was text-based, with no images, it was accessible to many who had limited online services. "There was also a simplicity about it that had appeal," she said.[22]

Around the same time, feminists began conversing with one another through text-based discussion boards. Some boards functioned mainly as sites for sharing news, while others provided forums for strategizing and preparing for UN conferences. "People act like Twitter and Facebook invented the ability for people to communicate for political or social change," O'Leary observed; in fact, the contributors to many of the earliest discussion boards devised a style of communication that was also conversational and highly interactive.[23]

Norms of engagement soon emerged. An unwritten rule required those who could easily access the internet to deliberately take breaks between their posts so that people who could not get online as easily had a chance to contribute. Many of these conversations were so rich that when new web-based technology became more widely accessible, the participants remained wedded to the discussion boards.[24]

One of the most exciting features of the universe emerging from the internet was that you didn't have to be a leader or an expert to create something new. When people planning to travel to Beijing complained about being unable to find basic information about the conference, a nightshift mainframe operator created a listserv. A single announcement for Beijing95-L resulted in her being "stoned" with subscription requests, and the list soon became one of the liveliest sources of information about the conference. Over six hundred people subscribed to the listserv.[25]

A more official and internationally oriented listserv, Beijing-conf, had sixteen hundred members and was sponsored by the UN Development Programme. But Beijing95-L served a particularly important function for US activists, who constituted half of its participants. In the months leading up to the event, Beijing95-L lit up with information about the conference, including the Chinese government's decision to move the NGO Forum from Beijing to Huairou; conference registration, visa, and hotel arrangements; the drafting of the Platform for Action; and the status of women in China. During the conference itself, the listserv posted continuous news and personal stories. At one of the workshops, the list's moderator received a standing ovation from an audience who viewed Beijing95-L as an "information lifeline."[26]

For the women who arrived at the NGO Forum not already hooked on the internet, a visit to the computer center usually converted them. Many relished learning how to discover new information online and send email updates to colleagues. Perhaps most important, they embraced opportunities to communicate with their families. It was September, the beginning of the school year in many countries. Those disappointed to have missed out on their children's first days of school took comfort in receiving email updates. Others used email instead of journaling, sending out reports of their daily activities to family and friends. Two weeks was a long time to spend in a foreign country and email helped alleviate some of the homesickness.[27]

Edie Farwell could relate to the thousands of mothers checking in on their youngsters. She had brought her one-year-old son with her to China so she could continue to breastfeed him and had hired her teenage niece to accompany her as a babysitter. In between feedings, Farwell's niece carried the baby around the grounds in a backpack carrier. Most of the activists the girl encountered assumed the baby was her son because they both had bright red hair. After hearing too many people muttering about the need for young girls to have better access to contraception, she put a sign on the backpack in nine languages: "It's my cousin."[28]

Awakened once or twice a night to feed her son, Farwell hardly slept for the three weeks she stayed in China. Yet she felt energized witnessing the skilled and determined women helping her to run the computer center. The majority of her team came from the Global South—they lived in countries such as Angola, Brazil, Ecuador, India, Tunisia, and Senegal. The eighteen languages they spoke included Arabic, Czech, Portuguese, Sinhala, and Wolof.[29] One of the US members had facilitated the transport of ten servers from Sun Microsystems in San Francisco to Huairou and the group had set up the two hundred workstations in the center by themselves.

Their ease in navigating this new technology presented a powerful model of female empowerment to the conference participants—and gave Farwell reasons to be optimistic.[30]

The technology center became one of the "hits" of the forum, with attendees opening seventeen hundred new email accounts and sending and receiving sixty-two thousand messages.[31] Some of the conference-goers felt so excited about the new skills they learned that they began teaching one another. For the staff, who were used to working in environments dominated by men, the opportunity to work collaboratively with other women was nothing short of exhilarating.[32]

A newspaper captured Edie Farwell helping a conference-goer navigate the internet at the computer center at the NGO Forum. *Courtesy of Edie Farwell.*

Barbara Ann O'Leary joined a group of technical specialists who worked through the night at the conference to extend access to information about the negotiations for the Platform for Action by translating documents and speeches and posting them online. She had recently left WEDO, and an independent UN reporting service had hired her as a contract worker and put her in charge of emailing its daily bulletin and posting it on the internet. The UN, the APC, and other outlets engaged in similar efforts and their work enabled people at home to track the drafting and lobbying and to send feedback via email to their representatives.[33] Discussions that would have once engaged only a few governmental delegates and leaders of major NGOs were now accessible to anyone with a modem and computer. Activists around the world responded eagerly, with the UN alone receiving 158,722 requests for files from sixty-eight different countries.[34] For those seeking to follow the happenings at the forum in Huairou, feminist websites and listservs posted updates and personal reports.[35]

Using new electronic tools in ways that foreshadowed the roles today played by Twitter and Facebook, people countered the mainstream media's lack of substantive reporting on the conference by developing their own world of alternative news coverage in cyberspace. "The volume of information was astonishing," said a journalist, after spending the good part of a day reading reports online.[36] The information available ranged from transcripts of the major speeches to descriptions of Bella Abzug's outfits. With a little digging, those who were interested in specific groups, such as lesbians or women of color, could find information about their particular activities. Even people who were at the conference began to depend on the internet for information about what was happening around them.[37]

When O'Leary was not posting documents, she was experimenting with online audio. She and a colleague recorded interviews with conference participants and posted them online. At the time, streaming audio was very new, and so O'Leary came up with a few strategies to make the information accessible. Because many people did not have the money or bandwidth to listen to a full audio interview, she broke them up into small sound bites. She also posted some text of the interviews next to the audio links so people could get a feel for the conversation without having to listen.[38]

Online feminism debuted at the Beijing conference. "We did it!" one of the technologists proclaimed afterward. What seems commonplace today—a vibrant alternative media offering a range of feminist perspectives on an event or issue—was unprecedented at the time. A Reuters reporter observed that there was "a simultaneous 'virtual' women's conference in cyberspace . . . giving Beijing '95 far broader reach and more immediacy than any global gathering in history."[39] That women were the ones navigating this technology made it all the more remarkable.

"Women's online activities soared throughout the world" as the result of Beijing, observed Shana Penn, author of *The Women's Guide to the Wired World*, one of the first feminist handbooks on digital organizing. The Beijing conference would spur thousands of US activists to build virtual communities that extended access to information and brought new voices into the movement.[40]

FOUR

HOW FEMINISM WENT VIRAL

The day after Sharon Rogers returned from the Beijing women's conference, she purchased a modem and called AT&T to have an additional phone line installed in her house. For several years, she had been using carbon paper to keep a record of the letters she regularly sent to close friends and family, the collection of which had become a de facto personal journal. She would send the top pages of the carbon to her mother, who would make photocopies and mail them out to her network. At the computer center at the NGO Forum, Rogers saw how email could streamline that process and also help her communicate more efficiently at her nonprofit job. When she got home, there was no turning back.[1]

Rogers wasn't alone in seeing the potential of the internet. By the end of the 1990s, anyone looking for feminism no longer needed to attend a march or a conference. All they needed was a modem, a computer, and a phone line. The internet enabled thousands of people—many of whom had been working and thinking in isolation, with no connection to established organizations—to become part of vibrant feminist communities. In chatrooms and on blogs, they created new worlds, interspersing fun and laughter with searing personal revelations and political analysis.[2]

Feminists' imaginative use of the internet prompted many of the same questions that arise in discussions of social media today: How can people create online communities without generating echo chambers? Can those who have full-time jobs afford to spend additional hours producing content for the internet with no financial compensation? How should internet forums handle disagreements, especially when conversations get nasty? To what degree do energizing and free-ranging online conversations translate into specific political victories? Even in the earliest days of the internet, activists foresaw and sought to grapple with these kinds of dilemmas.

Feminists' embrace of the internet in the nineties went largely unnoticed as the media focused the public's attention on a phenomenon called the "digital divide." People used this term to describe class, racial, and gender disparities in internet access, warning that if the divide was not addressed, those already disadvantaged would be left behind.[3] Although the disparities were real, commentators overlooked how quickly the gaps were closing. For example, the lack of mainstream news coverage representing African American perspectives on the 1995 O. J. Simpson murder trial drove many Black people to seek out and create alternative online news sources and discussions.[4] In 1997, one study found that African Americans were "online in impressive numbers." There were five million Black users, considerably more than press accounts emphasizing the digital divide suggested.[5] Similarly, whereas stark gender inequities persisted within the leadership of the technology sector, they weren't as dramatic on the ground: the proportion of women who were regular internet users skyrocketed from 15 percent on the eve of the Beijing conference to 50 percent in 2000.[6]

Beijing was a major catalyst in getting women online. It wasn't just the computer center that inspired them to turn to the internet in droves; many, like Sharon Rogers, were already looking for new, dynamic ways to engage with feminism. Rogers, for one, had been anticipating the Beijing conference for years, hoping it would help her transition to a career in international organizing. She had a Black father and a white mother; she identified as biracial, and later as a "woman of color." Going through life being perceived as someone from African descent, despite having ancestors who came over on the *Mayflower*, made her uncomfortable when civil rights leaders clung to "artificial" biologically based identities and opposed the inclusion of a "multiethnic" checkbox on the 1990 census. She gravitated toward "issue-based politics," where diverse people came together based on a shared commitment to a cause.[7]

Rogers's perspective had been fortified by the education she received as part of the "wave of women" that integrated all-male Columbia College at Columbia University in New York City in the late 1980s. She was one of the first students to graduate with a degree in women's studies. Learning how race and gender were social constructs helped her better understand her own identity and the world around her. After graduating, she entered the world of feminist policy advocacy, where she was disappointed to find organizations such as the National Organization for Women (NOW) and the National Abortion Rights Action League (NARAL) enacting agendas that did not fully address the experiences of women of color. Fighting for inclusion in these circles had grown tiresome; Beijing, she hoped, would point her in a new direction.[8]

Rogers's transition to international organizing happened in fits and starts over the decade, but the shift to using online communications was almost immediate. Before leaving for Beijing, her jobs with the YWCA and Planned Parenthood had required her to organize gatherings where supporters would pitch in by folding brochures and stuffing them into envelopes. For group communications, they relied on phone trees—a system where each person called would contact a few others. When important documents needed to be sent out, Rogers either mailed them or faxed them on machines that used rolls of thin thermal paper that darkened and curled after printing.[9]

But by 1995, post-Beijing, all of those methods were rapidly becoming outdated. Workshops held before the conference had trained activists to use the internet. Those who used the computer center in Huairou grew accustomed to using the technology daily. Rogers described the Beijing conference as a "critical turning point for my own use, and I think feminist use in general in the US, of internet technologies," with email and listservs quickly replacing phone trees and faxes. After returning to the States, she was able to blast email messages to many, many supporters with the click of a button.[10]

Established organizations such as NOW adopted new technologies in rudimentary ways. They still did the bulk of their fundraising through the mail (which many today continue to regard as the best way to raise money) but used the internet to streamline communications and share information about their activities. Early web pages for feminist organizations like NOW tended to be sparse. They outlined basic information, like the group's mission, history, upcoming events, and contact information, in a straightforward way, with few graphics and no space for site visitors to interact with one another.[11]

The growing numbers of websites representing marginalized groups opened new avenues for people searching for information about feminism. In the mid-1990s, Laila Al-Marayati, a gynecologist in Los Angeles, was thrilled to discover several websites discussing Muslim women's rights. It was a time when Muslim women's attempts to foster discussions about gender equality in their communities had been repeatedly shut down. Finding online spaces where other women were speaking their minds felt revolutionary—the internet felt like a place where people could not be silenced. Al-Marayati was so enthralled by the rich material she was discovering that when she took breaks between seeing patients, she would surf the web and print relevant articles to read in the evenings.[12]

She shared the most insightful ones with a group of Muslim women who had come together when the war broke out in Bosnia in 1992. After learning of the attacks on Muslim women and the ways rape was being used as a weapon of war, they felt compelled to act. Although Al-Marayati had a newborn and was starting her first job in a private medical practice, she carved out time to help form an interfaith group called the Women's Coalition against Ethnic Cleansing and traveled to Croatia to meet with other women's organizations. When she returned to the United States, Al-Marayati helped found the Muslim Women's League, an organization focused on dispelling stereotypes about the status of women in Islam.[13]

Al-Marayati's group organized a delegation of Muslim American women to attend the Beijing conference. They were united by their belief that too many people in the world assumed that Islamic laws were deeply misogynistic and that the women involved with the religion were complicit in their own oppression. After consulting scholars and conducting research on the internet, they drafted position papers about what the Koran actually said about the role of women in Islam. Their papers detailing Islamic teachings on topics such as marriage and divorce, women's health, and equal rights surprised many who assumed the Koran prescribed male domination. They created a website where they posted their papers so that anyone who was interested in these questions could find answers. Before long, people as far away as Asia had discovered the site—one of the few resources promoting faith-based arguments for Muslim women's rights.[14]

In anticipation of Beijing, Al-Marayati joined a few listservs discussing the UN event, at least one of which included Muslim men and women who felt uncomfortable with her group's efforts. They used the listserv to criticize some of the women in her group

Laila Al-Marayati (top center) with other members of the Muslim Women's Caucus at the NGO Forum. *Courtesy of Laila Al-Marayati.*

for not wearing traditional head coverings and for discussing domestic violence and the abuse of women by religious authorities. The critics believed that because Muslims faced so many attacks from people outside of their faith, they were all obligated to defend Islam in public. They considered the Muslim Women's League's airing of their "dirty laundry . . . a betrayal," said Al-Marayati. Witnessing how internet forums empowered people to say "slanderous" things that they would never have dared say to another human being in person gave her pause.[15]

After the Beijing conference, Al-Marayati grew increasingly weary of the tenor of the debates about Islam on the internet. She had a demanding full-time job, a young family, and was involved with the Muslim Women's League's efforts to organize summer sports camps for girls. She could no longer justify spending hours online fending off vitriolic attacks, particularly because doing so felt so unrewarding. Even some of the more cordial listservs had devolved into "shouting matches." The most frequent contributors and those who were the most aggressive and assertive set the tone.[16]

With online conversations among people who held different political perspectives bearing such little fruit, it is not surprising that most feminists who spent sustained time on the internet created self-contained communities. The 1997 handbook *The Women's Guide to the Wired World* devoted over a hundred pages to the growing numbers of websites for women, many explicitly feminist, with entire chapters listing those involving lesbians and women of color. Many of these sites posted feminist content but had little to do with organized feminism. The description of one such site, My Sistah's Room, said that it offered a space on the internet for women from the African Diaspora that included business listings, discussions of movies and politics, think pieces, and links to other Black women's websites. Another, Dykes, Disabilities & Stuff, offered a quarterly newsletter with news, reviews, essays, and art from lesbians with disabilities' perspectives.[17]

A host of lively personal websites and blogs penned by young people offered them new forms of community, augmenting and sometimes replacing the zines that had become mainstays for many budding activists. Young feminists had long prioritized producing and distributing their own texts as inexpensively and quickly as possible. In the 1960s and 1970s, they did this with mimeographed pamphlets and broadsides. In the early 1990s, they mailed out photocopied zines.[18] The internet seemed ideally suited to extending this kind of samizdat publishing. Feminist web pages sprang up. They were accessible at any time of day, from people's homes, schools, and workplaces, and they offered rich intellectual content, often coupled with humor and lighthearted banter. A 1998 *Ms.* magazine article found thousands of these sites addressing topics ranging from politics and poetry to sex and sports. Some young feminists remained committed to print, while others published print zines and e-zines simultaneously. Over time, growing numbers worked exclusively online, buoyed by the internet's capacity for publishing unlimited content and fostering immediate interaction with readers. At one online hub where eight zines linked their content, internet users could find a "BUST Lounge," where they could "talk to other Busties," and a "gURL palace," a graphic-heavy space filled with almost forty different web pages, many of them featuring chatrooms and interactive games.[19]

"The internet gave me brown people," recalled Elena Mary Costello Tzintzún. Born and raised in Columbus, Ohio, with a white father and Mexican mother, Tzintzún "grew up in extremes." In the mid-1980s, when she was six years old, her family lived out of a van. "My mother always says: . . . 'We weren't homeless. We had the van.'" After her father reinvented himself by becoming a stockbroker and then a vice president of a firm, the family settled in a primarily white community. In her high school of almost two thousand students, there were only a handful of Latinos, including two of her siblings, and around the same number of African Americans. Tzintzún struggled to find her place until she discovered the internet and started blogging. In the late 1990s, she became one of the founders of an informal community of "misfit people of color, trying to figure things out," several of whom identified as feminist. Calling themselves *Blogtitlan*, to signal the home they made for themselves online, they felt like a close-knit family, sharing intimacies and baring their souls online.[20]

Niche communities formed quickly online, as people seized opportunities to bond with others who they would never meet in person but who were going through similar struggles. In 1998, for instance, young women with disabilities discovered Gimp-Girl Community (GGC), a site geared toward teenagers who were grappling with what it meant to be a disabled person who was no longer considered a "cute kid." The founder of the site had left an abusive home and was struck by the number of other women who gravitated to the site who had either recently escaped abuse or were still experiencing it. GGC offered visitors information on disability as well as opportunities to take quizzes and participate in polls.

Questions ranged from "What was Einstein's disability?" to "Do you think the internet is a viable media for disability support and activism?" The liveliest parts of the site were the listservs and discussion forums, which divided the participants into even smaller identity-based groups. In the first year of operation, GCC launched Girlies, for young women with disabilities in transition to adulthood; QueerGirlies, for young queer women with disabilities; and QueerLadies, for queer women with disabilities.[21]

In these groups, the anonymity of the internet worked in people's favor; some took risks in sharing parts of their lives that they may not have felt comfortable discussing if they had to look one another in the eye. With such a unique subset of people participating in each forum, it was likely that even if no one else in the group had also had a particular experience, they would at least be understood.

As the sharing got deeper and more personal, people found it very hard to tolerate any dissent. Online communities often felt supportive because the participants empathized with one another and could relate to other people's experiences of feeling marginalized and disrespected by the outside world. A revealing incident happened on GimpGirl's QueerLadies listserv when a contributor opposed the inclusion of transgender people and bisexuals on the list, not recognizing that they had been integral to the discussions since the list's inception. "Is this not a site for LESBIAN women with disabilities?" she asked. "Why then are bisexuals and transgendered posting here?" A torrent of "vicious" opposition ultimately convinced the dissenter to permanently leave the list, but damage had been done. In a community that prided itself on being supportive, people had exchanged harsh words and many feared they would be excluded from participating. Activity on the listserv died off and it remained dormant for over a year.[22]

When the people managing some of the six hundred feminist listservs that sprang up during the 1990s realized how tense conversations could become, some tried to prevent conflicts by developing rules and standards of behavior to guide participants.[23] Most list-servs had a moderator, who was responsible for sending out each message and had the authority to reject contributions that did not adhere to certain standards. The moderator of the Feminists Against Violence listserv sent newcomers a message stating that she welcomed a diversity of opinions but would not tolerate "flaming" (personal attacks) or any statements that could be interpreted as misogynist. Anticipating snide remarks and overreactions, she urged list members to be patient with one another and to remember that many people were novices who were there to learn. She asked the experts on the list to take the time to explain why other people's statements were wrong rather than attack them for not understanding. For those just discovering the subject area, she encouraged asking questions rather than making assertions about topics they knew very little about.[24]

The early feminist web was in constant motion, with sites rapidly emerging, transforming, and disappearing. Some individuals would post content daily or weekly on their personal websites and then suddenly go dark. Others stuck around for years. In this free-wheeling environment, unheralded organizers such as Veronica Arreola emerged to help catalog the content and assist newcomers looking to connect. The eldest daughter in a Mexican American family in Chicago, Arreola had a strong work ethic that she attributed to being raised in an immigrant household. In 1985, when she was ten years old, Arreola's grandmother, who had not graduated from high school and who had a job in a factory, joined with Arreola's parents to save up money to buy the family a computer for Christmas. Arreola's father worked in a warehouse driving forklifts and her mother worked part-time as a receptionist, but they cobbled together the funds to buy a machine made by Texas Instruments. Arreola learned how to program simple games and honed her skills through high school classes in programming that her forward-thinking grandmother encouraged her to take.[25]

From a young age, Arreola had a strong sense of gender justice. One of the first protests she organized was in grade school, when the boys stopped allowing the girls to play soccer at recess. She talked her girlfriends into marching around the field chanting "Let us play! Let us play!" In high school, she identified with the character Lisa from *The Simpsons* as she fought for environmental protections and animal rights and served for three years as co-president of the Amnesty International club, organizing letter writing to free political prisoners.[26]

Entering college in 1993, she "dove right in" to the "resurgence of activism" inspired by the election of Bill Clinton. "This is it," she believed. "This is my time." She majored in biology but gravitated to women's studies and soon pursued it as a minor. Horrified by the Republican takeover of Congress in 1994 and the pledge made by the new Speaker of the House to enact a "Contract with America" that would lower taxes and shrink the size of government, she looked for guidance from a listserv she discovered called Women Leaders Online. It was the first listserv she ever joined and it connected her to a "vast network of amazing activists," including the writer Katha Pollitt, the media critic Jennifer Pozner, the organizer Bob Fertik, and the abortion rights activist Polly Rothstein.[27]

At twenty years old, she was too naive to be intimidated by these résumés. She dove right in, joining the chorus of complaints about the policies proposed by House Speaker Newt Gingrich. Arreola remarked that the kinds of things said in 2016 about President Donald Trump resembled the comments people made on the listserv in 1994 about Gingrich: "Can you believe what he just did!?" "How can we fight back?" The members of the list bonded over their hatred for Gingrich, but some differences of opinion emerged when discussing policy. Another woman on the list recalled that she received positive feedback when she discussed abortion rights or critiqued sexism in the media—the sorts of things on which everyone seemed to agree. But when she spoke about the threats facing poor women on welfare, the reaction was divided.[28] Those concerns weren't priorities for everyone; some of the middle-class women wanted narrower, more targeted agendas, which addressed the lived experience of people like themselves.

The online conversations of the late 1990s were informed by the mechanics of the technology. People did not have mini-computers in their hands 24/7, as they do in the social media age. Typing with ten fingers on full keyboards instead of with thumbs on a screen, feminists of the early digital era often wrote pages of text rather than snippets. Conversations could stretch on for days, even weeks, as people took breaks between posts and did not feel compelled to check in every few minutes. Sometimes this could diffuse a disagreement, and it gave ideas—and their authors—more room to breathe. Arreola, for one, preferred this slower pace to the "instantaneous" interactions that happen today on Twitter.[29]

Still, a place like Women Leaders Online was generative, and it inspired some women to pursue similar conversations offline, too. The discussions on the listserv, for example, spurred Arreola to volunteer with Planned Parenthood. The organization set up booths at street fairs and Arreola helped staff the tables, handing out information and free condoms. At several of these fairs, the Feminist Majority Foundation (FMF) had booths raising awareness about the Taliban's treatment of women. Rather than condoms, the FMF gave out packets of mesh from women's hijabs that fair-goers were asked to affix with a safety pin to their backpacks to draw attention to women's oppression in Afghanistan. (This was exactly the kind of rhetoric that Laila Al-Marayati was trying to counter.) Many years later, Arreola interpreted the FMF's depictions of helpless Arab women being forced to wear hijabs and needing rescue as disturbingly "imperialistic." At the time, she was so energized by the FMF's "Stop Gender Apartheid" campaign that she added a link to the cause to her personal web page.[30]

Arreola put up her website one year after joining Women Leaders Online. She began with one page documenting her love for the Chicago Cubs and another about the women's movement. In 1998, after a massacre at a middle school near Jonesboro, Arkansas, where an eleven-year-old boy and a thirteen-year-old boy fatally shot four girl students and a teacher and injured ten others, Arreola added a page on mass shootings. The Jonesboro massacre was the second deadliest school shooting in the United States up to that time, and Arreola's page linked to some of the writing about it that was emerging on the web, including analyses of the gender dimensions of gun violence. Jonesboro was followed the next year by an even deadlier incident at Columbine High School, where two seniors killed twelve students and a teacher before taking their own lives, provoking another moment of national mourning and self-reflection that played out on televisions as well as on people's computers.[31]

When Arreola needed a break from these heavy topics, she turned to lighthearted websites analyzing baseball and discussing the cult feminist television characters Xena the Warrior Princess and Buffy the Vampire Slayer. Both the baseball sites and the Buffy sites were linked to one another by "webrings"—a technological invention that people used to link similarly themed web pages. With the widespread adoption of search engines like Google still several years away, internet users relied on webrings to help them find sites that interested them. Each of the member websites in a webring had a navigation area at the bottom of the page that had "next" and "previous" buttons directing surfers to other sites in the ring.[32]

Arreola realized one day that while the webrings for Buffy and baseball were thriving, no equivalent webring for feminism existed. She set out to remedy the situation and appointed herself the moderator (or "ringmaster") for the country's first pro-choice webring. Arreola curated the content of the webring by approving and adding new sites. She called the webring "pro-choice," but it included sites featuring a range of feminist analysis, much of which was not directly connected to abortion. As long as the content supported women's control of their bodies, Arreola approved the site for inclusion. "These webrings that connected us were points of activism, especially for people who weren't in big cities like Chicago," Arreola said. She frequently received messages from people living in rural and isolated areas who did not know any other feminists and were thrilled to discover so many different perspectives.[33]

People needed ringmasters because the number of sites aimed at women was exploding. A host of them targeting the younger generation interspersed feminist consciousness raising with articles similar to those printed in women's beauty and lifestyle magazines. Their content included advice columns, television reviews, participatory polls (one asked readers if they shaved their pubic hair), and quizzes ("Are you over Your Ex?" and "What is your Skin Care IQ?"). On one such site, a voter guide for an upcoming election was presented alongside tips for beauty, fitness, and sex and a short-lived Dykes of the Month column, one of which featured the founders of the first mainstream clothing store aimed at lesbians.[34] Was this a clever way to introduce women who knew nothing of feminism to some of its ideas? Or was it a co-optation of feminism, a moderating of a radical movement to make a profit?[35]

"Our mission was to make pop culture . . . a feminist site of inquiry," reflected Andi Zeisler, a cofounder of *Bitch* magazine, which developed a major online presence in later years. Yet Zeisler and her colleagues could not stop other people from "watering-down" their ideas and turning women's empowerment into a brand.[36] One female entrepreneur who had a gift for catchy slogans started an initiative called *Webgrrls* to promote women's use of the internet. By 1998, Aliza Sherman had published *Cybergrrl: A Woman's Guide to the World Wide Web* and her website was receiving about two million hits each month. She was also making a good living through consulting work and paid speaking engagements. When people called Sherman's work feminist, she rejected the label. She cared about women's empowerment and took pride in refusing to work for the Miss America Pageant. Yet she got into the work "to make a living," not to contribute to a movement.[37]

As people lived more and more of their lives online, some of the problems they faced offline migrated to the internet. In 1993, for example, a young woman journalist penned a heart-wrenching article that brought to light the growing problem of online sexual harassment. Her account struck a chord with many readers because it described a scenario that was becoming increasingly common. The journalist was a member of an online discussion group that included men. In one of the conversations, she had posted a defense of the feminist punk movement known as the Riot Grrrls. A few positive comments inspired a stream of messages calling her an "evil cunt" who needed to "get a life" and "get fucked in the ass." Interspersed with the personal attacks came "reams of pornographic text detailing gang rapes." One harasser shared her email address under false pretenses with a web group for people interested in sexual bondage.[38]

Fearful that such incidents would deter women from the internet, feminists began offering advice for those confronting abuse and established websites to teach women how to avoid and curtail online harassment. It wouldn't solve the problem, but it would hopefully make women feel safer online. Women had been learning to regulate and self-surveil their behavior in public spaces for centuries, the thinking went, and the internet was a new public space. One of the first sites, named Working to Halt Online Abuse, offered tips to help people develop internet "street smarts" as well as guidelines for creating harassment-free zones on websites and discussion forums. The advice included using a gender-neutral username and gender-neutral email address so that others would not know whether users were women or men. Other tips included not entering too much personal information into online profiles and making those profiles accessible only to friends and family.[39] It was clear that life online was a funhouse mirror of life offline—and that likely the distinctions would only diminish over time.[40]

By the late 1990s and early 2000s, webrings had fallen out of favor. Yahoo had bought and altered the technology, and the company's efforts to route viewers through its own platform made webrings more difficult to access. In their place, feminists created specialized websites to catalog the rapidly expanding corners of the internet used by marginalized groups. For example, in 2001, the Grrrl Zine Network began cataloging over one thousand "grrrl, lady and trans folk zines" written in fourteen languages from more than thirty countries. One of the zines featured on the Grrrl Zine Network described itself as an "Italian grrrl distribution" featuring "female/aracha-feminist/queer/antisexist DIY stuff." Another was penned by a transgender man, who grew up in a rural, economically depressed and conservative area of Ohio. In 1999, as a college student in Athens, Ohio, he created the zine *Soldier,* which offered a personal take on trans and queer issues and critiques of mainstream society. He described online zines creating a "liberatory" space, free from the dictates of mainstream culture. Those participating in this alternative space were creating "pockets of resistance to a corporate-owned world."[41]

Many people's involvement in political debates took place almost exclusively in these liberatory spaces. Arreola's involvement in internet-based conversations spurred her to help out with Planned Parenthood, but many others did not volunteer for progressive organizations or pursue feminist careers as a result of their online activity. Most probably did not contribute money to social justice causes. What good were they doing for the movement? Were they even part of the movement at all?

A major goal of social movements is changing how people think. In that respect, the people contributing to the online conversations were extending feminism's reach. As a result of their efforts, more people than ever before were being exposed to feminist ideas—and generating their own. They were thinking critically about how their families and communities had shaped their identities and discovering how to interrogate norms that they had taken for granted. Some learned to embrace their marginalized identities, to become more comfortable and assertive at home and in their workplaces. The ideas promoted through women's studies courses and feminist nonprofits continued to influence people, to be sure. But more and more people were also caught up in the feminist dialogues happening online.

By the late 1990s, individuals from all backgrounds were encountering feminist politics, not through NOW or NARAL but through the online writings of women of color, activists with disabilities, and queer and transgender people. In blogs and discussion forums, these independent media producers raised people's awareness and established new networks and personal relationships. Their growing presence on the web contributed to a broader cultural shift in which people from all walks of life increasingly looked to the internet for community and cutting-edge analysis. When feminists embraced personal computers and modems, they chipped away at the power of mainstream organizations and corporate media outlets to define and shape their movements.

The internet was consciousness raising, and it could also be activating. Just as the twenty-first century's Women's Marches grew out of a single post that went viral, by the late 1990s, a small but growing subset of feminists had begun to use internet-based tools for collective action.

African American women were particularly adept at this kind of organizing, having established strong communication channels through two previous initiatives that relied on telephones and faxes. In 1991, Elsa Barkley Brown, Deborah King, and Barbara Ransby picked up phones to collect signatures and raise money to publish a statement expressing support for Anita Hill's testimony against Supreme Court nominee Clarence Thomas. "African American Women in Defense of Ourselves" ran in the *New York Times* with sixteen hundred signatures, each solicited individually. The statement condemned the racist and sexist treatment of Anita Hill and emphasized that the sexual abuse of Black women had been ignored and trivialized throughout the nation's history.[42] Three years later, a coalition of reproductive justice activists that included Loretta Ross and Toni Bond relied on the fax machine to send personal letters to a different but overlapping network of Black feminists. They collected over seven hundred signatures for a statement printed in the *Washington Post* detailing the necessity of including women of color in health care reform. Describing reproductive freedom as a "life and death issue" for many Black women, they called for universal health care coverage that included the full range of reproductive services, including abortion.[43]

When plans got under way for the 1997 Million Woman March, the organizers turned to the internet, hoping to tap into the growing number of Black women communicating with one another online.[44] The website for this African American women's march received more than a million hits in the months leading up to the event, with regional websites reporting additional traffic. Organizers urged those who had access to the internet to print copies of the text of their website and share the physical pages with friends, neighbors, and coworkers who were not yet online.[45]

As with Beijing, one of the takeaways from the Million Woman March was activists' realization that the internet made them less dependent on the mainstream media for publicity and endorsement—they could counter being overlooked by the media through their own channels. The grassroots mobilization that began online resulted in over half a million African American women from across the country marching from the Liberty Bell to the Philadelphia Museum of Art in the rain and cheering for speeches from the California congresswoman Maxine Waters, the South African political activist Winnie Mandela, and the actor Jada Pinkett—yet it wasn't a major focus of most media outlets. Foreseeing the disappointing press coverage, the march organizers took it upon themselves to solicit commentaries on the event and share the accounts through their networks. Several of the most striking stories included videos taken by attendees with camcorders. The leaders' success in mobilizing people online and crafting their own narratives about the event offered a model of internet organizing for the digital age.[46]

In the 1990s, most of the feminists who worked in established institutions and nonprofits, emboldened by the interactions happening on the internet, envisioned online tools supplementing, but not replacing, the human interactions that had long served as the bedrock of their organizing. When they dug into their work, whether at a domestic violence shelter or a reproductive rights advocacy organization, they still did most of it in person with other people, at workshops, meetings, and conferences. Emailing colleagues and sending messages to listservs did become part of their job description. But the labor involved in fostering the more freewheeling discussions and analysis happening on the internet remained largely uncompensated. People who made a living from organizing largely did so face-to-face—and more and more people were pursuing careers in feminism.[47]

FIVE

MAKING A LIVING FROM SOCIAL CHANGE

"We have accomplished a lot," Kata Issari, an antiviolence advocate, concluded at a conference organized by women of color in 2000. "But have we made a movement, or have we lost our way?" Issari put her finger on a paradox of organized feminism in the 1990s: While thousands were able to turn feminism into a career, promoting social change through jobs in the professions and the nonprofit sector, acquiring these new platforms came at a price. Activists needed to work together to forge broad-based coalitions to achieve their goals, but they were competing with each other for jobs and grants. And many feminists wanted to pursue ambitious initiatives that emerged from the grassroots, but most grant makers wanted to fund people with professional expertise and groups that offered discrete services and pursued specialized projects with short-term goals—initiatives that could be accomplished in a quick, targeted way. Although Issari and others warned that they were making too many compromises, once most activists got a taste for pursuing careers in feminism, they were hooked.[1] They might have had their doubts about the goals of the people who paid their salaries, but even the fiercest critics of professionalization were usually not willing to quit their jobs or forgo all forms of outside monetary support. Instead, they tried to make the most of their careers without compromising their principles or straying too far from their roots. It was a tricky balance to strike.

The nineties generation was not the first to earn a living from feminism. As early as the mid-nineteenth century, some women's suffragists and health reformers got paid for speaking to audiences on the commercial lecture circuit known as the lyceum. Though nominally middle class, many of them depended on the money they earned from lecturing to make ends meet. After the Civil War, the vast quantities of wealth amassed in what historians call the Gilded Age gave rise to a new form of charity that influenced the burgeoning women's movement. Wealthy individuals began to donate large sums of money to attack social problems. While Andrew Carnegie built impressive public libraries and John D. Rockefeller contributed millions of dollars to medical research, a small network of wealthy white women philanthropists (most of them single) gave money to promote white women's voting rights, access to higher education, and reproductive rights.[2]

Many of these elite women instructed the recipients of their monies on how to spend the funds. The same was true in the civil rights movement, where donors in the early twentieth century redirected the National Association for the Advancement of Colored People's focus away from combatting lynching and mob violence and toward equal education. Then, as now, the power of philanthropists to use their wealth to determine the direction of a movement often annoyed the activists who depended on their financial largesse.[3]

In the postwar period, growing numbers of feminists sought to promote social change through their jobs in the nation's professional workplaces. Small contingents of feminists had long fought against the sexism and racism they experienced while holding jobs in established institutions; by the 1990s, they were shaking up male-dominated professions, such as journalism and law, that underpinned modern life. Feminists carved out niches in academia and in churches, seeking to make these institutions more hospitable to women and minorities and to use their professional platforms to ally with people organizing for social justice in other arenas. Many feminist professors, for example, taught about social change in their classrooms and stood up for greater equality within the university while networking with local community groups. Some people even fought for equal opportunity and protection from sexual harassment and homophobia in the Armed Forces—the most masculine of all institutions.[4]

By 1998, the political scientist Mary Fainsod Katzenstein pointed out, with so many struggles arising from the nation's workplaces, the movement no longer relied solely on the "placard-bearing activists" whose pickets, sit-ins, and marches had attracted the attention of journalists in decades past. More and more people were learning how to collectively push back against injustices from within the workforce, whether it was by standing up to their bosses or finding ways to harness institutional resources to promote social change in the world at large. Although it is impossible to quantify the dispersed forms of activism that emerged from professional settings because they were rarely counted or reported in the mainstream media, they were "prolific" and multiplying.[5]

Those who held jobs in the exploding nonprofit sector experienced the contradictions Issari spoke of most acutely. Many of their organizations relied on volunteers to show up for events and disseminate information, yet by the 1990s, almost all of them also had paid staff who relished the opportunity to live out their politics by pursuing careers in social change. Many had concluded that sustaining organizations exclusively on volunteer labor was no longer practical. Some had become mothers and could no longer put in late nights and weekends for the cause. Even those without children had grown weary of fitting activism into their limited spare time, particularly because most had full-time jobs.[6]

Linda Burnham was typical of many. She joined the ranks of feminism's nonprofit workforce after spending the 1970s and 1980s as a volunteer in the Third World Women's Alliance and the Alliance Against Women's Oppression. Occasionally, a donor would "kick in a few hundred dollars" to help fund these Black women's organizations' activities, but no one received a paycheck. During this period of her life, Burnham distanced herself from a US feminist movement she considered too "far removed from the realities" of those who confronted poverty and racism. Over time, however, she joined many other women of color who were claiming feminism as their own and finding ways to earn a living from their callings.[7] In 1989, longing to live an integrated life in which her work was not separate from her politics, Burnham took a risk and cofounded a nonprofit in Oakland, the Women of Color Resource Center. At first, she supported herself with part-time work at the city attorney's office, but after putting together a board of directors and applying for nonprofit status, she made feminism her full-time job.[8]

Burnham lived paycheck to paycheck. Like many in her situation, she had mixed feelings about asking others for money. It was hard not to feel as if she was supplicating herself to elites who were patronizing and out of touch with the realities of working people's lives. Subsisting on only a few small grants, the Women of Color Resource Center amassed a modest annual budget of $25,000, which covered Burnham's salary as well as the center's every expenditure. For years, Burnham never took a vacation. She worked late nights and weekends just to keep the center afloat. Health insurance and most creature comforts were out of the question. "The place would have folded a long time ago, if I hadn't been stubborn and . . . really healthy," she reflected. Still, not a day passed when Burnham did not feel fortunate. She could have made more money and worked much less hard in another profession, but it would not have given her the sense of purpose she felt at her center.[9]

Others were making similar choices. The women's health activist Loretta Ross said that she felt eternally grateful that she no longer needed to join the millions working at soulless jobs to support herself and her son. In the 1970s, after attending Howard University, she had worked in Washington, DC, as a secretary by day and a waitress by night, staying up late in the evenings reading books for a storied Marxist-Leninist discussion group. On weekends, she participated in Black nationalist politics and tenant organizing. Discovering the writing of the Black feminist bell hooks was a revelation. In 1979, a job directing the DC Rape Crisis Center offered her an opportunity to put the theorist's call for Black women to claim feminism into practice. ("If ever a book built a movement, [hooks's manifesto] *Ain't I a Woman* did it for us in DC," she later said.) The crisis center that hired Ross was broke and she had to put some of the money she received from an insurance settlement into its coffers to keep the doors open. She supplemented her income by typing people's theses and dissertations in the evenings. Yet working full-time for a feminist organization felt like a gift. Compared to waitressing, being paid to fight oppression was a "privilege" that made her feel "like a rich woman."[10]

Ross went on to hold a variety of paid positions in social change organizations through which she became intimately acquainted with the growing number of philanthropic foundations that were subsidizing feminists like her. Between 1981 and 1996, the number of foundations in the United States nearly doubled from twenty-two thousand to thirty-nine thousand, and the value of gifts made to them more than doubled. Because the Internal Revenue Service required foundations to give away at least 5 percent of their assets each year, as their wealth grew, so did their grant making.[11] Established feminist organizations sometimes could get grants from longstanding funds such as the Rockefeller Foundation, but smaller groups were more likely to seek out independent "Women's Funds," which sprang up to compensate for the relatively small proportion of money given to feminist causes by mainstream philanthropies. By the mid-2000s, nearly 150 Women's Funds across the country gave approximately $60 million each year to groups working to improve the lives of women, people of color, LGBT communities, and people who were poor.[12]

Though it never seemed like enough, there was money to be had for those who knew where to look and how to get it. Between 1990 and 2006, established foundations responded to pressure from feminists to increase their giving toward gender equality by doubling the amount of money directed at women and girls.[13] Meanwhile, foundations focused on women such as the Ms. Foundation for Women and Astraea National Lesbian Action Foundation funded some of the most innovative grassroots social justice work in the country aimed at empowering marginalized groups.[14]

Ross herself had the most contact with the Ford Foundation, which had become a stalwart supporter of feminist causes. In the 1970s, a contingent of women employees had pressured Ford to address the sexism within its own workplace and to fund initiatives to eliminate gender disparities in the world at large. By 1980, Ford had dispensed more than $30 million to support projects aimed at increasing opportunities for women, with many focusing on minority and working-class women.[15] Ford cemented its reputation as a champion of gender equality with the appointment of feminist Susan Berresford as its president in 1996. During her twelve years at the helm, the foundation greatly increased its funding of organizations led by women of color, of groups addressing LGBT issues, and of initiatives targeting low-income women and their families. Women such as Ross, who had once seen major foundations as out of reach, were increasingly drawn into the fold.[16] But that didn't mean the money always went where the organization heads felt it was most needed.

A particularly telling interchange involved the UN conferences of the 1990s, which the Ford Foundation saw as crucial training grounds for activists confronting a globalizing world.[17] Ross was part of a group of African American, Asian American, Latina, and Native American reproductive health activists that Ford funded to attend the 1994 UN Conference on Population and Development in Cairo and the 1995 Conference on Women in Beijing. Ross, by then a seasoned international activist with many connections abroad, embraced the opportunity to attend these global conferences. But several of the people in her cohort, whose organizations faced pressing needs at home, were not as confident that spending thousands of dollars on international travel would pay off.

Ford was offering to foot the bill, though, so the women embraced the opportunity and hoped it would serve as a gateway to future funding. They returned home brimming with ideas about how they could use the lessons they gleaned from their sojourn abroad only to find that Ford would no longer fund them. Ross, rather cynically, wondered whether Ford preferred for them to be "political tourists" rather than rabble-rousers in the United States.[18]

Nevertheless, a few years later, Ross and some of her travel companions got together with several other women of color reproductive health activists to see whether a Ford program officer would take a chance on them. Although they had decades of experience and tremendous expertise on issues ranging from HIV/AIDS to the new implantable contraceptive Norplant, they seemed to have little chance of snaring a major grant. Some were the only staff members of small organizations. None had personal connections to major donors who could write them large checks.[19] They were caught in a catch-22: foundations typically required organizations to present a track record of managing substantial budgets before awarding sizable grants, but most organizations couldn't demonstrate ability to manage large amounts of money without grants from foundations.[20]

Ross had grown tired of watching organizations of women of color receive grants in the range of $5,000 while a "Planned Parenthood might get a $50,000 grant from the same foundation." It was particularly galling when foundations gave Planned Parenthood grants earmarked for "outreach" to women of color—instead of providing that money directly to the Black, Latina, Asian American, and Native American women's health organizations working in the field.[21]

Yet, lo and behold, at a 1997 meeting in New York City, representatives of these groups convinced a Ford Foundation program officer to put her entire $4 million budget toward the development of what became one of the most influential women's health organizations of the twenty-first century. Program officers have a tremendous amount of influence on how a foundation's money gets spent. Typically, potential grantees first have to convince an officer that their ideas are worthy of a proposal submission. If, after reading that proposal, the officer is still interested, the grantees work closely with them to fine-tune the approach. In a back-and-forth process that often takes several months, program officers advise grantees about the specific kinds of work a foundation will and will not fund as well as how they would need to assess and report back on their effectiveness. The goal is to anticipate any potential criticism so that when the officer brings the proposal to the rest of the foundation's staff, everyone agrees that the program should be funded.

Some program officers were extremely hands-on in soliciting and helping to craft the proposals they championed. Such was the case with Alexandrina "Reena" Marcelo, who asked a member of the Latina Roundtable on Reproductive Rights to convene a meeting of the leaders of grassroots women of color health organizations so she could consider possibilities for funding them. By the end of the meeting, Marcelo had concluded that they could do more together than apart. She helped sixteen organizations—four Latina, four Native American, four African American, and four Asian American—form a coalition through which Ford could funnel large sums of money. They eventually named the coalition Sister-Song: Women of Color Reproductive Justice Collective.[22]

The founding members of the coalition had impressive résumés and proven track records of pioneering new approaches to issues ranging from mental health to fetal alcohol syndrome.[23] They all had different specialties, but they united in their commitment to reproductive justice—a concept Black women health care activists had invented in the early 1990s to capture the essence of women of color's historic struggles for bodily autonomy. To them, reproductive justice meant the human right to have children, to not have children, and to parent in safe and sustainable communities. The coalition members embraced the concept because it encompassed their diverse efforts to help women achieve better health and greater control over their own bodies.[24]

Binding together as a multiracial collective rather than working along parallel lines in separate networks helped SisterSong members accomplish something most fledgling organizations could not: successfully push back against a program officer who suggested taking their work in a direction they felt was unwise. Marcelo asked them to develop a series of initiatives tackling reproductive tract infections, a women's health issue she believed needed much more attention. The organizations told her that before they could set their sights on programmatic goals, they needed to do bricks-and-mortar "capacity building": hire paid staff, recruit a board of directors, develop bookkeeping and budgeting systems, and file for 501(c)3 status to allow donors to make tax-deductible contributions.[25]

It was an audacious request for them to make. Nonprofits across the country had been complaining for years about program officers choosing only to fund high-profile new initiatives, leaving staff members scrambling to find ways to pay for the unglamorous, behind-the-scenes work of building their infrastructures. Ross described Marcelo as an "angel" for meeting their request and awarding them three years of funding for capacity building.[26]

One of the first things they did with those three years was practical and educational. They organized a series of trainings on the running of a nonprofit: how to write grant proposals, develop institutional policies and procedures, build boards of directors, set up account books, lead and manage volunteers and staff, and navigate the Internal Revenue Service. Doing this work collectively was more cost efficient than doing it separately and it helped them foster personal ties because it required them to spend extended periods of time with one another. They brought consultants in to speak with them and taught each other. Over time, they employed conflict-resolution processes to help them with some of the disagreements they were having as they considered how to structure the collective and work for change as a group. "Any time you form a coalition, you've got conflict," Ross observed. With so much money at stake, choosing which people would take on leadership roles in the running of the collective inevitably brought considerable tension and stress.[27]

Ford saw the value in the meetings and training, but the foundation initially drew a line when the organizations listed the purchase of electronic equipment as part of their budgets. Most of the activists were thrilled at the prospect of purchasing photocopiers, fax machines, and computers—all of which had become standard fare in many nonprofit workplaces (and, in fact, in many US workplaces of the nineties). When they learned that the foundation had a policy that precluded using grant money to purchase equipment, they were outraged. To some, it seemed like a racist practice that was preventing them from becoming technologically proficient; their better-off white peers would already have such machinery.

Marcelo was sympathetic and open. After listening to their concerns, she told them that she would ask her supervisors to look into the restriction on equipment purchases. With a little research, foundation officials discovered that the ban was a myth; no such policy existed. The result was a windfall for SisterSong, and for all the groups that have received funding from Ford to purchase equipment ever since.[28]

Ford funding made such a difference in Alice Skendandore's career that she referred to herself as "the poster child" for Sister-Song. She had taken an interest in the politics of women's health during her pregnancy in the 1970s, when she became part of an underground community of lay midwives in Las Vegas who helped deliver each other's babies in their own homes.[29] In 1992, she returned to Wisconsin, where she had grown up on an Indian reservation, and started a Native American women's health collective. They met weekly for entire days around her kitchen table, discussing topics such as parenting and alternative medicine. Invited to speak at a local health fair, she gave a passionate account of the benefits of home birth and midwifery that attracted Ford's attention, resulting in an invitation to participate in the SisterSong meetings. With a three-year Ford grant for $150,000, she rented a storefront and opened Wise Women Gathering Place to offer community health services and practical advice. One of her SisterSong colleagues described her as an "unstoppable" force. Making use of the skills she learned in the trainings, she applied for a variety of grants and was soon bringing in "all sorts of private and government funding."[30]

Skenandore had grasped a lesson learned too late by some of the other SisterSong members: relying on a single funder was too risky. After the three years of capacity building, Marcelo had promised them a second phase of support that would enable them to develop new programming. But before that phase even launched, Marcelo left Ford. The new program officer hired to replace her took the portfolio in a different direction, and SisterSong lost its funding. Without the Ford money, SisterSong almost folded. Several organizations did drop out and it took years for the collective to recover.[31]

Antiviolence activists learned a related set of lessons as they watched the infusion of grant monies change the character of their grassroots movements. In the 1970s, when Suzanne Pharr helped found the first domestic violence shelter in Arkansas, she never could have dreamed that, within a decade, such work would be funded by the government, and that people everywhere would become aware of and outraged by violence against women. This transformation began in the 1970s and early 1980s with small groups of feminists in cities and towns in every region of the country creating referral centers and crisis lines. Many took the victims into their own homes, making available their spare bedroom or their couch, providing food and clothing. Over time, the groups acquired separate apartments and houses to serve as shelters. The one in northwest Arkansas was purchased by three female professors and run by a group of volunteers, most of them white like Pharr. They helped the residents realize they were not to blame for their predicaments and taught them about the structural forces that made all women economically and socially vulnerable to male violence. Pharr and her colleagues believed that their movement would be stronger if it was led by people who had directly experienced such situations, so they encouraged abused women to participate in their advocacy work and join the staff of the shelters and crisis lines.[32]

Over the next two decades, Pharr watched the rise of free-market Reaganomics transform the antiviolence movement in an unexpected way. With the Republican president seeking to reduce the size of the government through tax cuts and the slashing of social welfare programs, while transferring previously federal responsibilities to the states, many state agencies offered contracts to nonprofits to provide human services. It was a windfall for those running or looking to start shelters and crisis lines. Yet Pharr was skeptical. She was glad that some of the money she paid in taxes was being used to provide people with essential resources, but she was left with a nagging question: Could such services put an end to the societal problem of violence against women or were they merely stopgap measures?[33]

Whatever the answer, Pharr's movement soon began to splinter, as some activists embraced governmental funding while others tried to maintain their distance from it. Pharr and her peers had learned about violence against women by talking to victims; they put their faith in community-based movements led by those most affected by these issues. The government, meanwhile, preferred to fund social workers, who had learned about domestic violence in graduate school. These professionals saw violence against women as a mental health issue and offered victims therapy and resources like food pantries and subsidized housing.[34]

As chair of the Lesbian Task Force for the National Coalition Against Domestic Violence, Pharr felt increasingly uncomfortable as she encountered growing numbers of people in the field with service-oriented rather than social change visions. Finding a safe place for victims to live was important. But what about treating all women as potential contributors to feminism? One disappointed activist put it starkly: feminism was becoming "a dirty and unspoken word" in the new, tamed antiviolence circles.[35]

Over time, Pharr bumped into another unintended consequence of the professionalization of social movements: competition. The more she extended her networks, the more she saw progressive groups fighting for "crumbs of money" instead of working together. Most disheartening was that activists were keeping secrets from each other instead of sharing their plans for the future. Many told her that they needed to hold their plans close to their chests because they feared rival organizations would steal their ideas. Opting out did not seem possible. How else could they pay for their work? "When you drop a basket of food among very hungry people, very few people stand back and say, 'Oh, I won't compete,'" Pharr later recalled.[36]

Pharr drew a line when she thought that activists had compromised their political principles to secure money. She had seen her colleagues in the antiviolence movement being particularly susceptible to this kind of compromise because of the availability of governmental funding, on which they were increasingly dependent. They learned that people holding the purse strings often got to dictate the message. In 1985, for example, when the Department of Justice granted the National Coalition Against Domestic Violence over half a million dollars to conduct a public education campaign, the coalition used some of the money to raise awareness of the links between domestic violence and other forms of oppression such as racism and homophobia. The first government-funded publication it released used the words *lesbian* and *woman abuse*. When the Justice Department insisted on the removal of those words (claiming they were too narrow because men are also abused), the request threw the coalition into turmoil. After heated debates, they refused to change the wording. The government withdrew the funding. It wasn't long before a rival group formed to take the money, leaving the coalition permanently weakened and the antiviolence movement deeply split.[37]

Growing numbers of activists agreed with the National Coalition Against Domestic Violence's refusal to rely on governmental funding. Ross's rape crisis center had received a few governmental grants in the 1980s, but after she left the center, she took pride in working for organizations that did not receive any governmental funds and could freely advocate against state policies they thought were misguided. "Not that I've asked [the government for funds] and not that they've offered." Ross laughed. "It's kind of like détente."[38] For some of those whose advocacy involved participating in international coalitions, rejecting US governmental funding was not only principled but also practical. Many activists from other countries saw the United States as a destructive and imperialist force in the world and refused to partner with US activists who received money from their government.[39]

For feminist media outlets, navigating the world of advertisements and sponsorships presented a similar set of moral quandaries.[40] Committed to working only with "like-minded organizations," the editors of *Bitch* magazine faced vexing decisions in their first decades. Started in the mid-1990s after its founders, Andi Zeisler and Lisa Jervis, were inspired by a panel they attended about zine publishing in the Bay Area, *Bitch* by 2001 had received assistance from a press association that helped its creators scale up the commercial side of their enterprise and make it into their full-time job. They weren't running a shelter or an advocacy group, but they had incorporated as a 501(c)3 and had to grapple with many of the same tensions between their values and their finances.[41]

In one instance, an independent record label asked *Bitch* to run an advertisement featuring an image of naked and bloody women that offended readers, who turned to the magazine for its feminist take on popular culture. A few years later, the editors faced another moment of reckoning when American Spirit cigarette company proposed a long-term funding partnership. The offer came at a time when they could barely cover their bills. A regular infusion of cash would have put them on stable financial ground for the first time in the magazine's history. Yet they knew many of their subscribers would feel uncomfortable supporting a publication funded by Big Tobacco. With the staff unable to come to a decision, *Bitch* put the question to its readers. The overwhelming response was for *Bitch* to reject the money. So it did.[42]

It was different for organizations with wealthy constituencies. The National Organization for Women (NOW) refused grants from foundations, corporations, and the government. Yet it could annually raise millions of dollars from direct mail campaigns and major donors. At best, most grassroots groups could expect a few thousand dollars from membership dues and individual donations. The proceeds they made from bake sales and car washes could not cover a single staff member's salary, or even a year's rent.[43]

What to do? Those grappling every day with the compromises involved in navigating the world of funding began to wrestle with this question practically and theoretically. They used the term "nonprofit-industrial complex" as shorthand to refer to the government's increasing reliance on nonprofits to provide human services and to the system of grants and funding that deterred people from pursuing ambitious and radical agendas.[44] In writings and public presentations, they analyzed how the growth of this nonprofit-industrial complex was fundamentally reshaping their movements.[45]

Women of color who worked in sexual assault and domestic violence prevention led the way in developing these analyses. After the passage of the 1994 Violence Against Women Act, much of the funding for their field came through the Department of Justice. This encouraged organizations to pursue solutions to violence against women that relied on the criminal justice system; some groups even located their offices within local police departments. Many of the women of color who were part of these organizations found such practices troubling. They believed imprisonment and fines did little to prevent abuse—in fact, such measures often made things worse by ensnaring people in a punitive and racist legal system. For years, they had urged their white colleagues to consider adopting strategies to end violence that didn't involve judges or the police. Instead of focusing on such punitive measures, they suggested programs devote resources toward organizing victims to press for broader societal changes. After making very little headway with most white colleagues, in 2000, they formed INCITE! Women of Color Against Violence. Within just a few years, this organization had modeled alternative forms of organizing against violence and fostered vital conversations among feminists about the policy implications of governmental funding on their work.[46]

At first, INCITE! opposed all governmental grants for antiviolence work but embraced the possibility of receiving funding from private foundations. A small grant from the Ms. Foundation helped launch the organization and its members continued to apply for grants from a range of philanthropic institutions.[47] However, seeds of doubt were planted during a trip that some members took to India, where they met activists taking principled stands against all forms of funding. Another formative moment occurred in 2004, when the Ford Foundation awarded INCITE! a $100,000 grant and then suddenly withdrew the offer. INCITE! believed Ford's about-face came because someone at the foundation read a powerful statement it had published on its website in support of the Palestinian cause (even though Ford provided financial support to Palestinian organizations as part of its overall grant making). Regardless of Ford's reasons, the power of a foundation to reshape an organization's agenda could not have been clearer.[48]

That same year, INCITE! organized a national conference of progressive activists to reflect on the implications of the nonprofit-industrial complex. "The Revolution Will Not Be Funded" conference in Santa Barbara, California, drew hundreds of community organizers, activists, service providers, and scholars. In one of the widely quoted speeches, Suzanne Pharr described how compressed funding cycles and grant givers' insistence on "deliverables" led too many nonprofits to focus on short-term measurable achievements (such as serving a particular number of clients) rather than meaningful long-term goals that would build movements that could press for more systemic change.[49] She and others echoed critiques of foundations that had been aired by activists for many decades, charging that the philanthropists behind them were invested in maintaining the status quo. Philanthropy was aimed at preserving a capitalist social order that engendered dramatic societal inequality, the activists suspected. Those with money doled out just enough to tame the rage of those who had the least rather than fund transformative initiatives that would put foundations out of business. Pharr ended with a rousing call for the crowd to look beyond the grant-seeking process and rekindle the joy and sense of possibility that first drew her and so many others to the movement.[50]

Though some assumed the speakers involved in the "Revolution Will Not Be Funded" conference were calling for people to quit their paying movement jobs and stop writing grant proposals, IN-CITE!'s position turned out to be rather more nuanced. The main takeaway was that the nonprofit-industrial complex was caught up in the system of global capitalism. Since it was not possible to organize outside of capitalism, almost every form of organizing would require activists to make concessions. INCITE! hoped the conference would help them think about how to preserve their integrity while navigating a fundamentally flawed system.[51]

By the mid-1990s, feminists recognized that every form of activism was "replete with its own contradictions," observed the sociologist Claire Reinelt. With so many now dependent on salaries or grants, there were no easy answers to questions about whether their work was "contributing to women's liberation or simply to more sophisticated forms of oppression." This was a world in which a program officer at one of the country's most influential foundations provided millions of dollars to launch a multiracial reproductive justice collective. But it was also a world in which feminists working on behalf of victims of violence were facing trenchant critiques of their reliance on the government and their entrenchment in the legal system. People were trying to forge coalitions, but they existed within a grant-making system that compelled many of them to compete with each other. Few people, it seemed, could engage in political action without compromising in some way. "Instead of denying this reality," Reinelt observed, "feminists . . . accept this as the condition of their activism."[52]

It was a lesson that successful activists of all kinds would have to learn.

SIX

"WOMEN'S RIGHTS ARE HUMAN RIGHTS"

When First Lady Hillary Clinton took the stage at the Beijing Women's Conference, the world was listening. Dressed in a powder-pink business suit with large gold buttons, she exuded confidence and a sense of purpose rarely on display at home. "If there is one message that echoes forth from this conference, let it be that human rights are women's rights and women's rights are human rights once and for all," she proclaimed. It was a triumphant moment for Clinton—a desperately needed win after her failed attempt to reform the US health care system. Few recognized that it was also a victory for the international networks of feminists who had dreamed up the slogan. They now witnessed it becoming part of a global lexicon.

Clinton never claimed she coined the phrase "women's rights are human rights," but many people in the United States assumed that she had. The First Lady's speech captured the public's attention. The international feminist movement that had come up with the slogan did not. Most journalists and pundits assumed that US feminists engaging in policy advocacy would focus their efforts on Capitol Hill. They missed the outpouring of feminist activity happening throughout the 1990s at the United Nations, in which US women joined forces with women from other countries. Some of the US activists who participated in this international lobbying were lesbians and women of color. Almost all of them had been part of US-based social movements fighting on behalf of those most oppressed. Yet in the global arena, they were all seen as privileged, representing a racist and imperialist country. Though the learning curve for these activists was steep, and people from other countries viewed them with suspicion, many ultimately grasped how to collaborate and develop common goals with people with very different life histories. They built lasting relationships across cultures rooted in shared histories of struggle, while finding joy and a sense of purpose in such work. "The way we change the world is we change ourselves," one activist said. The US feminists who joined international networks did both.[1]

The activists of the nineties knew that prior attempts at international coalition building among feminists had been rocky. Yet with the end of the Cold War offering new possibilities for alliances, they resolved that this time would be different. Some earlier failed efforts had pitted white North Americans, who emphasized the need for legal equality, against Africans, Asians, and Latin Americans, who focused on the problems posed by militarism and poverty. By the end of the century, though, the rise of neoliberalism and the growth of fundamentalist movements led many to believe that all their problems had similar roots—and that they shared common goals. Growing numbers of US activists followed women of color and other radicals before them in acknowledging their own country's history of imperialism and looking to chart a different course.[2]

Over time, increasing numbers of US feminists found ways to be part of the international women's networks that had been developing since the 1970s. In the early 1990s, these networks took by storm a series of major UN world conferences focused on the environment, human rights, and population and development. The world's governments had expected to address women's issues at the Beijing event in 1995; they had not expected gender to be on the agenda of these earlier conferences. But the feminists who entered these international spaces taught governments that women's issues were *everyone's* issues, bound up in matters typically considered to be "gender neutral" such as the environment and economic development. Implementing feminist agendas could improve conditions in entire countries, they believed, and so they lobbied for each conference's goals to include the promotion of women's rights. To achieve such lofty objectives, activists from different parts of the world worked together to present a united front.[3]

Charlotte Bunch considered the 1985 UN World Conference on Women in Nairobi to be a turning point for global feminist coalition building. In the 1970s and early 1980s, UN conferences and other international meetings had been instrumental in introducing activists to one another and providing them with opportunities to work together. Yet Nairobi was special because over 60 percent of the participants came from the Global South, and the cumulative effect of their presence on women from the rest of the world was undeniable. Bunch was familiar with the thriving feminist movements in many parts of Asia and Latin America, but this was the first time she encountered large numbers of activists from African countries other than South Africa.[4] Coming upon an international feminist movement with leadership from the Global South was powerful for a young woman who had grown up in a small New Mexico town and fantasized about world travel. In the early 1960s, as a student at Duke University, Bunch had participated in the campus YWCA and Methodist Student Movement, joining local civil rights and antiwar demonstrations. When Black Power advocates eclipsed the moderates in the civil rights movement, excluding potential white allies such as she, Bunch became one of the first female fellows at the left-wing Institute for Policy Studies in Washington, DC, and helped start the DC women's liberation movement.[5]

"The mood and era was one of people separating to create their own issues," Bunch recalled of her experiences in the early 1970s. In 1971, she joined a lesbian-feminist collective called The Furies, whose members included the photographer Joan E. Biren and the novelist Rita Mae Brown. Living communally and cutting ties with men gave The Furies a unique perspective on patriarchy that was reflected in the feminist theory they published, which rejected "male" values of competition, aggression, and acquisitiveness.[6] Soon, however, Bunch came to reject "the purist assumption" of separatism, which held that men or straight women could never join their revolution. A small group of people with exclusionary politics could never create change alone, Bunch realized. She began to think that it was more important to choose her allies based on their political commitments rather than their identities. As she moved into international feminist circles, where she represented a country with a checkered history, she hoped others would afford her the same courtesy.[7]

In 1979, Bunch moved to New York City, where she embarked on the international phase of her career, traveling the world to talk and learn about women's rights. When invited to attend a small international workshop in Bangkok sponsored by the Asia and Pacific Centre for Women and Development in preparation for the 1980 Second UN World Conference on Women, she was nervous about how she would be perceived there as an out lesbian. But she found that most people she encountered respected her for not hiding that part of her identity and some were curious to understand how it connected to her feminism. The experience reinforced the lessons she had learned while organizing for civil rights: it was impossible to work well with others without staying true to oneself.[8]

As Bunch considered how she could contribute to international feminism, the civil rights movement offered a model. People of color had long sought to collaborate and act in solidarity with movements for social justice in other countries, but many white activists were slower to catch on. In the 1970s and 1980s, however, Bunch saw US activists of all kinds supporting liberation struggles in Vietnam, Central America, and South Africa.[9] Recognizing that her US citizenship and degree from an elite university gave her certain privileges, Bunch—like many others coming into a greater consciousness—wanted to use her privilege to make a difference.

Bunch noticed that some of the US women participating in international feminist meetings seemed not to understand what many foreigners saw as the poisonous legacy of US imperialism. She cringed when they presented themselves as experts on international development rather than as feminist partners in a common struggle. Like the social workers who were increasingly staffing the domestic violence shelters, they had good intentions and academic pedigrees but had not been schooled in social justice and feminism. Bunch gravitated to a different group of US women working internationally who had similar backgrounds in progressive organizing. They resolved to create something different by interacting with feminists from other countries "as activists in parallel movements."[10] Instead of talking about women who weren't from the United States, Bunch and her cohort would talk *with* them.

It wasn't just talking. Being a good partner in a parallel movement involved a lot of listening, too. Bunch watched and learned as feminists from different regions of the world built coalitions that did not include or focus on North Americans. In Latin America, for instance, feminists from different countries gathered to debate issues and forge relationships in conferences called *encuentros*, held every two or three years. Likewise, members of the influential Global South coalition Development Alternatives with Women for a New Era (DAWN) cultivated bases of support within their own countries and then gathered to collectively develop policy recommendations for international development.[11]

Bunch thought hard about what it would take to create an international network in which feminists from North America and

Europe could participate fully, but not dominate. During the 1980s, she was watching for such opportunities as she pursued consulting work that kept her moving between national workshops on feminism and international meetings. On her travels, she noticed tense conversations across national lines involving US activists—but also several instances that inspired hope. The more hopeful discussions involved US activists finding ways to establish common ground with women from other countries, based on shared issues in which they all sought strategies for change. What made for a substantive, coalition-building dialogue? A lightbulb went off when Bunch realized that many of the most generative ones she had witnessed focused on control of women's bodies and especially violence against women.[12]

She landed on this insight at a perfect moment. In the leadup to the 1985 UN women's conference in Nairobi, activists from each continent had independently identified gender-based violence as a major problem; they succeeded in having it mentioned in that UN gathering's *Forward Looking Strategies*. In 1981, the first feminist *encuentro* for Latin America and the Caribbean, held in Bogota, Colombia, had declared November 25 as "International Day against Violence against Women."[13] Before a global movement that involved US feminists could coalesce, however, women like Bunch had to prove that they could listen to and learn from their counterparts in Asia, Latin America, and Africa. It wasn't easy, because they had centuries of history to overcome. Most activists across Asia, Latin America, and Africa were well versed in the history of Western colonialism and US imperialism, and their perceptions of the persistence of global power imbalances made them wary and suspicious.

US feminists learned about practices in other countries such as *sati* (the ritual burning of a widow on her husband's funeral pyre), dowry deaths (the murder or alleged suicide of women in response to harassment intended to elicit or increase family dowry payments), and female genital mutilation. Most viewed these customs as far more horrific than anything regularly happening to women in the United States. The Global South activists who opposed these practices in their home countries challenged such Western interpretations. What made these forms of violence worse or different from domestic violence, rape, and partner abuse/murder in the United States? They argued that gendered violence in the United States needed to be considered analogous to the violence against women in other places. Why did Bunch and her counterparts not view their country's high rates of wife abuse and murder through a similar lens?[14]

For many US activists who had been working on violence against women in the United States as part of local movements, this formulation was surprising at first, but the more they considered it, the more it made sense. The beginnings of a genuine dialogue took root, not by looking askance at other countries for their alleged backwardness but by sharing critiques of their own cultures. "The basis of working on feminism, in any kind of global way," Bunch said, is "realizing that you are going to be challenged, and you are there to learn and to grow as well as to share your own authentic experience."[15] As a white person working in the Black-led civil rights movement, she had learned not to abscond when faced with difficult conversations, especially when she was contradicted or felt uncomfortable. Some US activists became defensive when people from other countries challenged their beliefs. Bunch encouraged them instead to step back and listen. They could earn trust by responding genuinely to other people's concerns and acknowledging the privilege that they gained on the world stage simply because they lived in the United States.[16]

Rather than trying to solve other people's problems, Bunch encouraged US activists to think more deeply about how what happened in other countries connected to what happened in the United States, and how they could learn from others. She believed it was incumbent on them not to sensationalize what was happening elsewhere but to expose the terrors women faced in their own country in order to share approaches. The idea was that they were all trying to change their own cultures and stop the oppression of women and could benefit from hearing about each other's strategies rather than ranking oppressions.[17]

In 1987, a position as a visiting professor at Rutgers University gave Bunch a platform to put these principles into practice. As she ran events and seminars, she sought to foreground and learn from the voices of people from Asia, Africa, and Latin America whose experiences had been marginalized. Yet she tried to do this without silencing the North Americans or the Europeans. She believed their experiences and critiques of their cultures and governments were also vital. "We're all part of the problem; we're all part of the solution," she said. "All our voices have to be heard."[18]

When feminists from different parts of the world listened to each other, they kept returning to a question that would come to define their collective campaign: Why did appeals for human rights exclude the problem of violence against women? In focusing on human rights, they were invoking discourses that had served as powerful declarations of the dignity of all people for centuries. The civil rights claims that US social movements often promoted were more limited. Civil rights protected citizens from discrimination and granted specific rights such as equal protection and due process—but they could only be granted by nation-states. By contrast, human rights were universal, inalienable, and inherent for every person. Because every person in the world had dignity and worth, every person had fundamental rights that could be defined and defended independently of governments. What those fundamental rights were and how they should be articulated was—and remains—the subject of intense debate.[19]

In the aftermath of World War II, Latin American feminists had advocated for the inclusion of human rights in the UN Charter and successfully lobbied for that document to promote the equal rights of women.[20] Yet, in the 1970s, NGOs such as Amnesty International, as well as human rights–based campaigns against Latin

American dictatorships, had focused on offenses that were not gender specific and usually on men who had been taken as political prisoners.[21] Over the next decade, women in these human rights movements began to speak out. A 1981 issue of *Human Rights Quarterly* featured a collection of articles that explored the implications of women's human rights.[22] Mothers who had organized during Argentina's "Dirty Wars" to demand the return of their children and grandchildren (whom the regime had "disappeared") started to assert their rights as humans rather than as women. In Pakistan, when attempts to argue for women's rights in religious terms created controversy, activists reframed their demands in the context of human rights. Meanwhile, women from different parts of the world began to criticize the male bias implicit in definitions of war crimes that excluded rape and other forms of sexual torture. Bunch summed up what was happening: "Good ideas . . . [often emerge] simultaneously from more than one source."[23]

Bunch first heard the slogan "Women's Rights Are Human Rights" from a Filipino women's coalition called Gabriela. As part of the protests against the dictatorship of Ferdinand E. Marcos, they launched a Women's Rights Are Human Rights campaign in 1988. For Bunch, this "catchy and provocative . . . phrase . . . immediately clicked" as a succinct way of expressing what women around the world had been arguing. The slogan caught on, not because it came out of left field but because it perfectly encapsulated an ongoing conversation.[24]

Some feminists had to work hard to convince male-led human rights groups to address their concerns. Men had argued that violations against women such as rape and domestic violence fell outside their human rights purview because they happened in the private sphere, rather than being governmental crimes. US women presented their arguments to Amnesty International and Human Rights Watch, while women from other countries went to their national equivalents. They asked how these human rights advocates could claim to promote the "liberty and security of person" and the right not to be subjected to "torture or cruel, inhuman or degrading treatment" without taking seriously sexual assault and wife beating as well as the deprivation of food, clothing, shelter, and gainful employment to women. Meanwhile, feminists who were working within human rights agencies also put pressure on their male colleagues and bosses to address women's rights. By the late 1980s, they enjoyed some success. Several NGOs, including Amnesty International, launched women's task forces and initiatives.[25]

But for many women's human rights activists, the ultimate prize was the UN, and they set their sights on that. At first, they doubted whether they could take on such a towering institution. Who would listen to them? On what grounds could they testify? But they reminded each other that there wasn't a single successful social movement in the history of the world that had waited for permission before acting. Indigenous peoples had been using human rights paradigms to lobby the UN for decades—and no one had invited them to do so. The activists seeking women's equality resolved to enter halls of power and define human rights for themselves.[26]

They grounded their arguments in the Universal Declaration of Human Rights. Article 2 of the declaration protected everyone "without distinction of any kind such as race, colour, sex, language . . . or other status." Other sections of the declaration asserted that everyone has the right to "life, liberty and security of person" and "no one shall be subject to torture or to cruel, inhuman or degrading treatment or punishment." Today, the idea that the declaration includes the protection of women's rights and prohibits gender-based violence seems "logical—even undeniable," Bunch remarked. But when activists went to the UN making this demand, the idea that the declaration could protect women from rape and domestic violence felt revolutionary.[27]

In 1989, Bunch's visiting position led to a more permanent appointment as the founding director of the Center for Women's Global Leadership (CWGL) at Rutgers—thus also scoring a win for the women's human rights campaign, because the directorship gave one of the coalition members a powerful platform. Within two years, the center's annual budget was half a million dollars. One-third of the funding came directly from Rutgers, and alumni, other donors, and foundations made up the rest. Bunch used the money to pay for events bringing groups of people from different countries together at Rutgers to craft strategy and to fund international colleagues with smaller budgets to be present where social change was happening. Attending meetings around the world was an essential part of talking through and lobbying on these urgent feminist issues, and one needed a seat at the table to decide what was on the agenda. At a most memorable summit in 1991, Bunch organized the first two-week Women's Global Leadership Institute, where activists from across the world came together to share ideas and strategize about the future.[28]

Some of the invited guests viewed Bunch with suspicion; they felt uncomfortable organizing inside a country they still regarded as an empire. They appreciated the plane ticket but were disturbed by the fact that Bunch had the power to decide who got invited to meetings. It was not unlike the sentiment raised by some women of color activists regarding the selection of the Ms. Foundation delegation to Beijing. Bunch listened to the concerns, and acknowledged that her ability to choose the participants reflected a power imbalance. But she stressed that she was trying to wield her power in an ethical way by inviting activists representing different regions of the world, all of whom were connected to grassroots struggles in their own countries. As she saw it, her new position offered her a golden opportunity to raise large sums of money to advance their collective cause and put activists in the middle of developing conversations who might not otherwise be able to shape discourse. What good would it do for her to refuse to apply for that money? Waging an international campaign was going to be expensive. People from every continent would need to come together and spend days at a time working side by side. Only substantial cash infusions could make that happen.[29]

And there were large sums of money to be had. Major US foundations such as Ford believed social movements needed to be more globally connected and were funding activists to attend UN conferences. They were regularly awarding grants for hundreds of thousands of dollars to US-based feminist organizations working internationally, such as the International Women's Health Coalition and the Women's Environment and Development Organization (WEDO), which was run by the former US congressperson Bella Abzug.[30]

Bunch was no shrinking violet, but next to Abzug, anyone would seem demure. Abzug wore her trademark wide-brimmed hats, which gave her a bit of height and projected into others' space. In this final chapter of her storied career as a changemaker, she had turned her attention from domestic politics toward international feminism and environmentalism. Although some found her overpowering, she was also adored. When she traveled to international conferences, she drew a crowd. Women from all over the world approached her, showered her with hugs and kisses, and praised her courage at taking on world leaders. Abzug's daughter Liz observed that her mother connected with people who came from very different backgrounds because she loved to dance and sing and exuded "tremendous heart and compassion, particularly for underdogs and people who had to fight to survive and subsist."[31]

No one ever doubted who was in charge at WEDO, but Abzug hired a multiracial staff and chose an eminent global board of directors she knew would stand up to her. Their ranks included the Indian environmentalist Vandana Shiva and the Kenyan founder of the Green Belt Movement Wangari Maathai (who was awarded the Nobel Peace Prize in 2004). Abzug forged strong ties with them and many other international activists in part because she seemed "authentic." She did not try to hide the fact that she was "a brash New Yorker, Jewish," her assistant Jessica Halem explained. "She wasn't doing yoga and pretending to be Namaste."[32]

Bunch was a powerful public speaker, but behind closed doors, her manner was less abrasive than Abzug's. She had a unique talent for getting people to participate and be involved in any given conversation; the goal was for everyone to feel like they could be heard and contribute to specific strategies to push the movement forward. So many attempts at coalition building had been derailed by rival factions all looking to address fundamental problems concerning women's rights. Naturally, because the stakes were so high, tempers flared when people disagreed about the best way to protect women. In decades past, debates about prostitution and sex trafficking had elicited bitter fights, and those debates had never been resolved. When these issues came up at Bunch's leadership institutes, rather than try to gain a consensus, Bunch steered the groups to agree to disagree—and to focus their attention on initiatives they could all support. They left the first institute with a plan to promote women's human rights in their local communities and at the UN's World Conference on Human Rights scheduled to take place in Vienna in 1993.[33]

The plan included the launch of "16 Days of Activism Against Gender Violence" held between November 25 (International Day for the Elimination of Violence Against Women) and December 10 (Human Rights Day), in which activists in different parts of the world designed awareness-raising actions that suited their local contexts. Most of them also participated in gathering signatures on a petition calling on the UN World Conference on Human Rights "to comprehensively address women's human rights" and to recognize "gender violence, a universal phenomenon which takes many forms across culture, race, and class . . . as a violation of human rights requiring immediate action." "The petition was not just to be signed," said Bunch. It was an "organizing tool" for activists to raise awareness of the meaning and implications of women's human rights in their local communities.[34]

The human rights activists were not alone in aspiring to set a feminist agenda for a UN conference. The early 1990s played host to many such opportunities, with major conferences held in rapid succession addressing the protection of the environment as well as population and development policies. With big foundations offering significant financial support, several other burgeoning global feminist networks working on environmental protection and reproductive rights also saw these UN events as ways to advance their campaigns by inserting themselves into debates that typically did not include women's issues. Rather than spend their time only at the NGO forums, they would target the governmental meetings where delegates from every country gathered to produce platforms articulating shared goals. Feminists wanted their perspectives to be represented in those platforms.

Abzug blazed a trail by helping to organize feminist environmental groups to influence the 1992 UN Conference on Environment and Development in Rio de Janeiro. The first draft of the action plan referred to women's issues only a few times, in the poverty section. Abzug and her colleagues believed feminist goals were part of nearly every single issue. Emphasizing women's roles as stewards of the environment and their expertise in sustainable development, the activists argued that none of the conference's goals could be accomplished without promoting the rights of women. They began lobbying two years in advance of the conference. Rather than attempt to insert themselves in the policymaking process at that final event, which turned out to be mainly a formality, done after all the substantive conversations had already taken place, they learned that they could gain a hearing if they swarmed the earlier regional and international "Prepcoms." Prepcoms were where delegates drafted most of the language considered for inclusion in the conference documents.[35] Prepcom attendees set the tone for the conference.

At these meetings, Abzug introduced feminists to a vital tool for effecting policy change: the caucus. Modeled in part on the National Women's Political Caucus that she had helped found in Washington, DC, in 1971, those participating in the women's caucuses held at UN meetings devised language for UN documents.[36] A typical women's caucus was, according to economist Radhika Balakrishnan, an "amazing organizing place . . . totally global . . . whoever came from around the world, we'd meet, we'd strategize, and work." The problem they were addressing was that even authorities who were on their side did not know how to rewrite the UN's documents to reflect feminist concerns. Such meticulous work required specialized, insider knowledge. So these activists drafted hyperdetailed memos outlining the specific sentences and phrases they wanted deleted and added to the documents, dictating and debating as one member typed. Like lawyers arguing in front of the US Supreme Court, they gave the authorities "precedent-setting" information that showed how their demands built on accepted norms within the United Nations. Previous UN-based lobbying had mainly involved activists interacting with delegates on an ad hoc basis. By collectively giving voice to feminist needs in caucuses, drafting text, and distributing it to governmental representatives en masse, they achieved far better results. Sympathetic governmental delegates appreciated the strategy because they could advocate for the passages that the activists had drafted instead of having to write their own.[37] It saved time, but it also avoided confusion. Feminists were asking for exactly what they wanted.

One activist described drafting the memos as akin to "writing a collective term paper." Nearly every single word proposed for inclusion or deletion came under intense scrutiny around conference room tables and hotel room floors. Balakrishnan regularly stayed up well past midnight talking as her fingers flew across her keyboard, hoping to reach a consensus. Although she and other US activists benefited from English being the most widely spoken language among the coalition, they were not given any special treatment. "We were American women in a global movement, not American women separate from a global movement," Ritu Sharma reflected enthusiastically.[38]

Young and idealistic, Sharma struggled to find a place for herself in the caucuses. Several times, she approached women from other countries and told them that she was from the United States and wanted to help them. Some were "outright mean," while others tried to be tactful, but they all responded the same way: "We don't need you to come down . . . to try to help us." Many told her they were doing just fine addressing their country's problems and that instead of trying to get involved in matters she knew little about, she should devote her attention to addressing the destructive policies of her own government. It was an important lesson for a budding feminist eager to right past wrongs and promote greater equality on the international stage. "I . . . got . . . beaten up pretty good," she said. When she returned to the States, though, she took their words to heart. In 1998, she founded Women Thrive, an organization that influenced US foreign policy on behalf of women and girls living in poverty in developing countries.[39]

Even seasoned players who knew not to talk down to others needed thick skins to survive the caucuses. Tensions between activists from different regions of the world and resentments over US leadership and power simmered in the background. In the heat of the moment, some people said cruel and disrespectful things. Others blew off steam by gossiping and making snide remarks.[40] But there were also attempts to provide comfort. After a particularly contentious day in one of the WEDO caucuses, two of the participants tried to alleviate some of the stress by giving a shoulder massage to the woman in charge. At another, someone brought in a massage chair and hired a masseuse.[41]

Yet they returned every day, from early morning until late at night, energized by the fast pace of the work and sense of common purpose. The rooms buzzed with energy as people marked up official documents and tried to convince others to sign onto their proposals. Gallows humor emerged after spending hours holed up in windowless rooms. So did unexpected friendships. In Cairo, Balakrishnan seized the opportunity to work with a brilliant human rights lawyer she had admired from afar. In Copenhagen, she became "attached at the hip" to a Brazilian reproductive rights researcher. In Beijing, lesbians from across the world bonded when their caucus was assigned to a bordello-like room in an elite gentlemen's club that featured naked women etched into the glass doors. The intensity with which everyone approached the tasks at hand

and the incredibly fast pace at which they worked created a visceral sense of being in struggle together.[42]

The drama built when they fanned out to convince governmental authorities to support their recommendations. Some carefully placed stacks of memos on people's desks. Others, armed with binders and folders with pages spilling out, ran through the hallways tracking down potential supporters. One recalled a meeting in which governmental authorities were surrounded by activists sitting on the floor taking notes. When the officials took a coffee break, the women swarmed them and handed them stacks of documents. A select group of activists joined the official meetings of working groups convened to address certain sections of the documents. One described intense all-day negotiation sessions, fueled by handfuls of raisins and almonds.[43]

The bonds between the activists deepened outside of the halls of the conferences. Over meals in local restaurants, people would catch up on what had happened at the conference that day. They would get personal, too, sharing stories about their lives. Sometimes small groups would meet up in one person's hotel room, plotting strategy and eating snacks. Occasionally, they set out on adventures. In Cairo, a small cadre of Jewish women from Mexico, Brazil, and the United States gravitated to each other on Rosh Hashanah and found a temple where they could attend services. When they arrived, they were surprised to encounter fellow conference-goers from all over the world—including Bella Abzug. Few could understand the prayer books or service, which were in Hebrew with no translations. Yet they took comfort in the ritual and the mingling afterward over the traditional refreshments of apples and honey.[44] After one of the Prepcoms in New York City, a local activist introduced several Latin American colleagues to one of her favorite haunts—a Latin drag queen club called Escuelita near Port Authority bus terminal. They were delighted to learn that one of the Mexican women in the group was a "superb and indefatigable" dancer, and they partied until four in the morning.[45]

Working collaboratively to pull off special feats was particularly bonding. In Vienna, when the women's human rights network gained a spot on the main conference agenda, they made the most of the attention. They carted in stacks of the signed petitions they had been collecting (almost half a million signatures from 124 countries) calling on governments to address women's human rights at every level of the proceedings.[46] Bunch joined Florence Butegwa, the director of Women in Law and Development Africa, to deliver a rousing statement (from the Global Tribunal on Women's Human Rights held in the NGO area) describing their claims not as "an appeal on behalf of a special interest group but rather a demand to restore the birthright of half of humanity." The dramatic performance concluded with one of their Zambian partners calling for a minute of silence. With her stopwatch held high in

Left to right: Charlotte Bunch (USA), Asma Jahangir (Pakistan), and Florence Butegwa (Uganda), speaking at a press conference held by the Global Tribunal on Women's Human Rights during the 1993 UN World Conference on Human Rights in Vienna, Austria. *Reprinted by permission of the Center for Women's Global Leadership, Rutgers the State University of New Jersey.*

the air, she asked delegates to remember all the women around the world who would die or be badly injured by domestic violence during that minute. No one would ever forget the impact of that moment.[47]

As global feminist networks chalked up one victory after another at UN conferences, people began to realize they were part of something very special. Thanks to feminists, the final version of Agenda 21 (the plan from the 1992 Rio environmental conference that had, initially, barely acknowledged women) mentioned women in *hundreds* of places, stating that they played a crucial role in issues ranging from desertification and deforestation to the management of toxic chemicals and the protection of the world's oceans.[48] The same was true of the Vienna Declaration on human rights one year later. The preamble asserted that "the human rights of women and of the girl-child are an inalienable, integral and indivisible part of universal human rights" that should "form an integral part of the United Nations human rights activities." The body of the document included nine paragraphs on "the equal status and human rights of women" and identified women's human rights as a matter of importance in a number of other sections.[49] In Cairo in 1994, too, feminist reproductive rights activists built on work they had been doing for decades to successfully challenge long-held beliefs about population and economic development held by many governmental authorities. They poked holes in arguments assuming poverty could be alleviated partly through "population control," a practice that frequently involved coercing women to use contraceptives. The "Cairo Consensus" recognized the feminist argument that strong economies depended on the promotion of women's rights and reproductive health.[50]

The crowning achievement was the Beijing Platform for Action, which upheld the previous victories and made even more advances. The 132-page document asserted an expansive definition of women's human rights. It conceptualized women's empowerment and participation in decision-making processes as fundamental components of peace and global prosperity.[51] Women's rights were human rights, the Beijing Platform affirmed.

Still, it didn't please everyone; there were grumblings and disappointments. The Beijing Platform was framed around human rights, which some criticized for being Eurocentric and universalizing, unable to account for women's diverse experiences. Others emphasized that human rights were meaningless without economic rights. They argued that the women spending thousands of dollars on airfare and hotel rooms to lobby at the UN did not pay nearly enough attention to women's poverty.[52] The group of activists who stayed up until four in the morning trying to get the term "sexual orientation" included in the Platform encountered such intense opposition from conservative countries and the Vatican that they had to settle for a statement affirming women's rights to make sexual decisions free of coercion and violence.[53] But the way the entire UN works was changed as a result of feminist efforts; soon, other social movements modeled their strategies on the ones that had brought the feminists such success.[54]

Prepcom by Prepcom, conference by conference, feminists had shown what could be accomplished through the UN. When they returned home, many tried to use documents from the conferences to spark public conversations about women's rights and to extract concessions from their governments. The documents were nonbinding but could still be used as tools for raising awareness and political lobbying. Even in the United States, a country known for being hostile to UN directives, people developed recommendations for implementing resolutions in the Beijing Platform for Action in their communities, advocacy organizations, workplaces, and government.[55]

In a certain sense, the Beijing Platform marked the end of an era for feminists. Over time, much of the money for international conferencing dried up as donors moved on to new sets of priorities. Moreover, the rise of conservative and fundamentalist movements placed those feminists who remained involved at the UN increasingly on the defensive. Activists around the world still use the UN documents from the 1990s to spark conversations with ordinary people about their rights and to pressure governments to live up to their promises.[56] But while some remain committed to ensuring that the UN responds to feminist voices, the far-reaching UN-based activism of the nineties has also taken on new forms.

Maybe this is because what mattered was not just the documents themselves but the process of crafting and advocating for them. "It wasn't about the UN," explained Bunch, a remarkable statement from someone who had spent years of her life battling inside its hallways. "It was about women building a movement and utilizing the space that the UN brought to us . . . to affect ideas and policies more broadly." The ideas they promoted—that women play a role in every single international issue and that gender equality is a prerequisite for a flourishing nation—have lived on and transformed how people around the world understand and debate global politics.[57]

The ties between the activists who were on those front lines also persist. Today, when Bunch reads a concerning headline and wants to find out what is really happening in another country, she phones or emails one of her friends from the women's human rights network. One US activist observed that the friendships she forged with people from other countries at UN conferences would be there "forever" because of the intensity of the work they did together. Working side by side "deep into the night," sharing meals and swapping stories, they created relationships they continue to draw on and treasure. "The fact that you were in that struggle together," she said. "That's what builds a movement."[58]

SEVEN

TACKLING WOMEN'S POVERTY FROM GLOBAL PERSPECTIVES

In the 1990s, anyone who cared about women's poverty cared about the fate of welfare. Many were horrified to see President Clinton leading a full-scale assault on the Aid to Families with Dependent Children (AFDC) program, which had provided public assistance to single mothers for over six decades. Some activists tried to stop this speeding train, but opposition to the program had been growing for nearly half a century. Democrats had been its reliable defenders and so when the leader of that party decided to eliminate it, those who opposed that decision could not put on the brakes. In 1996, with bipartisan support, Clinton signed the Personal Responsibility and Work Act, eliminating single mothers' entitlement to welfare.

It was a crushing defeat, to be sure. But many of the feminists who fought for welfare were in it for the long haul. They saw the speeding train's path as just one vector of a worldwide system of global capitalism that was responsible for exacerbating the economic inequalities and hardships confronting women and girls throughout the world.

The pundits and journalists who fixated on the welfare battles on Capitol Hill did not report on the feminist researchers and organizers who believed a worldwide problem needed global solutions. These US activists understood that the practical experience of a peasant in rural India differed from that of a mother thrown off welfare in Baltimore. But many came to believe these problems had similar roots. What could activists learn from one another, across countries and circumstances? A great deal, it seemed.

There was, however, no consensus among US feminists on what the most effective strategies were. Some saw the greatest promise in the microcredit programs used in countries like Bangladesh, which tried to literally use capitalism to fund poor women, encouraging them to operate small businesses by offering them very small loans that helped them expand nascent money making ventures. Others gravitated toward a very different set of theories promoted by radical feminist economic thinkers from the Global South, who argued that capitalism had harmed poor women and sought to fundamentally reshape the world's economic order rather than adapt to it. Others, working at the grassroots, drew inspiration from an international movement for wages for housework—a bold declaration of the economic value of women's unpaid labor.

The activists who promoted these revolutionary approaches challenged conventional prescriptions of mainstream economic thinking. They also defied what the public understood to be conventional practices of feminism. Some organized in arenas, such as churches, that had long been important to subsets of feminists but that were not typically part of the public's perceptions of the movement. Stymied by politicians at home, many lobbied international institutions like the World Bank and the UN. Boldly tackling the worldwide problems of poverty and inequality, these feminists pushed for access to the world's most influential economic thinkers and tried to convince them to grapple with the human costs of global capitalism and its deleterious effects on women.

In the early 1900s, when state governments had provided pensions mainly to poor white single mothers, those programs hadn't raised much public ire. Most of the uproar and the ugly stereotyping emerged after World War II, when the federal program Aid to Dependent Children (the precursor to AFDC) became associated in the public mind with unmarried Black women migrating from the South to the North. Although more white women still received welfare than any other group, Black women had started pressing for equal access to the program.[1]

Over time, the idea that welfare primarily served African American women was promoted by the media and politicians alike. In 1965, Assistant Secretary of Labor Daniel Patrick Moynihan wrote a report on Black families that drew on racist stereotypes and set the terms for public debates. A liberal, Moynihan hoped his study would convince the Democratic president Lyndon Johnson that racial equality would never be achieved purely through civil rights legislation: economic policies were needed to address the poverty many Black families confronted. Yet what came to be known as the "Moynihan Report" charged that the roots of that poverty stemmed largely from the "pathology" of Black family structure—he singled out the high rates of African American single motherhood and welfare recipiency as particularly problematic. In 1976, when the former California governor Ronald Reagan was seeking the Republican presidential nomination, he introduced the specter of the "welfare queen," claiming that women abused the system and collected as much as $150,000 a year. That rhetoric caught on. People began to claim AFDC was a system of entrapment: Why would someone get a job, they argued, if the government paid them to do nothing? That argument ignored the economic contributions of women who worked full-time in the home. By 1989, 64 percent of Americans believed that welfare benefits "make poor people dependent and encourage them to stay poor."[2]

Welfare became even harder to defend as some white feminists emphasized the idea that a job outside the home could be liberating and the economic squeeze on families meant that middle-class mothers' employment became the norm. With more white middle-class families depending on two incomes, growing numbers of women began to face the reality of paid work as a requirement for survival rather than a choice. This shift underlay the increasing public antagonism to AFDC, which followed a similar logic to the blowback about so-called entrapment. If middle-class women had to sacrifice time with their children to enter the labor force, the reasoning went, why should the government support poor women to stay home?[3] During the 1980s, the "supply-side" (or "trickle-down") economic policies promoted by President Ronald Reagan reinforced this perspective. The core tenets of "Reaganomics" were that taxes, governmental regulation, and spending on social programs such as welfare hampered economic growth.

Meanwhile, the Democratic Party abandoned the Keynesian economic thinking that had protected welfare for decades. As early as the 1970s, conservative Democrats had joined Republicans in blaming high inflation and high unemployment on regulations that protected workers and instituted controls on markets. These "New Democrats," who gradually took control of the Democratic National Committee, promoted free-market capitalism and the reduction of the social safety net. Bill Clinton embodied this approach, which came to be known as the "third way." Believing that the Democrats needed to take votes from the GOP to reclaim the highest office, he neutralized Republican critiques of his party by declaring the "era of big government is over." During his 1992 campaign, Clinton promised a "new covenant" between citizens and government that would replace welfare "entitlements" with programs that promoted market-based "empowerment."[4]

Two years later, Republicans were able to form majorities in both the House and the Senate for the first time in forty years by intensifying their attacks on governmental spending. The "Contract with America" of House Republican leader Newt Gingrich promised support for small business owners and relatively well-off white married wage earners while disparaging governmental support for the poor, and particularly AFDC recipients. Clinton responded by doubling down on his attempt to chart a middle path. To win back white moderate and conservative voters, he supported a crime bill that led to increased policing of minority communities and secured support across the aisle for the elimination of AFDC.[5]

The AFDC cause seemed doomed, but supporters of the right to welfare continued to battle. A recipient-led welfare rights movement had emerged in the late 1960s, when chapters operating in nearly every state and major city fought against the stigma of public assistance and campaigned for more generous benefits, including a guaranteed annual income.[6] The National Welfare Rights Organization disbanded in 1975, but a decade later, welfare recipients resumed nationwide organizing. In 1987, representatives from twenty-five states attended the founding convention of the National Welfare Rights Union. Eight years later, four hundred delegates attended a convention in Houston to oppose federal welfare reform.[7]

Similarly, women from various faith traditions had been organizing to address poverty for decades. Like the welfare rights activists, they did not necessarily adopt the feminist label, but their efforts directly addressed the unique economic challenges faced by women and people of color. In 1987, as the welfare rights movement was kicking into a higher gear again, the multidenominational organization Church Women United launched an intensive five-year effort aimed at addressing the poverty of US women and children.[8]

These two streams of women-led antipoverty organizing were joined by networks of secular, predominantly white, middle-class activists, many of whom had been disparaged by women of color for neglecting the poor and who wanted to do better. For instance, the National Organization for Women (NOW), supported by the American Association of University Women and the Feminist

Majority Foundation, launched a campaign to defend AFDC. Supplementing these efforts, feminist scholars, writers, and political commentators formed a "Committee of 100" to lobby and intervene in public debates.[9] They held press conferences, hosted vigils, spread their message through mailings—they even went on a hunger strike. None of this changed public opinion or made a dent in the championing of the free market on Capitol Hill. In 1996, Clinton signed the Personal Responsibility and Work Opportunity Act, which eliminated AFDC and replaced it with a much more restrictive program called Temporary Assistance for Needy Families.[10]

The wall of resistance to AFDC led many of those who cared about women's poverty to cast about; they knew they would have to look elsewhere to make changes that would benefit those who had the least.[11] Some fought for structural reforms to make the global and US economy work for all women. Others followed the centrist Democrats' embrace of the market and sought support for initiatives promoting poor women's small business ownership.

Connie Evans was drawn to such programs, having witnessed how much of a difference it could make for a woman to run her own business. In the 1960s, Evans's widowed mother had run a successful independent catering company out of their family's kitchen in Franklin, Tennessee, which had paid for her four children to attend private schools and colleges. In the early 1980s, Evans had used her role as a project manager in Chicago public housing as an opportunity to help residents find jobs. Her efforts attracted the notice of ShoreBank, Chicago's progressive community development bank, which recruited her to direct a Women's Self-Employment Project (WSEP) in 1986. Evans saw the opportunity to become the head of an agency promoting women's entrepreneurship as a way to honor her mother's legacy and shake up the business world. At the time, "business was seen as something that only . . . white male college-educated folks did," she said. People did not consider women, and particularly low-income women of color like her mother, to be credit-worthy.[12]

Meanwhile, in parts of Asia and Latin America, institutions like the Grameen Bank in Bangladesh had also identified women's lack of access to credit as a major cause of poverty. By providing groups of women with small loans, stepped up over time, they helped some of the world's poorest people turn informal income-producing activities, such as selling handicrafts, into small businesses. The lending institutions preferred to give credit to women, viewing women as lesser credit risks than men, and believing women were more likely than men to spend money they earned on their families.[13]

In 1988, ShoreBank arranged for Evans to meet with the Grameen Bank's founder, Muhammad Yunus, in Chicago to discuss what it would take to import some of his lending practices to the United States. Energized by their conversation, Evans followed up a few months later with a trip to Bangladesh. In 1990, she won a fellowship from the Chicago Community Trust, which paid for her to travel to study microcredit projects in twelve countries in Asia and Africa. As part of this trip, she spent six months observing a $30 million microloan project in Sri Lanka.[14] When Evans returned to the United States, she developed two self-employment programs for women in Chicago, which became models for other US feminist initiatives. Both programs promoted women's microenterprise projects (small businesses that employed five or fewer people) through the provision of microcredit and other supportive services. The idea was that women would ultimately be able to provide for themselves and (hopefully) create jobs for other women.[15]

As WSEP took shape, Evans connected with major foundations and with other feminists running microenterprise projects across the country.[16] Between 1986 and 1996, the number of microenterprise programs had risen from just a handful to more than two hundred in forty-four states.[17] Philanthropic foundations supported the efforts (Ford was an early supporter of the Grameen Bank) and the Ms. Foundation for Women tried to encourage projects focused on women through a multi-million-dollar granting initiative geared to feminist practitioners.[18] A series of Ms.-sponsored Institutes on Women's Economic Development offered women like Evans opportunities for professional development and network building. They would come together for a few days to learn from experts and compare notes. Keynote speakers included women organizing economic development projects on Native American reservations and those working with immigrants and refugees. Friendships often formed among people who were pursuing similar kinds of projects in different parts of the country.[19]

Those promoting women's entrepreneurship found champions in the White House. Bill and Hillary Clinton had met Muhammad Yunus in the 1980s and were immediately attracted to his ideas. Microcredit programs fulfilled both the Democratic urge to provide a helping hand to persons who were poor and the Republican effort to extend free-market principles to all sectors of the economy, a perfect combination for a politician hoping to plot a third way in Washington.[20] In 1997, the president hosted an international microcredit summit in DC, attended by two thousand people from 110 countries. There, he promised $1 billion over the next five years to US community development programs that included microloans.[21] The summit introduced presidential awards for microenterprise. The first award went to Connie Evans.[22]

Eventually, some bankers and community development experts who witnessed the growth of feminist microenterprise sought to replicate them as profit-making ventures, untethering them from their social function. By 1999, microenterprise had become a multimillion-dollar industry. There were 341 microenterprise programs operating across forty-six states and the District of Columbia, with a clientele that was 75 percent female.[23] By 2006, there were more than 500 programs.[24] However, many of the feminist initiatives that targeted poor women and welfare recipients were unsustainable. Most programs needed philanthropic grants to keep them afloat. Yet foundations increasingly directed their funding elsewhere. Without the outside resources, pressure mounted for microenterprise programs to focus on being self-supporting economic entities rather than institutions of social change meeting the needs of poor women. Practitioners reduced spending on job training programs and selected the most educated and privileged applicants to receive loans, a process they likened to skimming the cream off the top of the milk.[25]

Pamela Sparr had warned that this would happen. The economist believed that microenterprise programs would never meaningfully tackle the problem of women's poverty because they did not address its roots.[26] Sparr had been deeply affected at age seven when her parents separated. As her fifty-something mother struggled to earn enough money to support her child, Sparr took on adult responsibilities such as cooking dinners and finding forms of free entertainment—the curious youngster typically gravitated toward getting books from the library. One summer, the family's major outing was a tour of a local Smucker's plant to learn how they made fruit jams, a far cry from the family trips to beaches and foreign countries she saw on television and read about in her library books.[27]

Sparr's world cracked open further after a pivotal experience when, while a student at Northwestern University, she spent a day in Chicago's Cook County Juvenile Court observing the proceedings. This episode solidified a lifelong interest in racial and economic justice and prompted her to switch majors and schools. After graduating from Oberlin College with honors in economics and a second major in government, she bucked her professors' guidance to go directly to graduate school and instead followed her heart with travel. In 1978, her understanding of the world again altered dramatically. She spent nine months in London, including a six-month research position at the London School of Economics. It was a tumultuous time in Britain's largest city—the capital of a country in the midst of great social unrest and high unemployment. Unionized coal miners were striking and the hard winter was brutal for them. South Africans fleeing apartheid and economic migrants from Southeast Asia were among those arriving in England seeking safety and new lives.

The Conservative Prime Minister Margaret Thatcher came to power in May 1979. Aiming to address the politically untenable levels of unemployment, Thatcher broke from decades of governmental investment in social welfare and economic regulation to promote privatization, deregulation, tax cuts, and reduced spending on social programs. The immediate focus of her solution to unemployment was to break the unions and keep out foreigners, ostensibly to save jobs for Britons. A burgeoning public hostility toward people of color was palpable and at times vicious. Sparr lived in a communal house in Tooting Bec, at the time, a largely South Asian neighborhood, where people talked about immigrant women of color being subjected to virginity tests at the airport and she heard of race riots with people of color and their allies being beaten, chased, and occasionally killed by white fascist groups and the police.[28]

In 1979, Sparr left England and entered a graduate program in political economics at the New School for Social Research in New York City, where she studied under the renowned Indian-born, Stanford-educated economist Gita Sen and reveled in being part of a diverse, international, and activist-oriented student body.[29] The early 1980s was a heady time, as the field of progressive feminist economics took off in locations such as the New School and the University of Massachusetts, Amherst. As faculty and graduate students collaborated with grassroots groups, their research agendas grew. Many identified a profound need to help ordinary people— particularly women—translate their economic experiences into cogent political analysis to strengthen their organizing and their ability to participate in public policy discussions. As Sparr's networks continued to grow after she graduated, she was particularly inspired by the 1988 founding of the Women's Alternative Economic Network, which brought together women of color and white women organizers alongside Catholic and Protestant feminist leaders from across the country.[30]

Churches had been instrumental to the success of the civil rights movement in the 1960s, and Sparr and her colleagues increasingly interacted with the legions of women turning these institutions into hubs of feminist activity. Sparr had attended Protestant churches in her youth and while in London had developed an interest in Buddhism and a yoga practice, but she did not identify as a person of deep faith. In New York, she was intrigued to encounter networks of Protestant and Catholic women activists who seemed to have "a deeper grounding, less anger, more fun, and more staying power over the long-run than many of the secular activists." Church Women United invited Sparr to participate in its efforts to mobilize Christian women to end women's poverty in the United States. "A huge, transformational agenda!" Sparr recalled. Inspired by their ambition, she joined them, and worked with a variety of other faith groups.[31]

With training as a journalist, Sparr had a knack for making academic theories and economic analysis accessible to ordinary people. Soon, her plate was full, with invitations pouring in asking her to write articles and lead discussions among women who wanted to change the world yet had never opened an economics textbook. In 1991, when the United Methodist Church offered her a full-time job as the Executive Secretary for Development Education and Action for the Women's Division, she was overjoyed. Earning a salary ("with benefits no less") to conduct the advocacy work for which she had been earning small stipends felt like she had hit the jackpot. The opportunity in front of her was tremendous: the Women's Division was the largest faith-based women's organization in the United States, with about a million members.[32]

Sparr understood what she was signing up for. She knew that every major faith tradition had shortcomings, particularly when it came to the treatment of women and gay people. But she also believed that people who fixated on the problems with organized religion were missing its potential to change the world. For an idealist looking to pursue an ambitious international political agenda, the global reach of the United Methodist Church and its financial resources and institutional connections were tremendous assets.

Religious institutions had real estate, long-term relationships, physical and financial resources, and members and staff at the ready. Above all, people from faith traditions had the ability to weigh in on politics with a certain kind of moral authority that others lacked. Sparr wished more feminists had gotten to know the church women she worked with: "Very loyal people who, if you called them with a certain kind of moral imagination, were in it for the long haul . . . putting their bodies and money on the line."[33]

As Sparr immersed herself in this spiritually driven world, her yoga and meditation practice felt increasingly insufficient. She yearned to be part of a community where she could be loved and inspired to grow. After asking around, she found an integrated Unitarian Universalist church with a Black minister that had a strong commitment to eliminating racism and a welcoming stance toward homosexuality—two key criteria for her. She immediately felt comfortable there and became a member in 1992. Over time, her deepening spiritual practice became a sustaining force in her politics: "A faith-rooted life helps me have greater courage, more resilience, greater staying power, a wider perspective, stronger and deeper commitments, and an ever-widening circle of loving connections and care—with humans and the Earth."[34]

Sparr's spiritual awakening was accompanied by continuous intellectual growth. She joined a group of US women working inside and outside of the churches who were frustrated with a field of feminist economics called Women in Development (WID). WID's adherents criticized international economic development programs for their focus on men and argued that the integration of women into the economy would foster economic development. Although Connie Evans did not identify as a WID disciple (she was not part of academic networks, and so not really affiliated with the economics field, per se), the microcredit programs she promoted were in line with its philosophy. Sparr and her colleagues took a much different approach: they argued that free-market capitalism would never be good for women. Why work within the constraints that would keep women in chains? Rather than integrate women into a fundamentally flawed system, they fought to change that system: constrain multinational corporations and strengthen labor unions and social welfare programs.[35]

The new network gelled one morning over bagels and cream cheese in the kitchen of the Center of Concern. Another stereotype-busting institution, this organization was rooted in the Catholic Social Thought tradition that promoted peace and economic equality. A group of feminists gathered at the center at the invitation of Sparr's friend and collaborator Maria Riley, a Catholic sister with a PhD in English and expertise in women's studies. Like Sparr at the United Methodist Church, Riley had found in the Center a powerful platform for promoting feminist change. She had invited her colleagues for breakfast so they could discuss the implications for US women of the critical analyses of global capitalism and structural adjustment programs being produced by Development Alternatives with Women for a New Era (DAWN), the Global South network that Sparr's teacher, Gita Sen, had co-founded. The rich and productive conversation convinced them of the value of working together. They were a diverse bunch, from several different faith traditions, but were united in their belief that they had to offer alternatives to the WID way. The name they came up with, Alternative Women in Development (Alt-WID), reflected that consensus.[36]

The signal contribution of the kitchen table group was that they linked the situation of poor women in the United States with that of those in Asia, Latin America, and Africa. This formulation came as a surprise to some of the Global South feminist researchers, who had assumed that US women were much better off than they were. Intrigued, one of them asked Alt-WID to flesh out the analysis. The result was *Reaganomics and Women: Structural Adjustment U.S. Style*, published in 1992. The title said it all. In thirty-three succinct pages of accessible text, and with numerous charts and graphs, Alt-WID showed how various policy shifts during the

Reagan administration dramatically increased income inequality and poverty, with women bearing the largest part of the burden, and women of color most harshly affected. The group documented various types of policies that the Reagan administration and congressional Republicans supported, such as steep cuts in governmental funding to social programs, the deregulation of industries (which promoted corporate concentration and wealth at the expense of consumers and workers), tax cuts for corporations and high-income households, and a dramatic devaluation of the dollar. They compared these policies and their outcomes with the standard policies the International Monetary Fund (IMF) and World Bank required of countries facing bankruptcy. Their conclusion: slightly different flavors of the same basic economic recipe ("neoliberalism") resulted in similar outcomes—tremendous social and economic hardship that was borne disproportionately by low-income women.[37]

Alt-WID members found an eager audience for their ideas among activists in their own country. Unless they had participated in international organizing, most US activists had never heard of structural adjustment programs. Even the term *globalization* was just starting to enter the public lexicon.[38] Alt-WID believed that needed to change.

Many others joined Alt-WID in spreading the word. In the 1990s, while journalists were covering the showdown over AFDC, networks of antipoverty activists working through organizations such as the Women's Alternative Economic Network were fostering conversations with ordinary people about economic inequality. Many were using the tools and methods of popular education, which had been employed in the early twentieth century by the Bryn Mawr School for Women Workers and the YWCA's Industrial Department when they were trying to advance women's labor struggles. The Brazilian Paulo Freire had captured the theory of this form of education in his 1968 treatise *Pedagogy of the Oppressed*. Marginalized people, he said, could come together to reflect on their conditions, imagine a better world, and create change.[39]

The activists of the 1990s put their own spin on these approaches in workshops that helped hundreds of thousands of ordinary people critically analyze the policies and structures that shaped their lives.[40] Some of the practitioners had read Alt-WID's analysis of Reaganomics and others had learned similar lessons elsewhere, at events like the Beijing conference. After the Women of Color Resource Center's Linda Burnham (the longtime activist who was part of the wave of women to start nonprofits) returned from the 1995 UN event, she and her collaborator developed a course for community groups called *WEdGE: Women's Education in the Global Economy.* Its eight modules included "Are My Clothes Clean? Women and the Global Assembly Line," "Don't Get SAPed: Women and Structural Adjustment Programs," and "Living on the Edge: Welfare, Low-Wage Work, and Homelessness." Their recommended role-play activities included a mock game show in which participants pretended to be people from different countries competing for loans from the World Bank.[41]

Sparr developed an eighty-five-page manual for a popular education course for United Methodist Women that included an exercise that asked participants to empty the contents of their purses and wallets and reflect on what the ID cards, keys, and stray receipts conveyed about their social and economic status. Another technique, the "World Trade Game," had them divide into groups representing countries around the world competing with one another by trading and manufacturing hand-cut paper shapes. When a "banker" periodically announced major swings in the monetary value of each shape, participants saw what could happen to a nation focused on the export of a single product. Though not every one of UMW's one million members took the course, Sparr said that a "significant chunk" of them received the training. Meanwhile, Riley was spreading the word in Catholic circles and others were doing workshops for labor unions and community groups.[42]

For the economist Marlene Kim, who worked with an organization aptly called Just Economics (which participated in WAEN), the beauty of popular education was that it helped people with no formal background in economics grapple with the structures that shaped their lives. In one of Kim's favorite exercises, she set up a table with one person sitting in a chair on top representing a CEO. Two people sat directly on the table below, representing management, and a larger group sat on the floor in front of the table, playing the part of people who held lower-paid service and clerical jobs. Kim asked the participants to strategize about how to improve the situation of people at the bottom. Was the answer to move them up and expand the number of people sitting on top of the table or to give them more money through measures such as increasing the minimum wage? Another exercise compared the "flat tax" (a single taxation rate for all people, regardless of income, that had been championed by Republican presidential candidate Steve Forbes) to the existing system of progressive taxation in which those with higher incomes paid more. Participants held poster boards filled with removable pictures, with one board representing the possessions of people in rich families and the other showing the possessions of poor families. The exercise helped participants to see that when a flat tax was imposed, the rich might have to give up a single sequined dress, whereas a poor family could lose their automobile and furniture.[43]

Alt-WID's interpretation of Clinton's welfare reform as a form of structural adjustment resonated with the members of an international network of grassroots activists who were taking their fight directly to the UN. Their leader, the Barbados-born Margaret Prescod, had been agitating for the rights of welfare mothers since the 1960s, when she was inspired by their organizing during the struggle over the Black community's control of education in Ocean Hill-Brownsville, Brooklyn. After the New York City school board's firing of white teachers set off a months-long New York City teachers' strike, Prescod, who worked in one of the affected schools, learned about community organizing from the welfare recipients working behind the scenes to keep the children fed and ensure that their education did not get interrupted. A few years later, a chance encounter with a table promoting "Wages for Housework" at a conference struck a chord. The idea that women's unwaged work had economic value "made immediate sense," she said, "because of the work I'd done with the mothers on welfare." A friend from a Black feminist study group, Wilmette Brown, was also intrigued, and so, in 1974, the two women borrowed money to travel to England for a Wages for Housework Conference. They were completely inspired by the potential for international working-class women's activism they saw there. When they returned home, they established a Black Women for Wages for Housework group.[44]

Over the next two decades, from her home in Los Angeles, where she had moved with her husband, Prescod grew Black Women for Wages for Housework into a transnational network that included squatters in the UK, Dalit women in India, and domestic workers in Trinidad. Drawing on the teachings of Malcolm X, a subgroup formed the International Women Count Network and took their demands to the UN, where they lobbied the world's governments to include unpaid labor in official calculations of gross national products and to remunerate women for their work. "In the US we were very small fry," Prescod said, but at the UN, her global network "had some clout."[45]

Prescod knew some of the members of Alt-WID and said it was not a "difficult leap" for her network to recognize that "welfare reform [was] a kind of structural adjustment," one that forced poor women to take on greater responsibility for unpaid labor to keep their families functioning. She and her network called on governments around the world to measure and value this growth of unwaged work performed by women, believing it would offer for the first time a "true measure of what it really takes for a society to function." Such statistics would also enable "realistic evaluations of how much cutbacks in the US and other industrialized countries—and 'structural adjustment programs' in non-industrialized countries—are costing women and communities."[46]

At UN meetings, a surprising number of people gave the International Women Count Network (which was founded and coordinated by the Wages for Housework Campaign) a hearing. The network achieved its greatest victory at the Beijing conference. At the official governmental meeting, members watched as Charlotte Bunch and her peers confidently strode down the hallways, delivering succinct talking points and handing out "nice little packets" of information to governmental delegates. Prescod joked that the members of her group looked like the "riffraff" in comparison—whereas other feminists blended into the crowd with their tailored slacks and jackets, Prescod and her friends stood out with their matching T-shirts proclaiming "Women Count, Count Women's Work" in English and Chinese. Their goal was to use their outsider status to their advantage: the presence of multiracial and global working-class women added an element of surprise and human interest to proceedings typically dominated by the middle class and elites. Also working to their advantage was a newly released UN Human Development report that estimated the value of women's unwaged work as $11 trillion internationally and stated that estimates of global output were off by 70 percent because they ignored this vital labor. The report thus linked the devaluation of women's work to their poverty and unequal status in all regions of the world.[47]

The paragraphs Prescod's network wanted inserted into the platform, committing nations to measure and value unpaid work and include it in national accounts, inspired fierce debates in tense, closed-door meetings. To put pressure on the negotiators, they convinced representatives of fourteen hundred NGOs to sign onto a statement endorsing their demands, staged silent vigils outside of the conference rooms where the officials were meeting, and issued frequent press releases about the progress of the negotiations. The message to those inside the meeting room was clear: women around the world were watching.[48]

To nearly everyone's surprise, the riffraff left the conference victorious. The Platform for Action highlighted women's disproportionate responsibility for unwaged work as a major contributor to their poverty and as a hindrance to girls' pursuit of education.

Two paragraphs in the platform specifically recommended that governments measure unpaid work and include it in national accounts. Another paragraph called on development institutions and donors to provide the resources and technical assistance countries in the Global South needed to fully measure all of the paid and unpaid work that people performed on a daily basis.[49] Prescod's group returned to their countries to share the good news, raising public awareness about the value of women's unpaid labor in the process. Prescod herself served as a consultant for activists in Trinidad who were teaming up to count women's unwaged work in that country's gross national product. She traveled to Barbados to lobby her country of origin's governor general. When she returned to the United States, she received an invitation from Hillary Clinton to participate in a workshop at the White House.[50]

In Beijing, while Prescod's team was staging silent vigils, Sparr joined an international group of colleagues in a sit-down session with James Wolfensohn. That the president of the World Bank was even at the UN women's conference was a victory—a signal that the bank could no longer ignore the growing body of feminist economic research. Wolfensohn gave a speech at the conference in which he acknowledged feminist criticisms of the bank's support for structural adjustment and promised to do more to address women's poverty. Following the speech, the activists solicited nine hundred signatures on a petition outlining the steps they believed necessary to ensure that Wolfensohn's pledge would become a reality. These included increasing the participation of activists from the Global South in policymaking and placing more women from diverse backgrounds in the bank's senior positions. They demanded increased investments in women's access to health services, education, agriculture, land ownership, employment, and financial services and called for each one of the bank's policies and programs to be evaluated according to its impact on women.[51]

Feminists recognized that the World Bank "was going to be a really, really tough nut to crack," said Sparr. Several of the most committed petition-signers formed a group called Women's Eyes on the World Bank to continue the pressure after the media coverage from Wolfensohn's public proclamations had subsided. They stood watch as Wolfensohn created a gender advisory board, which included a member of DAWN, and instituted a rule that required every single policy crafted by the bank to be evaluated to see whether it promoted women's interests. A series of progress reports issued by the bank outlined how Wolfensohn's commitments were being carried out. Ultimately, though, as Sparr predicted, the inner workings of the bank did not radically change. Beneath the World Bank's new "gender-friendly exterior," one 1997 study concluded, still "lies an institution lacking in sensitivity to the impact its work has on poor women."[52] It was mostly lip service.

Yet feminist pressure still made a difference. Wolfensohn ordered the creation of Gender Action Plans for each region that outlined strategies to address gender inequalities within all World Bank policies and projects. By 2002, the bank had issued a "Gender Mainstreaming Strategy" that outlined a set of policies geared toward ending gender inequality throughout its operations.[53] The degree to which the staff implemented these policies varied widely; success depended on the level of commitment of the employees working in various countries.

No one in the World Bank ever seriously considered alternatives to free-market capitalism; their reforms were much more in line with WID and Connie Evans's microcredit practitioners than the ideals of Alt-WID and Just Economics. Nevertheless, among the World Bank's leaders, it was now a matter of fact, not debate, that gender inequality hampered economic development and that development policies should serve the interests of women.[54]

The World Bank "didn't crumble," Sparr later reflected. Nor did microcredit lift women out of poverty. Popular education workshops didn't give struggling families more money or safer housing. The UN had said that unpaid labor should be valued, but women were still deprived of welfare benefits and governments were not considering anything resembling wages for housework. But there were still incremental victories that felt important. Feminists from around the world had forced the man in charge of one of the world's most powerful economic institutions to listen to their ideas and respond to them. UN documents now explicitly addressed the struggles of the world's poorest women and recognized the economic value of their unpaid labor.

Above all, thanks in large part to feminists, people from all walks of life began to grapple with what it meant to live in a world shaped by global capitalism. These ideas were brought down from the Ivory Tower, and the results have been lasting. Today, there is a growing consensus that income inequality is a problem, and people in the United States know that their access to cheap T-shirts depends on the exploitation of women overseas. They increasingly understand that women's labor in the home keeps families functioning and is rarely adequately compensated. Feminists had primed the pump for a revolution in thinking that coalesced in the twenty-first century in the wake of the global financial crisis and Occupy Wall Street. "Things have changed," Marlene Kim observed; "we were the first trickle in a dialogue . . . that is now a wide river, or a larger lake, or perhaps even a sea."[55]

EIGHT

ENVIRONMENTAL JUSTICE
AND LABOR ACTIVISM

Pamela Chiang could not believe her luck. In 1992, the young environmentalist had received an invitation to participate in a weekend gathering organized by the Southwest Network for Environmental and Economic Justice (SNEEJ). This new network brought together the growing numbers of people of color who were defining environmentalism not as the preservation of pristine natural habitats but as the assurance of ordinary people's health and safety everywhere they lived, worked, and played. The leaders of the network had heard about Chiang, a rising star in the student movement at the University of California at Berkeley, and had invited her and one of her fellow organizers to fly to Albuquerque, New Mexico, for the meeting. For Chiang, the SNEEJ meeting was quite a culture shock. She had participated in numerous initiatives led by people of color on Berkeley's campus. But in California, home to one-third of the nation's Asian Americans, multiracial spaces looked much different from the one she encountered in New Mexico. The SNEEJ group was primarily Latino and indigenous, with smaller numbers of African Americans and very few Asian Americans like her.[1]

Yet Chiang almost immediately felt comfortable. Looking around, she saw other women of color confidently assuming leadership positions and integrating gender issues into the agendas. She had arrived at the meeting assuming she would be challenged and intimidated. But in SNEEJ, she found feminism.

It was a form of feminism that looked much different from the popular images. The labor and environmental justice campaigns led by immigrant and working-class women called for jobs that did not force workers to breathe toxic fumes or subject them to sexual harassment and that offered regular hours and decent pay. Their organizing began locally, with domestic workers talking with one another on park benches and factory laborers gathering in worker centers. They extended their efforts internationally by participating in global coalitions protesting against the North American Free Trade Agreement and the policies of the World Trade Organization. Many of these activists did not call themselves feminists; they didn't feel connected to the white women's movement they had heard about. Yet as one Latina organizer put it, they promoted feminist goals and led "objectively feminist lives."[2] It was just the label they didn't identify with. By the end of the nineties, they had forged global networks that were shaking up the world's environmental and labor organizing movements and furthering feminist change-making across the United States.

Pamela Chiang had entered the University of California at Berkeley in 1987 with an ambitious agenda. Twice during high school, she had become seriously ill. When the medications prescribed by MDs did not help, her mother had taken her to a traditional Chinese doctor, who had cured her. Chiang bristled when people dismissed Chinese medicine as "hocus-pocus," and she envisioned a career in which she would study its relationship to Western forms of healing. She excelled in her science courses and loved conducting experiments in the campus laboratories. Yet the young researcher surprised herself by enjoying her electives in ethnic studies and anthropology even more than her pre-med classes.[3]

Chiang started questioning her chosen career when the Loma Prieta earthquake hit her hometown of San Francisco in 1989, severely damaging buildings and infrastructures, including a major freeway artery through Chinatown. She had grown up immersed in Chinese culture, watching her mother play chief advisor to the steady stream of immigrant families who came to their door looking for guidance. Her mother helped newcomers find apartments to rent and taught them how to settle parking ticket fines and acquire licenses to operate acupuncture clinics.[4]

After hearing about the earthquake, Chiang turned to an environmental group she had recently joined (called the "Campus Greens"), hoping they would be organizing relief efforts. The leaders looked puzzled when she asked about their plans. They told her that looking out for the environment meant protecting nature and that they were engaged in an important campaign to save the redwood trees in California. Chiang was disappointed. In her mind, the earthquake was an environmental disaster.[5]

As fate would have it, Chiang then came across the newsletter of an environmental justice organization called the Southwest Organizing Project (SWOP). Cofounded in Albuquerque in 1980 by Richard Moore and Jeanne Gauna, SWOP was an organization of poor people of color fighting for safe jobs and clean air and water. From the newsletter, Chiang discerned that SWOP had been launching protests against large corporations, such as computer giant Intel, charging that their production facilities damaged the environment in poor communities and harmed workers' health.[6]

Chiang felt as if a whole new world opened up to her. She had not known there were so many environmentalists who cared deeply about the fate of communities of color and poor people. She shared the newsletter with some of her friends and they started to check books out of the library and scour newsstands to learn more. Their excitement grew as they discovered that SWOP was part of a burgeoning grassroots environmental justice movement led by people of color that had been publishing all kinds of literature.[7]

The eager students pieced together a timeline of recent history not yet covered in their textbooks and created an alternative curriculum that delivered one "aha" moment after another. They learned that in 1982, when state officials erected a hazardous PCB disposal site in Warren County, North Carolina, the National Association for the Advancement of Colored People (NAACP) led a series of protests and five hundred people were arrested. The demonstrators argued that it was no coincidence that 60 percent of the residents of the county were African American, 4 percent were Native American, and nearly everyone was working class. The campaign helped stimulate a landmark study prepared by the United Church of Christ's Commission for Racial Justice, under the leadership of the civil rights activist Ben Chavis Jr.

Chiang and her friends read every word of "Toxic Wastes and Race in the United States," which surveyed twenty-five cities and found "a striking relationship" between the location of commercial hazardous wastes dumps and the racial backgrounds of the people who lived there. In naming these practices an "insidious form of racism," the study and the activism surrounding it helped give birth to the concept of environmental racism. Environmental hazards did not just fall from the sky, this line of thinking went. Such problems were created by human beings. Just as the policies and decision making of state authorities created situations in which poor Black neighborhoods were less likely than wealthy white communities to have public parks and adequately funded schools, it was no coincidence that minority communities were disproportionately used as dumping grounds for toxic chemicals and hazardous waste.[8]

Suddenly, events happening around the students made more sense. Chiang had heard of people protesting proposals to place a toxic waste incinerator in Kettleman City, a small rural town of low-income Latinx in the San Joaquin Valley that they claimed petroleum companies had been using as a dumping ground for PCBs, benzene, and asbestos. But she hadn't realized that these actions two hundred miles south of Berkeley were part of a broader environmental justice movement.[9]

Though Chiang did not give up on her dreams of integrating Chinese and Western medicine, a persistent voice in her head was growing louder. Instead of trying to cure people's illnesses, why not attempt to prevent them from getting sick in the first place? All around her, she saw groups addressing the environmental causes of poor people's health problems. Chiang and her friends started their own campus group to support such local struggles.

A flyer calling on students of color who cared about the environment to attend a meeting drew a small, racially mixed group. They called themselves Nindakin, Students of Color for the Environment. Their organizing helped spur the formation of the Berkeley Environmental Justice Coalition, in which students of color worked alongside white students. Taking advantage of the common belief that President George H. W. Bush was undertaking an invasion of Iraq to gain access to its oil, they convened a symposium: US Energy Policy: Who Bears the Burden? Hundreds listened to speakers discussing the consequences for poor people of their country's dependence on foreign oil. Interest in these issues was so high that Chiang and several others applied to participate in a program called Democratic Education at Cal, which enabled them to design and teach a fifteen-week course on environmental justice with support from a few professors. Chiang and her fellow students then reached beyond Berkeley and joined a campaign against the Chevron oil company. They charged that Chevron's facilities in Richmond, California—one of the poorest cities in the state—were exposing its mainly nonwhite residents to toxic spills and leaks as well as fires and explosions.[10]

It was news of this activity by students of color at Berkeley that prompted the invitation to Chiang and Vivian Chang, another

Nindakin member, to participate in the Albuquerque meeting of SNEEJ, the umbrella organization coordinating the activities of environmental justice groups in the region. In Albuquerque, Chiang found many other women who, like her, were not afraid to speak their minds. Some of them had been infusing feminist perspectives in SNEEJ since its founding. In fact, one of the organization's first published documents included a paragraph stating that women, especially women of color, were the "poorest of the poor" and paid the "highest price" for environmental and economic inequities.[11] Chiang could feel in her heart that SNEEJ's emphasis on women's struggles and women's prominent roles in the organization weren't "tokenism." They reflected the gender dynamics at play in local struggles. In many working-class communities, immigrant women—often mothers and grandmothers—were "the ones leading the fight."[12]

Chiang eagerly joined their ranks. Near the end of the weekend, the delegates divided into caucuses by states, and the California group nominated the assertive newcomer to be their representative. The twenty-one-year-old felt honored to be on a steering committee for a new organization that was planning on making waves at the White House. She was particularly pleased when, soon after the November 1992 election, SNEEJ members met with staffers on the Clinton-Gore transition team to discuss the need for policies rectifying how pollution disproportionately affected minority communities. The result was a commitment from the federal Environmental Protection Agency to address environmental inequalities.[13]

After her frustration with the Campus Greens, Chiang also took particular satisfaction in joining an organization standing up to the major players in the national environmental movement. This had begun in 1990, when SWOP sent a highly publicized letter to the "Big Ten" environmental organizations, criticizing them for their laser-like focus on protecting wilderness areas and endangered species. Signed by a hundred cultural, arts, community, and religious leaders—all people of color—the letter pointed out that

Native Americans, African Americans, Latinos, and Asian Americans were defining the environment as encompassing everywhere that ordinary people lived, worked, and played. In addition, it charged that such venerable groups as the Sierra Club, the National Wildlife Federation, and the National Audubon Society had a history of "racist and exclusionary practices" that included a lack of racial diversity in their staffs and a lack of accountability toward communities of color. A year later, the United Church of Christ's Commission for Racial Justice responded to the wave of organizing in those communities by convening a National People of Color Environmental Leadership Summit, with at least three hundred representatives of African American, Latino, Native American, and Asian American organizations from all fifty states as well as participants from Puerto Rico, the Marshall Islands, Canada, and Central and South America. The seventeen-point "Principles of Environmental Justice" that came out of the meeting has guided the movement ever since.[14]

Chiang turned out to be in the right place at the right time. In response to the criticism, the leaders of Greenpeace, one of the largest environmental organizations in the world, created a fellowship program to pay for people of color to hire new staff members for their own organizations. One of these grants went to SNEEJ, whose leaders, highly impressed by Chiang, hired her to a full-time post. Any lurking thoughts Chiang had about medical school dissipated. Shortly after graduating from college, she accepted the job.[15]

The SNEEJ post offered Chiang an opportunity to hone her networking skills and learn more about grassroots organizing. She was supposed to spend 50 percent of her time helping local groups work with one another and connect to the Southwest network. The other 50 percent was to be spent working with Fuerza Unida, a Mexican American women's organization in San Antonio, Texas, demanding better treatment for workers in sweatshops.[16]

Some might have wondered how Fuerza Unida had anything to do with the environment. But from the perspective of Chiang and her environmental justice colleagues, supporting women who were speaking out against sweatshops was exactly where the movement needed to be. Decades earlier, US reformers and unionists thought they had eliminated sweated labor when they gained the right to a minimum wage, overtime wages, and laws guaranteeing safer working conditions. But in the late twentieth century, the exploitation of workers had taken on new forms.

Some of the worst conditions were in the tens of thousands of small garment factories caught up in a subcontracting system that forced them to compete with factories in other countries where workers could be paid much less. Corporations such as Levi Strauss required smaller US shops to bid for their contracts. To succeed in this system, many independent shops promised to produce more goods for rock-bottom prices. To turn a profit, they sweated their workers, who were mainly women, forcing them to work at breakneck speeds for long hours with little pay.[17] The laws mandating minimum wages and maximum hours offered little protection because the government did not fully fund the agencies responsible for enforcing labor laws and some of the workers in the new sweatshops were immigrants who lived in fear of deportation. By the 1990s, the US Department of Labor itself estimated that more than half of the nation's twenty-two thousand garment factories violated wage, hour, and safety laws.[18]

Factory workers were not the only ones who suffered. As the US economy transitioned from manufacturing to service work, sweatshop conditions also existed in restaurants, nursing homes, and hotels—all of which paid workers very little and put tremendous strains on their bodies. Like the garment workers Chiang was sent to work with, women in these other lines of work were also starting to organize.[19]

Immigrant women led many of the campaigns in factories because they were the ones with the most backbreaking jobs. Confined in small spaces and engaged in the repetitive motions of sewing and manufacturing caused muscle strain in their hands, backs, and shoulders. Breathing the thick dust in cramped shops caused allergies and asthma. When those who worked in garment factories blew their noses, the colors of the fabrics appeared on the tissue.[20] How could such conditions not be considered environmental hazards? Chiang asked.

When Chiang encountered Fuerza Unida, the group was reeling from wages lost due to plant closures ordered by Levi Strauss. In 1990, when the clothing company, previously known for its liberal policies, had closed a San Antonio factory and moved its production to Costa Rica; 1,150 people, 92 percent of them Latino, lost their jobs. Nearly all of the displaced workers were mothers; many had been with the company for more than fourteen years. After the shock settled, close to half of them began meeting in a local church to see what could be done to recover their severance pay and secure compensation for work-related injuries. These meetings led to the formation of Fuerza Unida (which means "United Force").[21]

Fuerza Unida was part of what historian Dorothy Sue Cobble has called the feminization of organized labor. This happened after World War II, when increasing numbers of women entered the workforce and some of them looked to male-dominated labor unions to solve their problems. They brought a unique perspective to union organizing, pushing for pay equity and child care as well as paid maternity leave and greater job flexibility. Although they were not always welcomed by their male peers, many fought to eliminate sex discrimination and racism in the workplace.[22] In the 1970s and 1980s, antiunion legislation and declining employment in the traditional bastions of industrial unionism eroded the male-dominated unions. Meanwhile, membership in the public sector and service industries, much of it female, rose. In particular, the Service Employees International Union (SEIU) began to organize workers previously considered outside labor's purview, including janitors, home care attendants, and day care workers. By the end of the century, unions were reaching out to sites they had previously considered completely "unorganizable," from Walmart to fast-food restaurants. The predominance of immigrants in these occupations also led major unions in the AFL-CIO to reverse their decades-long opposition to undocumented workers and embrace a path to citizenship.[23]

Union leaders believed they had a chance to attract these new constituencies because they had witnessed the success of independent organizing efforts led by women like those in Fuerza Unida. These groups joined a tradition of "poor workers' unionism"— employed and unemployed people organizing for their rights outside of traditional labor unions, a longstanding practice undertaken by those whose struggles union leaders had overlooked (including domestic workers and welfare recipients).[24] Fuerza Unida helped hundreds of Latinas fight for emergency aid from the government and English as a Second Language (ESL) and GED classes to help them get other kinds of work. They staged local tribunals documenting the injustices they had suffered and sent representatives to testify before Congress. Their protests, held in cities across the Southwest and in Seattle, Portland, Chicago, Albany, and New York, helped them cultivate a network of committed allies.[25]

As part of her fellowship with SNEEJ, Chiang signed on as Fuerza Unida's national campaign coordinator, promising to help the group attract more supporters and media coverage. Fuerza Unida members had been showing up from time to time to picket outside of Levi's headquarters in San Francisco and had called for a national boycott. They also asked their supporters to cut the leather patch with the brand name off the back of their jeans and send it back to the company. The fact that they were outraged by the conditions in US garment factories yet still wanted to keep their jobs from moving overseas was a sign of how hard it was for them to make a living doing anything else. Their efforts to expose the terrible conditions in garment factories were aided in 1995 when television cameras covered governmental agents storming a sweatshop in El Monte, California, and freeing seventy-two Thai "sewing slaves." Viewers were outraged by the images of the women's terrified faces, lending support to the efforts of women's organizations such as Fuerza Unida to raise awareness of the problem.[26]

When Chiang first came to Fuerza Unida she felt privileged to discover a group of women who had been crushed by a huge corporation who were now building a life-affirming movement. Rather than imposing her own agenda, she gathered the women to cocreate a plan that involved two or three Fuerza Unida members coming to live in San Francisco for six weeks at a time to enrich their leadership skills and make use of the space and tools offered in the Greenpeace office. The women stayed with host families and rode the bus to the office each morning. If they weren't heading out to network with the National Lawyers Guild or groups of college students, they were standing over the fax machine or lining up in front of the photocopier. The more they accomplished, the more capable they felt. Chiang described the women's six-week stints as "life-changing."[27]

One of the most moving events Fuerza Unida organized with Chiang was a twenty-one-day hunger strike scheduled to coincide with Dia de los Muertos (Day of the Dead), the Mexican holiday that honors people who have passed away. Chiang joined them in going without food and camping on the plaza of the Levi Strauss headquarters. As they fasted, they paid tribute to those who had given their lives in service of sewing clothes for Levi Strauss and had died, they said, of broken hearts, injuries, and poverty.[28]

One Fuerza Unida member summed up SNEEJ's contribution to the group's campaign against Levi's: "They gave us the link between the environmental and the economic." SNEEJ leaders consistently sent representatives to support Fuerza Unida's demonstrations, showing that they understood the women's labor struggle to be part of the environmental movement. They also told the garment workers about the environmental toll of Levi's excavation of pumice in the Jemez Mountains, where Native Americans lived, and shared stores about factories in which workers were secretly taken to the hospital because they were passing out from exposure to toxic chemicals. Fuerza Unida members described unsafe working environments at the Levi Strauss factory and their own struggles with carpal tunnel syndrome and herniated disks.[29]

Chiang also connected Fuerza Unida to the burgeoning networks of women labor activists. Many of these women were organizing in worker centers: community facilities that provided working-class people with resources such as free legal advice, ESL classes, and popular education. By the turn of the twenty-first century, more than a hundred such centers existed across the country, funded by foundations, churches, labor unions, and individual donors. Some of them catered exclusively to female factory workers, while others addressed issues faced by those working in jobs primarily performed by women, such as childcare and housekeeping. Several had leadership development goals and programs explicitly geared toward women of color.[30]

Through SNEEJ, Chiang nurtured a connection between Fuerza Unida and Asian Immigrant Women Advocates (AIWA), a worker center in Oakland where she had volunteered while at Berkeley. "Sisterhood solidarity" was practically "instinctual" for these women workers, she recalled, and they made it a point to attend one another's rallies and pickets.[31] In 1992, AIWA launched a Garment Workers Justice campaign after a factory that had produced clothing for the designer Jessica McClintock shut down and did not provide its workers with back pay. One of the leaders of the campaign described working at the factory as akin to "being a prisoner in a sealed cage." She had found it suffocating to work ten hours a day, seven days a week, in a building where all of the windows were locked, but she had desperately needed the job and was now prepared to fight for what the company owed her. The garment workers received support from AIWA, which helped mobilize networks of Asian American organizations, women's groups, students, church groups, and labor unions across the country to support the pickets and consumer boycott. The outpouring of support and a spot on the CBS news program *60 Minutes* forced McClintock to negotiate. The workers ultimately won a cash settlement, an education fund for garment workers to learn about their rights, a scholarship fund for workers and their children, and a bilingual hotline for workers to report violations of their rights. This helped inspire a campus-based antisweatshop movement and protests against large corporations such as Nike and Guess.[32]

Over time, many immigrant women labor organizers came into contact with feminist popular educators such as the United Methodist Church's Pamela Sparr and the Women of Color Resource Center's Linda Burnham. After participating in popular education workshops, some of them were so inspired by the feminists' teachings that they sought out trainings so they could start to lead classes themselves. Most of them had already been raising gender issues such as sexual harassment in their campaigns and so they did not need to be convinced that gender inequality mattered. The educators encouraged them to further explore how sexism and international economic forces were shaping their lives. During the sessions, they talked about how women were affected by changes in the structure of manufacturing as the world became more connected, debated the federal push for anti-immigration legislation, and studied the history of women's labor organizing. A handout used in one workshop informed women of the price of the clothing they sewed, the low cost of materials, the meager wages they received, and where the bulk of the profits went. Educators prided themselves on their ability to use such tangible, real-world examples as springboards for discussions of abstract concepts such as neoliberalism.[33]

Meanwhile, several worker centers were developing projects to support immigrant women who held jobs as domestic workers. Unions had traditionally regarded them as unorganizable, working as they did for individual employers in isolated workplaces. Yet as far back as Reconstruction, domestic employees had formed their own associations to help secure better working conditions, and they have found ways to organize collectively ever since.[34]

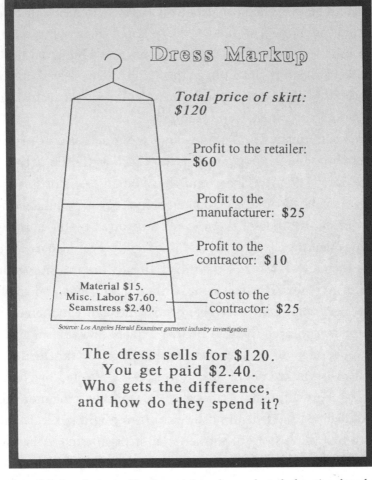

One of the handouts used by the activists who conducted educational workshops with garment workers. *Courtesy of Miriam Ching Yoon Louie Papers, Sophia Smith Collection of Women's History, Northampton, Massachusetts.*

"It was really hard to get six women in a room together," recalled Ai-Jen Poo of her first months as one of the lead organizers in New York City. Born in the United States and raised in a multigenerational immigrant household, Poo spoke Mandarin as her first language. Her mother joked that her fundraising career began in the first grade, when she stood outside a grocery store and sold homemade cookies to raise money for people suffering from a famine in Ethiopia. As a student at Columbia University, Poo felt she learned as much from her community organizing as she did from her courses. She was particularly moved when, working as a volunteer at the New York Asian Women's Center, she saw women taking refuge in a domestic violence shelter who were unable to rebuild their lives because they had small children and could not earn a living wage. What came first, she asked herself, being a victim of violence or being poor?[35]

It was a question similar to the one Pamela Chiang had posed about treating people's illnesses versus preventing them from getting sick, and Poo came to a similar answer about the need to address one of the roots of the problem. Her time at the shelter led her to believe that poor women were trapped in violent relationships in part because they did not have enough money to move away. If they had more money, they could leave abusive men and sometimes avoid getting involved in such relationships in the first place. Poo understood that women's greater financial security would not eradicate domestic violence, which affected women in all social classes, but she saw it as a vital first step in the struggle.[36]

In between waiting tables and finishing her undergraduate coursework, Poo joined a campaign to organize Asian women who worked in the service sector to advocate for their rights. Within a year she was hired as a full-time staffer and had launched an ambitious project to organize Filipino domestic workers. Lacking a shop floor on which to mount a campaign, Poo visited the parks and playgrounds where women gathered with their charges. She set up booths at local health fairs and put on "know-your-rights workshops." When women showed even a spark of interest, she invited them to gatherings in the basements of familiar churches, yet she struggled to convince even a dozen women to gather in the few hours they had free during the evenings. With each new member added, it seemed like another disappeared. But Poo dedicated herself to getting to know the women as individuals and could not imagine building a movement in any other way. "I don't think there's any shortcuts around face-to-face relationship building," she reflected.[37]

Organizers need a target, a place to direct their energies where they can win tangible benefits. Fuerza Unida's members had Levi's, but the nannies and housekeepers all had different employers. From her conversations with the women on the park benches, Poo learned that prior to moving to New York City, many of them had worked in Hong Kong, where a strong domestic workers' movement had established a standard contract for employers that defined acceptable labor conditions and mandated benefits such as paid time off. Upon immigrating to the United States, they were shocked to find the labor market was a "free-for-all" and that they had to individually negotiate with employers in a foreign language. How about campaigning for labor standards in their new country? asked Poo.[38]

The nannies' and housekeepers' enthusiasm ignited a powerful statewide campaign. The Filipino women reached out to Andolan, a group of South Asian domestic workers, and to household workers from the Caribbean and Latin America. They also forged ties with a worker center in Long Island that served Central and South American migrants, many of whom also worked as domestics. In 2000, this multiethnic workforce formed an organization they called Domestic Workers United (DWU). They embarked on a decade-long effort that in 2011 resulted in passage of New York's Domestic Workers' Bill of Rights.[39]

Organizing in a single state was a good start, but Poo and other labor organizers were learning that in a rapidly globalizing economy, the fate of US workers was bound up in that of workers around the world. Domestic work exemplified these connections. When relatively well-off mothers in the United States entered the paid labor force and needed childcare, they hired women from Asia and Latin America. These care workers' own children were being looked after by family members or by even poorer women in their home countries. What bound all of these women together was that none of them lived in nations that recognized care work as productive labor.

With that in mind, Poo and others forged a coalition with domestic workers in other countries, with the goal of convincing the

International Labour Organization to establish global standards for domestic work. In their organizing at this UN agency, which resulted in a 2011 victory, they argued that domestic laborers should receive the same kinds of rights as all other workers, including days off, social security, and a minimum wage.[40]

The factory workers in organizations such as Fuerza Unida had been arriving at similar conclusions about the need for transnational organizing. It was hard to gain any leverage with employers who could so easily move their factories to other countries. During the 1992 presidential campaign, the women of Fuerza Unida vehemently opposed Bill Clinton's promise to put his signature on the North American Free Trade Agreement (NAFTA), bringing Mexico into the Canada–US free trade agreement.[41] They called the 1990 plant closing in San Antonio that had left them unemployed a "precursor to NAFTA" and said that people on both sides of the border would suffer if Clinton signed the pact. They predicted that the wages and living conditions of the majority of Mexican workers would not improve as a result of NAFTA, while the economic prospects of US workers like themselves would further deteriorate. They also did not believe that trade agreements would ever address the environmental protections that were needed along the southern US border.[42]

Women from the United States and Mexico began to hone a distinctly feminist critique of free trade when they organized side by side. Such interactions had begun as early as 1985, when a group of US women living in Mexico formed Mujer a Mujer to facilitate popular education and worker exchanges. At a 1991 meeting in El Paso sponsored by the Women's Alternative Economic Network (one of the popular education groups that Pamela Sparr belonged to and helped launch), representatives from Mujer a Mujer joined activists from Appalachia, New York, San Francisco, and Mexico to tour *maquiladoras*, Mexican factories set up in border free trade zones, and to learn about one another's lives. The economist and popular educator Marlene Kim (the one who put chairs on a table to illustrate the pyramid structure of wage earning to community groups) led a workshop for them, and they ended up calling for better conditions for women workers on both sides of the border and opposing agreements like NAFTA that they believed would exacerbate all of their struggles.[43]

The conversations continued at the 1992 First Tri-National Conference of Women Workers on Economic Integration and Free Trade in Valle de Bravo, Mexico. There, 120 women from the United States, Mexico, and Canada collectively explored the effects of NAFTA on their countries. Through small group sessions that encouraged them to discuss differences in their experiences, they decided that NAFTA would harm them all—but in different ways: the female Mexican factory workers would receive meager pay and labor in conditions that were harmful to their health; the US women would find it increasingly difficult to find any kind of gainful employment at all.[44]

Their vociferous opposition to NAFTA established women labor organizers as major players in the debates over free trade. Fuerza Unida members were interviewed on CNN and their oft-repeated chant calling on governmental leaders to "Give NAFTA the shafta!" made for good sound bites.[45] Growing numbers of organized working-class women from the United States and Mexico joined them. One conference in McAllen, Texas, included La Mujer Obrera, a group of Chicana garment workers from El Paso, AIWA (the organization condemning Jessica McClintock where Chiang volunteered), and the Comite Fronterizo de Obreras, a Mexican women's worker organization.[46]

Grassroots networks helped coordinate a four-day "Human Face of Trade" trip for a bipartisan group of congresswomen in 1993. Traveling with several US activists, the politicians met with Mexican women working in US-owned factories and witnessed the devastating environmental conditions in the women's neighborhoods and workplaces. When the representatives returned home, they issued a scathing critique of free trade that reflected the feminist perspectives they had encountered. Those "most affected by trade policy" were women, the group observed. A report they submitted to the US House of Representatives described workers surviving in "desperate living conditions." "Supporters of NAFTA claim that each Mexican consumer buys $450 worth of U.S. exports each year," one of the congresswomen pointed out in a subcommittee hearing. "I can tell you that none of the Mexican workers I met with, as hard-working as they are, earn wages high enough" for such purchases.[47]

Feminist economics researchers supported these worker-driven efforts with academic studies and popular education. Pamela Sparr recalled people asking, "What does . . . trade policy have to do with . . . women's liberation?" She and other members of Alt-WID responded by asserting that trade was "the cutting edge of the next part of the struggle for women." Their studies questioning the benefits of open markets showed that the integration of national economies into a global economy through free trade shifted labor force participation rates for women and men and changed the kinds of work each sex performed in ways that often disadvantaged women.[48]

It is hard to overstate the intricacy of the social webs women formed as they tackled the major economic and political issues of their day. SNEEJ connected grassroots environmental justice leaders with labor activists and published articles analyzing the struggles of women in the *maquiladoras*.[49] Sparr was instrumental in having United Methodist Women support Fuerza Unida's campaign against Levi Strauss and express strong opposition to NAFTA.[50] The Chinese workers in AIWA were invited by Charlotte Bunch's group to testify about economic human rights at the UN World Summit on Social Development in Copenhagen in 1995. Pamela Chiang had helped found the Asian Pacific Environmental Network with Peggy Saika, who had led the meetings of Asian Americans in the tent in Beijing. Meanwhile, Ai-Jen Poo was being mentored by Linda Burnham, who had a host of connections in these labor and environmental justice networks, and decades later took a job organizing with the domestic workers.[51]

Thanks to such networking, working-class women who had identified feminism as white and middle class now saw the movement in a different light. Veterans like Linda Burnham had come to embrace the feminist label and now offered newcomers examples of organizing under the banner of feminism that they could get behind. When working-class women were invited to participate in events such as the Beijing conference, they discovered feminist spaces that showcased the activism of women of color. Funders such as the Ms. Foundation increasingly supported their campaigns, signaling that even some feminists with money cared about their struggles.[52]

After NAFTA passed in late 1993, several feminist coalitions turned their attention to the most powerful force for free trade—the new World Trade Organization (WTO). In 1994, the WTO replaced the decades-old General Agreement on Tariffs and Trade (GATT) as the arbitrator of trade disputes between nations and promoter and enforcer of international trade agreements. An exceptionally influential institution, the WTO ensured that its decisions were carried out by permitting sanctions on states that refused to abide by its rules.[53]

An international coalition of environmental, labor, religious, and consumer organizations set their sights on this powerful institution and organized a massive protest scheduled to coincide with the WTO's meeting in Seattle in 1999. Over five days, as governmental representatives attempted to hammer out the agenda for a new round of negotiations aimed at trade deregulation, they were impeded by a group of thirty thousand to forty thousand activists from around the world who demanded that a host of considerations, including standards for environmental protections and workers' rights, be incorporated into international trade agreements.[54]

In Seattle, feminists did not lead the largest demonstrations or attract much media attention, but behind the scenes, their fingerprints were everywhere. The international coalition of feminists working on poverty and development issues that was so active in Beijing drew on their analysis of neoliberal trade policies and their history of collaborative relationships to engage in planning for this

WTO meeting. Much was made of the historic alliance brokered between labor organizations such as the AFL-CIO and environmental groups such as the Sierra Club (a partnership often referred to as "the teamsters and the turtles"). But few recognized that this coalition could take shape only because the participants had listened to grassroots organizers, particularly women and people of color, who had been organizing at the nexus of environmental and labor justice for years and had urged the mainstream groups to broaden their agendas. Having moved beyond a focus on the shop floor, on the one hand, and the natural world, on the other, the two movements could finally establish common ground.

Media coverage of the Seattle protests focused on the civil disobedience and vandalization of Starbucks and Nike storefronts, but more effective in changing hearts and minds were the five days of peaceful events that resembled an NGO forum at a UN meeting. Feminists organized several of the panels and teach-ins held in universities, theaters, churches, and union halls across the city, sharing their analyses of the effects of free trade and globalization on women. At one feminist-inspired "mini-conference" that lasted a full day, the audience listened to testimonies by an Afro-Brazilian domestic workers' union leader, a Dominican garment worker activist, and a Colombian labor and women's rights activist.[55]

Pamela Sparr helped organize a marquee event that brought low-income immigrant women together with economic justice advocates from other countries. Their daylong meeting, "Women, Democracy, Sovereignty, and Development," included panels and strategy sessions led by activists and a march through the streets accompanied by an African women's drumming group. Around fifteen hundred people attended, including many representing NGOs that had not had much previous exposure to organized feminism.[56]

The teamsters and the turtles released public statements that revealed that they had been listening to the feminist researchers and garment workers who had described how international trade policy was harming women and people of color. A public letter signed by NGOs from around the world criticized the WTO and GATT agreements for benefiting "transnational corporations at the expense of national and local economies; workers, farmers, indigenous peoples, women and other social groups." They called for WTO compacts that did not interfere with multilateral agreements protecting human rights, the environment, health, food security, indigenous rights, and women's rights.[57]

Whereas today it might seem unremarkable that women and people of color were included in such statements, at the time such mentions were a milestone that revealed how far the ideas of these groups had traveled. "To blow open the notion that 'free trade' is gender neutral . . . was really a huge intellectual and political . . . contribution," observed Sparr.[58] The immigrant women resisting their local plant closures and the researchers working late at night in their carrels could never have predicted that one day their ideas would help shape in a massive worldwide protest.

"We were all feminists," said Ai-Jen Poo, describing a movement that did not always organize under that banner. Whether they were camping out in front of the headquarters of a large corporation or informing members of Congress about the effects of toxic chemicals, activists saw themselves advocating on behalf of women workers around the world. Care work was a global feminist issue, Poo asserted. So was factory work, free trade, and the protection of the environment, many others argued. Feminism could be a broad umbrella.[59]

NINE

HEART COMMUNITIES: SISTERSONG, SONG, AND INCITE!

Social justice was "in the fabric of my family for generations," recalled Beth Richie, whose parents' involvement in the civil rights movement offered a model of political commitment. "Engagement in social movements carried me through . . . elementary school, high school, undergrad, graduate school," she said. "It's . . . felt like a very natural pathway . . . the only pathway that I've known."[1]

In the early 1980s, Richie took a job as a social worker in a neighborhood health clinic in Harlem. She was attracted to the clinic's approach, which considered medical care as a racial and economic justice issue, just like housing or education. The longer she worked there, however, the more she realized that the list of services offered by the clinic was not comprehensive. In particular, she wondered if they could be doing more to address domestic violence. Many of the women she counseled felt trapped in abusive relationships.[2]

Struck by the magnitude of the problem, Richie started a domestic violence support group at the clinic and began attending meetings and conferences with feminists who were opening shelters and crisis lines in New York City and other parts of the country. She was impressed by white feminists' analyses of how patriarchal systems encouraged and tolerated sexual and domestic abuse.[3] And she felt inspired by the other women of color in the field who were networking with white activists and organizing independently. They were emphasizing how poverty and racism shaped intimate violence and calling attention to victims' reluctance to seek assistance from a criminal justice system they viewed as racist. White women were not yet paying much attention to their analyses. But the women of color felt optimistic that the more they shared their ideas, the more their white colleagues would learn. They felt similarly confident about the men they worked with in racial justice organizations. Perhaps naively, Richie reflected, "we expected that people we considered 'natural' social justice allies would meet our efforts with enthusiasm."[4]

What they were saying seemed obvious: Both sexism and racism shaped domestic and sexual abuse. Therefore, violence against women was both a feminist and a civil rights issue. To their surprise, neither the men nor the white women could accept this proposition. The men kept insisting that intimate violence had little to do with racial justice. And the women refused to consider racism as a major factor in shaping abuse. The title of a classic women's studies textbook summed up their challenge: *All the Women Are White, All the Blacks Are Men, But Some of Us Are Brave.*[5]

Richie and her colleagues were not the only ones in this predicament. Women of color health activists and lesbian rights activists had similar hurdles. Many white women focused on sexism, whereas women of color tended to see issues more holistically, linking the barriers people faced on account of sex to their struggles with racism and economic inequality. During the late 1980s and early 1990s, in the field of women's health, women of color attended all of the major meetings and conferences but could not shake the feeling that they were appendages to white organizing. White-dominated pro-choice organizations focused on abortion and did not support women of color's approach, which connected their right to terminate a pregnancy to their right to raise children and avoid sterilization abuse. The white men spearheading campaigns for gay rights had a similarly narrow focus. They prioritized fighting discrimination against homosexuals and did not welcome Black and white lesbians who insisted on also addressing economic inequality, sexism, and racial justice.

In the face of such resistance, women of color and lesbians who had been organizing independently joined forces and created multiracial coalitions of their own: INCITE! Women of Color Against Violence, the SisterSong Women of Color Reproductive Health Collective, and Southerners on New Ground (SONG). "To be in the margin is to be part of the whole but outside the main body," the Black feminist theorist bell hooks had observed in 1984. INCITE!, SisterSong, and SONG grew out of the margins of feminism, part of it, but not *of* it. The women who formed these organizations often interacted with white activists but always remained moored in communities of color. Because they were coming at feminist issues from their own perspectives, they were reimagining and inventing new ways of organizing around abortion, lesbian rights, and violence against women. Their holistic approaches sought to build coalitions among movements. They linked the struggle against domestic abuse with campaigns against militarism and police brutality and integrated the fight for sexual rights and reproductive health with efforts to achieve racial and economic justice. The more these women focused on building their own bases of power, the more those in the mainstream noticed—and felt compelled to respond.[6]

Most white feminists genuinely wanted to work with women of color—but on their terms. They prided themselves on opening up their meetings and offering women of color positions on boards of directors, but their attempts at outreach were too often clumsy afterthoughts. One admitted in retrospect that in making overtures, they had arrogantly expected women of color to "drop everything" to attend their events and fight for their issues.[7]

"It seemed like we were speaking different languages," Richie said. Her white colleagues had succeeded in convincing the public to take intimate violence more seriously by insisting that "any woman could be a battered woman" and that "rape is a threat to every woman." In conference papers and at meetings, Richie and her peers responded with evidence suggesting that such slogans, though well-intentioned, were harmful because they did not recognize how women's experiences of abuse differed along racial lines. White feminists nodded their heads but continued to repeat their own talking points. Richie participated in a variety of forums in which white women and women of color tried to team up. But the white women kept asking Richie and her peers to hold "diversity" training sessions to help facilitate "outreach" among women of color rather than engaging seriously with their ideas.[8]

White feminists persisted in emphasizing women's commonalities even as women's experiences increasingly diverged. During the late 1980s and early 1990s, people of color in many parts of the country were feeling the effects of the politicians' efforts to reduce homicides and the use of illegal drugs through stricter law enforcement. In New York City, where Richie lived, the number of officers patrolling the streets increased by nearly 50 percent between 1990 and 1997, with people of color most likely to be targeted by authorities. "We saw people being arrested, we saw police everywhere, we saw schools change," Richie recalled. Many white feminists fought for the 1994 Violence Against Women Act, landmark legislation that increased the funding of social services for victims, permitted undocumented immigrants to petition for legal-resident status, and suspended the deportation of some abused women. It made intimate partner violence a federal crime if it crossed state lines and imposed automatic and mandatory restitution by those convicted. But the act was passed as part of a conservative crime bill and most of the major remedies proposed relied on the criminal justice system—an institution that women of color distrusted.[9] It didn't fully take the experiences and perspectives of women of color into account.

White feminist leaders' support for legal remedies went hand in hand with their embrace of professionalization and turning away from the grassroots toward the nonprofit-industrial complex. As early as 1982, founders of the antiviolence movement had warned that their efforts were becoming depoliticized. Over the years, many women of color pointed out that to move toward a sort of "legitimate" activism—one that offered feminists paychecks and that cooperated with legal authorities—was increasingly to move away from the kind of activism that stood up for the needs of their communities.[10] Lines drawn became fractures.

A breaking point occurred at a board meeting for the National Coalition Against Sexual Assault in the late 1990s. During the coffee break, a group of women of color huddled in the hallway, grousing about how their opinions were once again being discounted and ignored. They had convened their own conferences on violence against women and had been talking for years about forming an independent organization. But this time, they started to make some real plans. One of them grabbed a pen and a napkin from the coffee stand and jotted down the names of the prominent women of color working in the field. (Beth Richie was not at the meeting, but her name was on the list.) The blurry writing on that crumpled napkin was the genesis of INCITE![11]

SONG's founders told a similar story of coming together during a national meeting where they felt alienated. It was a feeling Pat Hussain had experienced repeatedly in her youth. As a ten-year-old in Atlanta in the 1960s, Hussain had walked into a Krispy Kreme donut shop where people were sitting-in against Jim Crow. Upon witnessing a white man purchasing a hot cup of coffee and pouring it down the back of a Black girl, she recalled shaking with anger.

"I wanted to leap from that stool and attack him." With the police waiting to pounce on any Black person who made a wrong move, she got up from her chair and walked out. Hussain never forgot that moment. She believed that her inability to contain her rage and withstand humiliation was a "tremendous failure." As she watched the sit-ins spread across the South on her television screen, she felt "ashamed" at being "too weak to sit at a counter."[12]

Hussain also felt like a disappointment to her mother, who wished for a "girly-girl" instead of a tomboy who loved to ride her bike. At eighteen, however, she surprised her family by marrying and letting her mother plan a big wedding that included brides-maids and a honeymoon. A "virgin bride," she had trusted her husband when he told her she would grow to love him. After a few years, when she still felt empty inside, she went to the library and discovered a book called *The Bisexual Option*. "Well, maybe that's me," she thought as she turned the pages; she decided to visit a gay bar to find out. For months, every Friday and Saturday night, she stood outside of the bar feeling shaky and nauseous. "Calm down, Pat. Just go in. Have a drink," she told herself. But she could not muster up the courage to open the door.[13]

Finally, one evening her sister-in-law marched Hussain down to the bar and watched as she went in. Later that night, in the back of her van with a woman she had met, Hussain said she learned that she was definitely "not bisexual." She resolved to tell every member of her family that she was a lesbian, including her mother. One by one, they surprised her by accepting her sexual identity.[14]

Coming out made Hussain feel increasingly uncomfortable in the social justice campaigns she had joined. Having discovered new parts of herself, she felt as if the movement was forcing her to choose between identities. "I could work on civil rights . . . or I could work on issues of feminism . . . but they weren't woven together," she said. She had hoped to find refuge in the gay rights movement, but that turned out to be equally disillusioning: "My friends, my comrades, were killing me with their racism and sexism."[15]

In 1993, at the Creating Change Conference of the National Gay and Lesbian Task Force, Hussain found several other women who shared her frustrations. One of them, Mab Segrest, had been invited to give the keynote address at the conference. Segrest had recently taken a position with the World Council of Churches, which had introduced her to the networks of ecumenical activists like Pamela Sparr, who were fighting against the unregulated spread of global capitalism.[16] Segrest felt inspired by their work and wanted to share what she had learned with her fellow organizers in the gay rights movement. Her keynote movingly described the brutal working conditions she had witnessed on a recent trip to the *maquiladoras* and urged the crowd to join workers in the fight against global capitalism and white supremacy and in opposing NAFTA.[17]

The progressives in the audience loved Segrest's speech, during which she heard some hooting and hollering. But, as Hussain put it, most of the others were "muttering in the halls," claiming that NAFTA was an economic concern rather than a gay issue. Disheartened, Segrest, Hussain, and several others clustered together in one of the meeting rooms to discuss how to respond.[18]

Plans for SONG emerged in that room and in a series of conversations afterward. The founding group of the new organization was purposely interracial, with equal numbers of African American women and white women. The Black women were the Atlantan Hussain, the Durham-based Mandy Carter, and Joan Garner from Atlanta. The white women were the Arkansan Suzanne Pharr, the North Carolinian Segrest, and the Kentuckian Pam McMichael. Their résumés included Hussain's work as a cofounder of the Gay and Lesbian Alliance Against Defamation (GLAAD), Garner's role as director of the Fund for Southern Communities, Pharr's position as founder and director of the Little Rock Women's Project, Segrest's role as founding coordinator for North Carolinians Against Racist and Religious Violence, McMichael's position as cofounder of the Kentucky Fairness Campaign, and Carter's work as southeastern staff member of the War Resisters League.[19]

Five of the SONG founders (left to right): Mandy Carter, Suzanne Pharr, Pat Hussain, Pam McMichael, and Joan Garner. The sixth founder, Mab Segrest, is not in the photo. *Courtesy of Suzanne Pharr.*

It was a group of friends, most of whom knew one another already, who all shared a strong commitment to transforming the South. Calling the South their activist home, they saw themselves as part of a proud tradition of progressive movement building in a region many outsiders considered backward and incurably racist. In terms of sheer numbers, the South was crucial to any political fight. In the 1990s, three out of every ten Americans lived there. By 2015, it was four out of ten. Many believed if a progressive movement could succeed there, the rest of the nation would follow. "When the South is in motion for justice the whole country shakes," explained Hussain. The time had come for them "to step up" and do "our Southern work, in our Southern way."[20]

SisterSong formed a few years later in 1997, when the Ford Foundation responded to the burst of reproductive justice organizing among women of color by bringing some of the leading organizers together to create a national coalition.[21] From HIV/AIDS activists to midwives, everyone attending the Ford meeting could see their work as part of the struggle for reproductive justice, which they defined as the human right to have children, to not have children, and to parent in safe and sustainable communities.[22] On the eve of Ford's invitation, mainstream white women's health activists were "letting a few women of color in, one here, one there," recalled Luz Alvarez Martinez. One of twelve children born to Mexican immigrant parents, Martinez had grown up in the Bay Area, where her family spent summers harvesting plums and living in farmworker camps. In the early 1960s, after graduating from high school and getting a clerical job, she rebelled by moving out of her house and renting an apartment with a few friends instead of remaining at home or getting married. Another rebellion happened in a confession booth a decade later after she had married and given birth to twin boys. She told the priest that she was using birth control so she could wait a few years before having more children. He told her she could not use birth control and stay within the good graces of the church. "Forget it, that's over," she said, and left the church.[23]

That all happened before Martinez had even discovered organized feminism. In the late 1970s, once all four of her children were in elementary school, she began taking university courses to become a nurse midwife. Through her college's women's center, she met several members of the Berkeley Women's Health Collective who were running a feminist clinic. Martinez learned that they were part of a national network of feminist health activists whose work was guided by a conviction that medical care was a universal right—and one that could be delivered in large part by women who were not trained as physicians administering to other women. Soon Martinez was helping them establish a women of color clinic and attending training sessions and feminist conferences. She met several prominent African American activists, such as Byllye Avery, who took her under their wings and invited her to their events. Inspired by the First National Conference on Black Women's Health Issues at Spelman College in 1983 and the delegations African American women sent to the UN women's conference in Nairobi in 1985, Martinez began to think that Latinas needed to create their own health care network. In 1986, she cofounded the National Latina Health Organization in Oakland, the first national feminist health organization for Latinas.[24]

When white reproductive health advocates heard about Martinez and started inviting her to their events, she used it as an opportunity to highlight the lack of diversity in the pro-choice movement. She and several other women of color began refusing to participate in boards of directors, panels, meetings, and conferences unless the organizers asked more than one of them. If white organizers needed suggestions, she was happy to provide them with a long list.[25]

The tokenism was felt acutely in 1992, during the national pro-choice march held in Washington, DC. When planning for a march got under way, women of color called on the leaders to broaden the scope of the protest beyond abortion and to highlight the multifaceted struggles to exert bodily autonomy experienced by women who were not white or middle class. When NOW and other national pro-choice groups refused to go along with this, women of color organizers called on their supporters to march together wearing green armbands as a sign of protest. A frustrated Martinez yearned for an independent organization that would enable women of color to "call NOW to our table."[26]

Yet in 1997, when the Ford Foundation asked Luz Rodriguez, the executive director of the Latina Roundtable on Health and Reproductive Rights, to issue an open call to Native American, Latina, African American, and Asian American health activists to attend the meeting in New York City, many of them approached the occasion with skepticism. When Ford had sponsored women of color delegations to attend the 1994 UN Conference on Population and Development in Cairo and the 1995 Women's Conference in Beijing, the women's experiences of meeting one another and interacting with activists from other countries had been exhilarating, but their efforts to collectively draft statements about reproductive health had been challenging. Many had also been disappointed when Ford's funding dried up after the conferences.[27]

Rodriguez was not a nationally recognized reproductive justice leader and had not been part of those earlier efforts. Recognizing that most of the group did not trust her and that some felt wary of the prospect of working together under Ford's stewardship, she opened the meeting by asking the attendees to consider the collective power amassed by flocks of geese flying south for the winter in V formation, with each bird creating an uplift for the bird immediately behind. She said that the same was true of people and that a group effort could be particularly valuable when the going got tough. Geese rotated their positions as the leaders grew weary, sharing the burden of flying out front. And when one got sick or wounded, two others would "fall out" to lend their help. The more Rodriguez spoke, the more the energy in the room changed. Things began to feel lighter. She followed the speech with an ice-breaker that required each person to describe their most recent Pap smear. The answers brought forth gales of laughter and even a few tears. As the tension lifted, they began to appreciate the historic opportunity in front of them.[28]

A new organization could not be built from scratch in a single meeting or through phone calls or email. What came to be known as SisterSong, SONG, and INCITE! emerged after their founders spent extended time together in close quarters. INCITE! founders did the bulk of their planning over several intense weekends. Because they all lived in different parts of the country and could not afford hotel rooms, they would choose one person to host and then the rest would descend on that person's city. After everyone arrived, they typically spread their sleeping bags out on the floor and began talking, rarely taking a break. The conversations lasted late into the night, filled with an energy and passion they found intoxicating. These were no ordinary slumber parties. They were making

INCITE! into what one of them called a "heart community"—an intellectual and spiritual home.[29]

The INCITE! founders used their time together to further develop the analyses of violence against women that they had been promoting in their communities for decades. They determined that because women of color were just as victimized by state violence (enacted by institutions such as the legal and immigration systems) as they were by interpersonal violence, their organizing would have to address both. They pledged to do so through political organizing rather than social service delivery. Their goal was to treat survivors as potential activists rather than clients.[30]

The planning sessions for SONG happened at a more leisurely pace. "We always had great fun together," Pharr reminisced. During weekends at one another's homes, they laughed, flirted, and took long breaks for meals and walks. After years of running between meetings for different causes, the opportunity to sit down and share a meal felt symbolic. Hussain realized she had spent years grabbing snacks in the car and suffering from splitting headaches because she was too busy to eat. Wondering why their movements overlooked something as human as food, she determined that SONG would be different. "Eating food became a force in our organizing," she said.[31]

Inspired by the principles laid out in the 1977 statement by the Black feminist Combahee River Collective, SONG founders shared a commitment to tackling the interlocking systems of oppression that they believed made it impossible for gay people to live authentically. Fed up with civil rights activists prioritizing racism, feminists prioritizing sexism, and gay rights organizers prioritizing homophobia, they planned for SONG to address people's "whole selves" and fulfill their longings to live fully integrated lives.[32]

This would not be a reworking of Charlotte Bunch's experiment with separatism, which had called on lesbians to organize only among themselves. For decades, SONG's leaders had been forging alliances with other progressives that they had no intention of severing. With right-wing politicians such as North Carolina senator Jesse Helms using racism and homophobia to sow divisions among people who could have been allies, they believed coalitions were needed more than ever to fight back. Most SONG members were veteran activists who had worked on a variety of Southern social justice campaigns as out lesbians, and they saw themselves as uniquely well positioned to knit diverse groups of people together.[33]

Like SONG, SisterSong also had a focus on the South, and determining its guiding principles seemed straightforward at first. Black women had shared their vision of reproductive justice and delighted in how the others could see their work contributing to that far-reaching struggle to ensure that all women could secure bodily autonomy and achieve the right to choose whether and how to parent. Asian Americans who were facing an influx of toxins in their neighborhoods could define reproductive justice as encompassing their fight for safe food and a clean environment. The Native American activists could use the term to describe their quest for sovereignty and self-determination.

Some of the biggest stumbling blocks emerged when people who were not part of SisterSong meetings began using the label "reproductive justice." Over the ensuing years, Black women were dismayed to see that almost anything could be called reproductive justice—from pro-choice activism to breast cancer screenings. Some were so annoyed by this appropriation that they considered copyrighting the term. Others proposed requiring people to be officially trained before they could use it. One activist tried to help the organization navigate this morass by drafting a concept paper outlining what she saw as three equally crucial lines of work that were happening in the field: *reproductive health* (service delivery), *reproductive rights* (legal and advocacy work), and *reproductive justice* (organizing to identify and change broad structural power inequalities). She had hoped the paper would inspire activists to claim niches. Yet there was so much buzz about reproductive justice that a surprising number of people misconstrued her list to be endorsing that one method of organizing over everything else.[34]

Ultimately, SisterSong members decided that rather than police other people's interpretations of reproductive justice, they should focus on promoting their own definition, particularly through organizing conferences. The organization's executive director, Loretta Ross, had gotten her start as a paid organizer at the Rape Crisis Center in Washington, DC, and had participated in the UN events in both Nairobi and Beijing. Those experiences had taught her about the power of conferences to set agendas and define movements. In 2003, and again in 2007, she put on major national conferences that showcased the creative forms of reproductive justice activism happening across the country and highlighted women of color's expertise.[35]

Both SisterSong and INCITE! used national conferences to energize and connect the growing numbers of women of color

Loretta Ross speaking from the podium at the first SisterSong conference in 2003. Setting up the stage as a well-decorated altar honoring the ancestors and representing all four racial-ethnic groups became a SisterSong tradition, as did decorating the rooms in which panels took place. They modeled this practice on the National Black Women's Health Project's 1983 conference. *Courtesy of SisterSong.*

activists who were toiling at the grassroots. White people were used to attending conferences in which they were in the majority, but most women of color had never had such an opportunity. The experience was like discovering a well of cold water during a trek across the desert. The inspiring intellectual exchanges and personal interactions replenished them and readied them for the hard work ahead.[36]

SONG organized hundreds of smaller meetings in places where no gay rights groups had gone before. When they ventured into some of the most rural and isolated communities in the South, they found that even a small workshop or a film screening could change a person's life. Most other gay rights activists assumed rural people were ignorant. But SONG members who had been raised in such communities, like Suzanne Pharr, considered them "smart and knowledgeable," just lacking exposure to new ideas. Even people in SONG who had not grown up in the rural South embraced the challenge of organizing there. Whenever an opportunity to conduct outreach in a small town arose, Mandy Carter was known for jumping in her Volvo, turning on her radio, and driving for hours to make it happen.[37]

This was not the kind of work that attracted major New York City funders. While INCITE! and SisterSong were navigating their relationships with the Ford Foundation, SONG was reaching out to smaller and more specialized foundations and cultivating individual donors. After Hussain and McMichael took on roles as paid staff members, they headed up these fundraising efforts. The prospect of raising money filled Hussain with dread. Every time she asked a white person for money, she felt as if she was "going back to master with my hat in my hand" and "begging" for support. The lyrics of a James Brown song played in the back of her head: I don't want nobody / To give me nothing.[38]

Hussain never did enjoy fundraising, but over time, she became skilled at asking for donations. People felt better about themselves after they gave to SONG, she realized. This was particularly true of gay people who were keeping their sexual identities under wraps. "There's a slot in the front of that closet door," Hussain reminded them, promising to keep their secret while they slid their check out.[39]

SONG placed a huge emphasis on relationship building, a process Hussain likened to cooking a brisket. "You've got to take your time," she said. The organization became known for its weekend retreats, which melded popular education with time for the arts and self-reflection. At a 1998 People of Color Leadership retreat at a lakeside conference center in Little Rock, Arkansas, for instance, twenty-six participants from nine Southern states got to know one another by sharing their "transformation stories"—moments in their lives that had fundamentally changed them. Other sessions helped them envision a place for themselves in the "People of Color LesBiTrans movement" and consider how they could collaborate on joint projects. Offering participants a much-needed break from the frenetic pace of their daily lives, SONG retreats included time for people to relax and, when facilities were available, to swim, hike, and canoe. In the evenings, they had dinner together, often accompanied by poetry readings and musical performances.[40]

Nowhere else in the South could queer people of color experience such nurturing. "SONG operates by a format that I can only describe as building family into the movement," one participant observed. "When you step into a SONG space it's like going back to your favorite aunt's house for a special family gathering full of the type of deep conversations and face-splitting laughter you've longed for all year."[41] After two days soaking up the atmosphere, another activist described leaving a SONG retreat feeling "happy and over-joyed to be gay."[42]

Relationship building among gay people was important, but the SONG founders knew they could not win their fight alone. They reached out to people in other movements, offering workshops that helped other activists envision building multi-issue campaigns and analyze how the rise of conservatism was hurting women and minorities of all kinds.[43] Leading by example, SONG

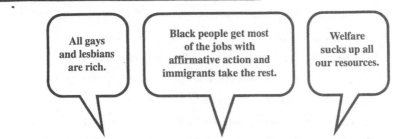

These quotes from the Right try to divert attention from...

Let's focus attention on real causes, not scapegoats, in a participatory workshop

THE ECONOMY

AND LESBIGAYTRANS LIBERATION

Thursday, September 12, 7:00 - 9:30 pm, White Rabbit Books, 309 West Martin, Raleigh

Hosted by White Rabbit Books

We often hear that the only thing lesbigaytrans people have in common is our sexual orientation, but beyond loving differently, we also share in common a basic need to make a living. At whatever level our jobs, we all are feeling the tremors of economic insecurity.

This economic climate affects our work for social change, economic issues help to fuel the fear tactics and divisive agenda of the Right, and conservative campaigns are not just homophobic, but driven by a system which seeks to shred the social safety net and values profits over people. Particularly in the soundbite scapegoating of a presidential and senatorial election year, we need to be better informed to challenge the platforms of those who oppose justice and to develop a better understanding of economic fairness.

On Thursday, September 12, 7:00 - 9:30 p.m., White Rabbit Books is hosting an economic workshop presented by SONG, Southerners on New Ground. The workshop for lesbigaytrans people and allies will explore our current economy and how it got that way, who benefits and who loses, connect the economic terrain to our struggle for lesbigaytrans liberation, and help develop methods to decode economic language and policies.

Workshop facilitated by SONG Co-director Pam McMichael
To register, call 856-1429

(see reverse)

A flyer advertising a SONG-sponsored workshop linking economic justice and queer rights. *Courtesy of Mandy Carter Papers, David M. Rubenstein Rare Book & Manuscript Library, Duke University.*

members joined the five-year Mount Olive Pickle boycott on behalf of immigrant farmworkers and backed the 2003 Immigrant Freedom Rides—caravans of buses that traversed the nation advocating for legal status for undocumented people. Their participation in these campaigns sent out two related messages. First, Southern organizers could only combat the right wing's divide-and-conquer strategy by supporting one another. Second, gay people were also immigrants and farmworkers; their struggles were one and the same.[44]

For INCITE!, the war in Afghanistan offered an opportunity to lend a feminist voice to the progressive organizing against the US invasion. When President George W. Bush gave a speech claiming that US troops would help save Afghan women from the Taliban, INCITE! members were horrified. They were even more distressed when the Feminist Majority Foundation supported the invasion on similar grounds. Several INCITE! members had met feminists from Afghanistan who opposed the US military presence. The Afghan women saw the US military and the bombing campaigns introducing new forms of fear and violence into their daily lives.[45]

In the moment of intense patriotism that followed September 11, what could INCITE! do to counter the bombs being dropped in the name of women? They devised a striking set of posters for members to distribute. One featured a peace sign with "Not in Our Name! Women of Color Against War." Another presented a portrait of a woman wearing a headscarf with the caption: "We Are Not the Enemy." From Santa Cruz to Chicago, feminists ordered the posters by the hundreds. INCITE! supporters brought the posters to antiwar marches, stapled them to signposts, hung them in windows, and displayed them on porches and front doors.[46]

Why would an organization concerned with violence against women join the opposition to the war in Afghanistan instead of welcoming the attempt to overthrow one of the most misogynist regimes in modern history? That was precisely the question INCITE! hoped their comrades in antiwar protests would ask. During

Posters from INCITE!'s campaign against the US invasion of Afghanistan. *Courtesy of INCITE!*

the weekends they had spent bunking up together, they had talked about how the professionals who sought to solve the problem of violence against women by relying on the criminal justice system failed to recognize the ways the state also perpetrated violence. INCITE! members saw violence in the home and violence enacted by the state (police, immigration officials, and the military) as two sides of the same coin. The Feminist Majority Foundation focused only on the former. From INCITE!'s perspective, how could feminists resolve to protect women from domestic violence but not care about those women's homes being destroyed by bombs and their country becoming the target of a military occupation? Predicting that the war would exacerbate poverty in Afghanistan and result in the destruction of schools and medical facilities, they feared these conditions would only heighten Afghan women's risk of experiencing interpersonal violence. In short, the military was part of the problem—not the solution.[47]

Like many of the US activists participating in the transnational feminist networks that were lobbying the UN, INCITE!

believed that it was not enough to say that they stood in solidarity with women in Afghanistan; they were obligated to seek change in their own country and exert pressure on their own government. The posters were part of that vision, as were the campaigns they launched against US military recruitment in working-class communities of color.[48]

INCITE! deepened its analysis of the connections between state and interpersonal violence through a partnership with Critical Resistance. Several of the founders were members of this national organization cofounded by Angela Davis in California in 1997 with the goal of ending what they called the prison industrial complex—the way that the government and industry work together to use policing and imprisonment as solutions to economic and social problems. Critical Resistance had an outspoken feminist at the helm, but most of its initiatives did not address violence against women. INCITE! urged it to consider a different approach.[49]

In 2001, representatives of INCITE! and Critical Resistance spent a weekend together to hammer out joint priorities. They went home triumphant, having coauthored a "Statement on Gender Violence and the Prison Industrial Complex." The statement included a stinging critique of mainstream feminists for relying so heavily on the criminal justice system to prosecute cases of domestic and sexual abuse and a call for the prison abolitionists in Critical Resistance and other organizations to address the multiple forms of violence that women and LGBT people faced in prisons, on the streets, and in their own homes. As academics and activists circulated the statement gathering signatures, they heralded it as a model of intramovement collaboration.[50]

Even the National Coalition Against Domestic Violence signed onto the statement, revealing how INCITE!'s presence had shifted power dynamics in the antiviolence movement. Over a decade earlier, white activists had refused to follow recommendations made by women of color. INCITE!'s emergence on the national scene had clearly shaken things up.[51] Although most of the white women running domestic violence and sexual assault programs would continue to rely on the criminal justice system, INCITE!'s organizing had forced them to acknowledge that theirs was not the only approach. Some of them even acknowledged that their "overreliance" on punitive strategies had been a "mistake."[52]

Even more dramatic shifts occurred in the abortion rights movement as SisterSong became a powerful force. In 2003, representatives from NOW, Planned Parenthood, the Feminist Majority Foundation, and the National Abortion Rights and Action League (NARAL) traveled to the SisterSong conference to ask women of color to support their upcoming march in Washington. In response, women of color came up with a set of demands. To signal that the protest was not just about abortion, they asked the organizers to change its name from the "March for Freedom of Choice" to the "March for Women's Lives." The leaders honored that request and also granted women of color seats on the march's steering committee and provided funding to pay for them to travel to the event. Loretta Ross agreed to serve as codirector of the march after the organizers met her demands, which included adequate compensation and a promise that she could focus her energies on mobilizing people of color.[53] It became the largest national demonstration the feminist movement had ever held, with over one million people estimated to have attended the 2004 event, at least 250,000 more than at the march held in 1992.[54]

While Martinez's dream of forcing NOW to come to their table had come true, the degree to which the white-led organizations had changed was an open question. After the march, NARAL hired SisterSong to conduct a "training" session on reproductive justice, but whether such education would produce any tangible changes in the organization remained unclear. The following year, Planned Parenthood sponsored a conference named "Reproductive Justice for All."[55] Were white women changing their approaches or practicing new forms of tokenism and appropriation? Would they ever really consider foregrounding the struggles of women of color? SisterSong's leaders could have easily gotten caught up in such hand-wringing. Instead, they joined activists in SONG and INCITE! in continuing to blaze their own trail.

EPILOGUE

During the 2000s, the founders of SONG, SisterSong, and INCITE! encountered a new generation of activists brimming with energy and ideas, and they decided that it was time to pass the baton. Decades on the front lines had alerted them to the perils of "founders' syndrome"—a hesitancy on the part of creators of nonprofit organizations to empower new leadership and allow organizations to change.

"We love SONG, but we're going to step back," Mandy Carter recalled thinking. Some of her colleagues stayed involved to ease the transition by providing support for the new team. Others left, finding it difficult to assume a position "halfway in and halfway out." "It's hard to let go of control," Mab Segrest acknowledged. But she did.[1]

Their departures allowed the organizations to incorporate ideas about gender and sexuality that many younger activists held dear. Although veterans had fond memories of their women's "heart communities," the new leaders believed that woman-only and lesbian-only spaces excluded people who did not fit rigid binary definitions of gender as male or female, and of sexual identity as either gay, bisexual, or straight. Welcoming fluidity, they threw open the doors. Before long, SisterSong had a Black male staff member. INCITE! revised its mission statement to include transgender and queer people of color. SONG's codirectors were a Black woman and a Latino man, who both identified as queer.

In the 2010s, all three organizations extended their founders' commitment to addressing pressing issues of the day by forging common cause with Black Lives Matter, the mass movement against racist police violence. The Black-led movement was sparked by the 2013 acquittal of a vigilante Florida homeowner, George Zimmerman, for killing an unarmed Black teenager, Trayvon Martin.[2] Black feminism was—and remains—the "intellectual lifeblood" of Black Lives Matter, observes historian Barbara Ransby. Rooted in nineties activism, the movement recognizes the interlocking systems of oppression people face and centers the concerns of those most harmed by these systems, including incarcerated women of color and their children. Feminists who were active in the nineties have been part of Black Lives Matter from the start and, in turn, the movement has empowered a new generation of activists.[3]

In 2013, INCITE! and SisterSong helped spearhead the Free Marissa Now campaign, which highlighted the struggles that women of color face. They called for the release from prison of Marissa Alexander, a victim of domestic violence who had been prosecuted for killing her abusive husband under the same "Stand Your Ground" laws that had exonerated Zimmerman. The campaign emphasized the connections between state and intimate violence first articulated by INCITE! It also drew on the theories developed by SisterSong to highlight how the assaults on Alexander's body and the legal system's restrictions on her ability to raise her children violated her reproductive freedom.[4]

Four years later, SONG followed up with Black Mamas Bail Out, a campaign to get Black mothers and caregivers out of jail in time for Mother's Day. This effort drew public attention to African

American women's disproportionate presence in jails and the injustices of the cash bail system.[5] Black Mamas Bail Out emphasized how regularly poor people of color are sent to jail simply because they cannot afford to post cash bail. Many lose their jobs and housing in the process because they can't make it to work and they can't pay rent.[6] SONG focused on bailing out Black mothers, codirector Mary Hooks explained, because African American women comprise 44 percent of the women in the nation's jails.[7] How was cash bail also a queer issue? SONG pointed to the "queer and trans mothers" who rarely captured public attention: "As a Black lesbian mother, as someone who has spent time in a cage, I know the feeling of being snatched away from my babies," Hooks told reporters.[8] By humanizing female prisoners as mothers cut off from beloved children, the action sought to expose the senseless cruelty of the system.[9]

The speed with which the Black Lives Matter movement emerged from the grassroots and articulated a clear set of goals has served as inspiration and a model for all kinds of feminists today. One white feminist remembered growing up and wondering: "Why isn't there anything like the Civil Rights Movement?" To witness Black Lives Matter creating a "public media storm" was "incredible." She had been an activist for decades, but it was the first time she felt like "real change is happening."[10] Some white feminists who were not directly part of the movement have tried to build coalitions with Black Lives Matter activists and to integrate issues of policing and criminal justice into other forms of organizing. Almost everyone sees Black Lives Matter as a powerful example of what a social movement can accomplish. "We need a Black Lives Matter for abortion," one said.[11]

Such a new mass movement surrounding abortion seems improbable at the moment. Even as most of the public supports the right to terminate a pregnancy, the longstanding power struggles between mainstream abortion rights activists and reproductive justice organizers that activists tried to work through in the nineties have not gone away.[12] Many other social justice campaigns, however, increasingly rely on broad-based coalitions that foreground the experiences and leadership of women of color. This is evident in the current immigrant rights movement's campaigns for legal protection and a path to citizenship, and it was part of the protests against the Dakota Access Pipeline staged by Native Americans and their supporters at Standing Rock in 2016. Drawing on matriarchal tribal structures, indigenous women "water protectors" were the core spiritual leaders and main strategists of the campaign against the pipeline and they frequently spoke out about the abuse they suffered from a police force they believed put the interests of oil corporations ahead of ordinary people.[13] In 2016, a broad-based coalition of unionized nurses, environmentalists, clergy, and Black Lives Matter activists, who came together to support the protests, insisted that "everything is connected—minimum wage, racial justice, climate change, women's rights, LGBT rights." They believed that their movements would rise or fall together.[14]

Many of the feminists participating in contemporary political campaigns continue to build and draw on the international networks that took shape in the nineties. In 2014, at the historic People's Climate March in New York City, over forty groups marched together under a banner proclaiming "No Climate Justice Without Gender Justice!" The women's contingent included Development Alternatives with Women for a New Era (DAWN), the Global South organization that had produced the research on gender and structural adjustment that had sparked many US feminists' intellectual awakening. The US-based Women's Environment and Development Organization founded by Bella Abzug also participated, as did Madre, one of the organizations that had helped connect women workers from Mexico and the United States. Activists emphasized the dramatic effects of global warming on women, especially indigenous women and women from the Global South. Women are 80 percent of the world's small-scale farmers and they bear unique burdens when there are crop failures or other environmental damage to local agriculture. As the world's primary caregivers, they shoulder the heaviest load as climate change spurs the spread of disease and makes illness more extreme.[15] These insights and activism drew directly on the feminist research and international networks of the nineties.

"Millennials were not born intersectional feminists," remarked Veronica Arreola, who had helped initiate the rise of online feminism through her blog and her creation of the first pro-choice webring. "They were raised in an environment that was already seeded with intersectional feminism." To miss that history is to forget all of the work that made the activist world of today. Erasure of the learning and intense labor of the past scripts a myth that the younger generation is somehow naturally more enlightened than previous generations, missing how much they are able to take for granted thanks to the work of their forebearers as well as how they share many beliefs with the activists who came before them. Such forgetting elides how movements of today are always building on and reacting to the activism of yesterday to meet today's conditions even as they build the groundwork for the future.[16]

It is not just the ideas promoted by older activists that contemporary feminists draw on—it's also their networks and personal relationships. When people engage in activism, they often forge connections that endure. Participating in a monumental event like the Beijing conference can bond people for life. But so, too, can the everyday work of organizing, be it arranging a panel discussion with new collaborators or sharing donuts on a subway while heading to a protest. Even when activists participate in campaigns that fail, the experience is rarely for naught. In 2018, feminists understood that they had little chance of stopping the appointment of Brett Kavanaugh to the Supreme Court. But that did not keep the National Abortion Rights Action League from allying with MoveOn.org to forge a coalition of seventy-five organizations that included the American Federation of Teachers, the Center for Popular Democracy, and the National Domestic Workers Alliance to stage demonstrations across the country.[17] Although they weren't able to halt the appointment, the next time a similar fight arises, the networks formed through the anti-Kavanaugh demonstrations will already be in place. The activists' personal connections will deepen when they engage in subsequent campaigns and they will bring new people to the movement. Disagreements or personal conflicts may emerge during this work that will need to be addressed if those activists wish to try to ally with one another again. We cannot understand the opportunities and challenges confronting feminists today without reckoning with both the bridges people burned in the past and those they built. Activism is social and the social is powerful.

Activism also requires money. A few feminist organizations still attempt to forge their own paths by relying solely on volunteers. But even Black Lives Matter (which is, in many respects, the epitome of a twenty-first-century grassroots movement) counts paid activists among its leaders. Critiques of the nonprofit-industrial complex such as those voiced by INCITE! have been heard, though, and there is a greater awareness of the problems that arise when foundation officers try to drive movement strategies rather than follow the lead of those working at the grassroots. Yet contemporary organizers continue to feel the contradictions articulated by the feminists of the nineties. They can't do their work without money, but they are constrained when the demands of the funders do not align with their vision of social change.[18]

Whereas many 1990s feminist organizations turned to email for communication and some groups established websites, many of the leaders of today's movements see online and in-person organizing as of a piece, with each dimension being equally important. Through Facebook and Twitter, they can drive national news cycles and raise thousands of dollars in a single day. In 2012, when the Susan G. Komen for the Cure Foundation, the largest and best-funded breast cancer nonprofit in the United States, announced that it would stop funding Planned Parenthood (which conducts breast exams and provides sexual and reproductive health care in addition to abortions), the outpouring of outrage feminists drummed up online forced reporters to cover the story. By the time the Komen Foundation reversed its decision and apologized, Twitter users had sent over 1.3 million tweets mentioning Planned Parenthood and it had raised $3 million.[19]

As in the nineties, the internet remains a place where all kinds of people share feminist ideas, often without receiving any kind of monetary compensation. Many see their online commentary as advancing their paid work in professions such as journalism and education, whether they post as individuals or as members of organizations. Some of these feminists do not need a platform like Planned Parenthood to drive national news cycles; they have created their own networks that can be activated with a single Tweet. In 2011, for instance, when the Missouri representative Todd Akin told KTVI-TV that pregnancy from rape is rare because "if it's a legitimate rape, the female body has ways to try to shut that whole thing down," online activists made sure the statement became national news. Todd Akin became a trending topic on Twitter while thousands posted on Akin's Facebook page, demanding that he withdraw from the Senate race that he had entered. Mainstream media outlets such as the *New York Times* picked up on the story, as did Akins's colleagues in Congress (many of whom also urged him to withdraw). Three months later, Akin lost the election.[20]

Feminists also increasingly use social media to hash out disagreements among themselves. In the 1990s, they were mostly finding one another online and creating niche communities of like-minded people. By the 2000s, some were also often engaging with other activists who failed to incorporate their perspectives. In the early 2010s, for instance, US women of color expressed their dissatisfaction with feminist "SlutWalk" marches, which began in Toronto following a police officer's statement that women should try to prevent rape by avoiding "acting like sluts." Feminists of color agreed that women's safety should not be tied to their appearance, but many felt uncomfortable with using the word *slut* as a rallying cry in the protest marches held around the world. Because the term *slut* had distinct historical meanings for women of color, the politics of reclaiming it were fraught. "We don't have the privilege to walk through the streets . . . either half-naked or fully clothed self-identifying as 'sluts' and think that this will make women safer in our communities," one collective of Black women wrote in an open letter to the SlutWalk organizers.[21]

Feminist online networks widely shared and debated these critiques by women of color. Yet the call for SlutWalk to fully integrate women of color's perspectives and choose a new name went unheeded. Though ever-increasing numbers of white feminists have recognized women of color's perspectives, many still resist prioritizing these views. They are not alone in foregrounding their own issues. Some middle-class feminists of color, for example, feel no obligation to lift up the views of working-class women, particularly if they are white. Activism from the margins is more vibrant and influential than ever—but that does not mean that feminism has suddenly become a monolith in which everyone supports the same agenda.

Yet in some cases, women of color have changed public conversations with remarkable speed. This happened in 2017, when the actress Alyssa Milano asked survivors of sexual violence to reply with the hashtag #MeToo. Through social media networks that had been decades in the making, women of color pointed out that Tarana Burke had come up with the slogan over a decade earlier in her work with survivors of sexual abuse. Like many feminists, Burke had decided that the best way to address a social problem—in this case, that of sexual harassment and assault of young low-income women of color—was to create a nonprofit. She had started Just Be Inc in 2007 and used the slogan "Me Too" to foster empathy among women from different walks of life. Ten years later, after women of color drew attention to her activism online, mainstream news reporters picked up the story. After Milano learned of this history, she acknowledged Burke's efforts and shared the spotlight.[22]

A few months later, when reporters shifted their focus to the sexual harassment of women in Hollywood, feminists of color again redirected the narrative. The farmworker organization Alianza Nacional de Campesinas issued a public letter that expressed support for their Hollywood sisters while calling attention to the sexual abuse suffered by the seven hundred thousand women who worked in the fields and packing sheds. Their complaints echoed those voiced by nineties organizations such as Fuerza Unida and Asian Immigrant Women Advocates (AIWA). While Fuerza Unida and AIWA had used conferences and face-to-face meetings to tell white feminists about their struggles and secure support, the farmworkers posted their letter on the online website of *Time* magazine and shared it through social media. After attracting a great deal of attention online and off, the letter prompted celebrities to create #TimesUp, an initiative to eliminate harassment and abuse in all workplaces that has raised over $21 million to fund legal assistance for victims.[23]

The #TimesUp cause made a public appearance at the 2018 Golden Globe Awards ceremony, where women wore black and many men sported pins to signal their support. Seven celebrity women brought women of color activists as their dates, including Burke and the domestic worker organizer Ai-Jen Poo. In interviews on the red carpet, the activists galvanized support for their causes, resulting in an additional $700,000 raised within thirty-six hours.[24]

As with almost all highly publicized feminist activity, this display of solidarity drew criticism from others in the movement. Some charged that it was not real activism because it involved wearing fancy clothing and going to galas rather than advocating for tangible policy changes. Others questioned the depth of celebrities' commitments and faulted them for lacking connections to low-income communities.[25]

Into this dust-up stepped Rinku Sen. The racial justice feminist who had been a bridge builder at the Ms. Foundation orientation in Beijing in 1995 penned a widely shared post on social media that was reprinted in *The Nation*. Sen reminded those who criticized the action as not being radical enough that #TimesUp was rooted in decades of grassroots organizing. The core ideas of the campaign—that sexual abuse and harassment were problems also faced by women who were not wealthy and white and that those who worked in low-paid occupations were at great risk—were not glib slogans, but rather ideas that had been expressed for decades by activists, so it was good to see them receive broad publicity. "No one knows exactly what formula will ward off the authoritarianism looming over our country and the world, but that formula probably doesn't include the word 'only,'" Sen observed. Too often organizers got trapped in binaries, thinking they had to choose between policy change or cultural change, civil disobedience or voter registration, showing up at a celebrity gala or organizing in local communities. In fact, social movements needed to pursue all of those tactics— and more. She reminded the critics that no single strategy, idea, or demonstration had ever changed the world by itself.[26]

Sen's "humble 33-year view of social change" had taught her that it "takes *everything* to build a movement in the millions. . . . Everything we've got. Every member, every leader, every ally, every platform, every tactic and every dime—all directed toward specific goals at specific moments." Movements did not produce their strategies and foot soldiers at the flip of a switch. They activated personal networks and ways of thinking that had been decades in the making—only becoming visible to the mainstream in particular instances when people turned to look. "The moments when your big ideas have the potential to become reality don't come around that often," Sen warned. "When they do, we have to move."[27] The feminists of the 1990s, the change-makers no one had seen coming, had put in place what was needed for the surge.

ACKNOWLEDGMENTS

This book grew out of my conversations with activists who took a leap of faith and trusted me to tell their stories. Although many of their names do not appear in the text, everyone I interviewed shaped the narrative and changed the way I think about the world. It was a privilege to learn from so many inspiring people.

Archivists across the country welcomed me into their reading rooms and patiently helped me locate crucial documents. I am especially indebted to the staff at the Sophia Smith Collection of Women's History at Smith College, who hosted me year after year; they are building a rich repository of the records of grassroots feminists, especially of women of color. I also took particular pleasure in working with the feminists running the Sallie Bingham Collection at Duke University and the Schlesinger Library at the Radcliffe Institute.

Without financial support, this book would have been much longer in the making. The American Philosophical Society, Linda Arnold Carlisle Grant, Princeton University Library, Rockefeller Archive Center, Sophia Smith Collection, Southern Association for Women's Historians, and the University of North Carolina Greensboro helped fund my research. I spent an unforgettable year at the National Humanities Center, where I received expert assistance from librarians Brooke Andrade and Sarah Harris and enjoyed cultivating relationships with scholars from other institutions, including David Johnson, Kunal Parker, and Nan Woodruff. A yearlong fellowship from the American Council of Learned Societies came at another perfect moment, enabling me to hunker down and finish drafting the book.

I relied on a network of college students to drive my children from place to place while I typed. Several of them became trusted friends and role models: Mady Morton, Caroline Medlock, and Amira Shehata. Madeline Huey became part of our family.

For assistance both personal and professional, I am grateful to Jennifer Ash, Pete Carmichael, Tamar Carroll, Marisa Chappell, Nan Enstad, Crystal Feimster, Susanna Lee, Katherine Marino, Jennifer Mittelstadt, Jocelyn Olcott, Anne Parsons, Peter Willets, and Leandra Zarnow. I am also fortunate to have Wesley Hogan and Rachel Seidman as friends and colleagues—both of them shared parts of their own books with me prior to publication.

Several people generously offered astute comments on the entire manuscript: Eileen Boris, anu Jain, Grey Osterud, and Judy Wu. For helpful feedback on chapters and articles, heartfelt thanks to Paul Adler, Keisha Blain, Jason Brent, Dorothy Sue Cobble, Nan Enstad, Benjamin Filene, Daisy Hernandez, Kate Masur, Joanne Meyerowitz, Premilla Nadasen, Claire Potter, Robyn Spencer, Heather Thompson, and Lisa Tetrault. I also benefited from the many activists who sent me primary documents and fact-checked passages.

My writing group of Nancy MacLean, Jacquelyn Dowd Hall, and Laura Edwards read the book chapter by chapter and Tera Hunter joined us for a year when she was living in North Carolina. Tera's friendship has been a lifeline and she continued to help with the book from Princeton. Laura took me on invigorating walks around her neighborhood and helped me gain perspective. No question was ever too small for Jacquelyn, a meticulous editor who spent hours patiently contemplating word choices while sneaking in the hardest questions. Nancy MacLean read multiple drafts on short notice. Her brilliance is evident on every page. A loyal and trusted friend, Nancy pushed me to make this a better book while generously sharing the tools to make it happen.

I relished working with Deborah Mitchum, a talented transcriber with a remarkable eye for detail. Vaughn Stewart and Lane Ridenhour offered technical assistance with photographs and Skype. Tiffany Holland, Hannah Dudley Shotwell, and Kelsey Walker were excellent research assistants. Kristina Wright and Sheila Washington offered vital practical support. Linda Gordon started me down this road decades ago and remains an inspiration. For many years, Grey Osterud and Eileen Boris have been personal and professional mentors and I am thankful for their wisdom and their friendship.

Many trusted colleagues at the University of North Carolina Greensboro have been inspiring players in the struggle to preserve the core values of higher education and to resist the corporatization of the university. Without people like Asa Eger, Jennifer Feather, Veronica Grossi, and Anne Parsons, I would despair. My summer reading group reminds me of why I became a historian in the first place and the faculty in my new home of Women's, Gender, and Sexuality Studies are reminding me of what still can be accomplished.

Heather Thompson has been my advocate and confidante since the day I met her. She introduced me to Geri Thoma, who has expertly helped me navigate the world of publishing. Kate Masur and I were campus feminists together in the nineties and she has remained a vital part of my life ever since. Kate put me in touch with Leah Strecher, who acquired the book for Basic and encouraged me to think in more expansive ways.

Working with my editor Claire Potter has been one of the greatest experiences of my professional career. She astutely helped me develop my vision and taught me how to execute it on the page. Claire's enthusiasm and faith in my abilities have made this a better book than I could have ever dreamed of writing. She is also a kickass feminist. Christina Palaia was a tremendously insightful copyeditor, and Stephan Przybylowicz was an excellent indexer. Brynn

Warriner's patience and meticulousness made a huge difference. Thanks also to Lara Heimert, Basic's publisher, and the entire team at the press.

This book owes a lot to the people who cared for me during challenging times. Phone calls, text messages, coffee dates, and visits with Tera Hunter, anu Jain, Kate Masur, Nancy MacLean, Lisa Tetrault, and Heather Thompson have sustained me. Shira Neuberger patiently helped me navigate the minutiae of the day to day as well as life's biggest questions. Spending time with Tiffany Holland never ceases to fill me up and delight me. I will always be grateful to Benjamin Filene for his steadfast support, particularly when things seemed bleak. Susan Davis is my faithful companion in grappling with matters of the heart—and so much more. Ann Newman's kindness and moral compass is a guiding light on and off the tennis court. Nights on the porch with Watson Jennison and Jeff Jones make me incredibly happy—I treasure our unique and life-affirming bonds.

In addition to chosen family, I have the good fortune to have two incredibly loyal and hilarious parents. Mona Levenstein, my generous and kind-hearted mother, has modeled feminist values and given me the space I needed to chart my own course. When things got down to the wire, my father, Harvey, left retirement to help me with the book, deftly editing every chapter. Their steady presence has made all the difference. My life is also greatly enriched by members of my extended family, particularly Cindy Croatti, Alan Patrick, Nick Brown, Sam Brown, and Donna DiFillippo.

During periods of intense writing, my son, Owen, would regularly inquire about my progress and cheer whenever I completed a chapter. When I announced that I had finally finished writing the book, no one celebrated more than Owen, and his enthusiasm meant a lot to me. Every day, Owen's hugs and sense of humor enrich my life and nourish my soul. It has been moving to witness him becoming a force for good in our world and to watch him bring joy to those around him.

My daughter, Anna, has challenged my ideas and helped me to see the world in new ways. She even got hold of a draft of the introduction to the book and marked it up with helpful suggestions. To watch Anna decide for herself to embrace the work of feminism has been amazing, particularly since so many of the lessons taught by the people in this book are the foundation upon which she and her friends are building. Anna's passion for life and determination to make the world a better place fills my heart and gives me hope.

For over twenty years, Jason Brent has cared about me, and cared about feminism. We have delighted in one another and weathered many storms together. Through it all, Jason's boundless curiosity has made my life more interesting and his sense of humor makes it a lot more fun. Jason never once questioned the time I spent on this book or expressed any hesitation in tackling the labor that fell to him. He set the tone for the family and for that, and so much more, I will always be grateful.

BIBLIOGRAPHY

PRIMARY SOURCES

MANUSCRIPT COLLECTIONS

Archives of the American Friends Service Committee, Philadelphia, Pennsylvania
  National Women's Party Records
  Saralee Hamilton Records
Arthur and Elizabeth Schlesinger Library on the History of Women in America, Radcliffe College, Cambridge, Massachusetts
  National Organization for Women, Additional Records, 1970–2011
  NOW Legal Defense and Education Fund, 1968–2008
  Records of Legal Momentum, 1978–2011
  Records of the National Organization for Women, 1959–2003
Atria Institute on Gender Equality and Women's History, Amsterdam, the Netherlands
David M. Rubenstein Rare Book and Manuscript Library, Duke University, Durham, North Carolina
  Bitch: Feminist Response to Pop Culture Records, 1996–2008
  BUST Magazine Records, 1993–2007
  Mab Segrest Papers, 1889–2014
  Mandy Carter Papers, 1970–2013
  Robin Morgan Papers, 1970–2000
  Sisterhood Is Global Institute Records, 1979–2013
  Southerners on New Ground Records, 1993–2003
  Third Wave Foundation Records, 1992–2011
  World Conference on Women (4th: 1995: Beijing, China)
Department of Rare Books and Special Collections, Princeton University Library, Princeton, New Jersey
  Kristen Timothy Papers, 1990–2000
University of Notre Dame Archives, Notre Dame, Indiana
  Center of Concern Records

Department of Special Collections and University Archives, Stanford Librar-
    ies, Stanford, California
    Papers Relating to the United Nations 4th World Conference on Women,
        Beijing, 1992–2001
Dolph Briscoe Center for American History, the University of Texas at Aus-
    tin, Austin, Texas
    Women's International News Gathering Service (WINGS), 1978–1999
General Commission on Archives and History, the United Methodist
        Church, Madison, New Jersey
    Church Women United Records
Iowa Women's Archive, the University of Iowa Libraries, Iowa City, Iowa
    Dorothy Paul Papers, 1955–2014
    Lonabelle Kaplan Spencer Papers, 1931–2007
    Judy Polumbaum Papers
Laila Al-Marayati Personal Papers, Los Angeles, California
Lesbian Herstory Archives, Brooklyn, New York
    Beijing Conference 1995
Rare Book and Manuscript Library, Columbia University, New York City
    Amnesty International of the USA, Inc.: National Office Records,
        1966–2003
    Women's Environmental and Development Organization, 1980–2018
Rockefeller Center Archives, Sleepy Hollow, New York
    Ford Foundation Records, 1936–2011
    Office Files of Marcia Smith, 1992–1995
Sophia Smith Collection, Smith College, Northampton, Massachusetts
    Amy Richards Papers, 1995–2012
    Black Women's Health Imperative Records, 1983–2016
    Charon Asetoyer Papers, 1985–2008
    International Women's Tribune Centre Records, 1970–2000
    Lora Jo Foo Papers, 1980–2009
    Loretta Ross Papers, 1956–2013
    Luz Alvarez Martinez Papers, 1978–2007
    Miriam Ching Louie Papers, 1970–2012
    Ms. Foundation for Education and Communication Records
    Ms. Foundation for Women Records, 1973–2008
    National Asian Pacific American Women's Forum Records, 1995–2010
    National Congress of Neighborhood Women Records, 1974–1999
    Saralee Hamilton Papers, 1911–2013
    SisterSong Women of Color Reproductive Justice Collective Records,
        1996–2010
    Undivided Rights Book Project Records, 1992–2002
    Voices of Feminism Oral History Project, 1990–2014
    Women of Color Resource Center Records, 1984–2011
Special Collections and University Archives, Rutgers University, New Bruns-
        wick, New Jersey

Center for Women's Global Leadership
Urban Archives, California State University, Northridge, California
> Coalition for Women's Economic Development Collection, 1980–1999
William J. Clinton Presidential Library Archives, Little Rock, Arkansas
> Clinton Presidential Records: White House Staff and Office Files

ORAL HISTORIES BY AUTHOR

Liz Abzug, June 6, 2013, New York City.
Laila Al-Maryati, August 20, 2014, Chapel Hill, North Carolina, to Los Angeles, California, by Skype.
Luz Alvarez Martinez, January 7, 2014, Richmond, California.
Veronica Arreola, September 8, 2017, Chapel Hill, North Carolina, to Chicago, Illinois, by Skype.
Byllye Avery, May 16, 2017, Chapel Hill, North Carolina, to Provincetown, Massachusetts, by telephone.
Radhika Balakrishnan, June 18, 2015, Chapel Hill, North Carolina, to New York City, by Skype.
Carol Barton, March 24, 2015, Durham, North Carolina, to New York City, by Skype.
Carol Barton and elmira Nazombe, March 17, 2015, Chapel Hill, North Carolina, to New York City, and Highland Park, New Jersey, by telephone and GoToMeeting.
Alison Bernstein, March 29, 2016, Chapel Hill, North Carolina, to New Brunswick, New Jersey, by Skype.
Susan Berresford, March 8, 2016, Chapel Hill, North Carolina, to New York City, by Skype.
Melissa Bradley, April 6, 2015, Durham, North Carolina, to Washington, DC, by Skype.
Ellen Bravo, May 27, 2014, Chapel Hill, North Carolina, to Milwaukee, Wisconsin, by Skype.
Charlotte Bunch, March 20, 2013, Chapel Hill, North Carolina, and January 5, 2015, Durham, North Carolina, to Lima, Peru, by Skype.
Sally Burch, March 23, 2014, Chapel Hill, North Carolina, to Quito, Ecuador, by Skype.
Sarah Burd-Sharps, August 20, 2013, Chapel Hill, North Carolina, to Brooklyn, New York, by Skype.
Linda Burnham, July 11, 2013, Chapel Hill, North Carolina, to Oakland, California, by Skype.
Eliza Byard, June 13, 2014, Chapel Hill, North Carolina, to New York City, by Skype.
Elizabeth Campbell, March 7, 2014, Chapel Hill, North Carolina, to New York City, by Skype.
Mandy Carter, September 9, 2016, Durham, North Carolina.
Ellen Chesler, July 16, 2014, Chapel Hill, North Carolina, to New York City, by Skype.

Pamela Chiang, December 3, 2014, Durham, North Carolina, to Belgrade, Montana, October 9, 2018, Chapel Hill, North Carolina, to Belgrade, Montana, by Skype.

Alicia Contreras, January 18, 2015, Chapel Hill, North Carolina, to Oakland, California, by Skype.

Cinnamon Cooper, October 4, 2017, Chapel Hill, North Carolina, to Chicago, Illinois, by Skype.

Edwina Davis and Susan Davis, May 9, 2014, Chapel Hill, North Carolina.

Susan Davis, June 7, 2013, New York City.

Beth Dehghan, May 13, 2015, Raleigh, North Carolina.

Dázon Dixon Diallo, April 11, 2017, Chapel Hill, North Carolina, to Atlanta, Georgia, by Skype.

Julie Dorf, May 6, 2014, Chapel Hill, North Carolina, to San Francisco, California, by Skype.

Mallika Dutt, February 11, 2014, Chapel Hill, North Carolina, to New York City, by Skype.

Connie Evans, July 16, 2014, Chapel Hill, North Carolina, to Washington, DC, by telephone.

Cynthia Eyakuze, August 29, 2014, Chapel Hill, North Carolina, to New York City, by Skype.

Edie Farwell, April 15, 2014, Chapel Hill, North Carolina, to Hartland, Vermont, by Skype.

Lora Jo Foo, January 8, 2014, Oakland, California.

Marilyn Fowler, July 17, 2014, Chapel Hill, North Carolina, to San Francisco, by Skype.

Joan Ross Frankson, May 21, 2013, Chapel Hill, North Carolina, to London, England, by Skype.

Jo Freeman, March 20, 2014, Brooklyn, New York.

Kim Gandy, May 28, 2017, Chapel Hill, North Carolina, to Silver Springs, Maryland, by Skype.

Adrienne Germain, January 7, 2015, Durham, North Carolina, to New York City, by Skype.

Yma Gordon-Reid, August 8, 2018, Chapel Hill, North Carolina, to Long Island, New York, by telephone.

Sara Gould, July 17, 2014, Chapel Hill, North Carolina, to Brooklyn, New York, by telephone.

Sarah Granger, October 17, 2017, Chapel Hill, North Carolina, to Los Altos, California, by Skype.

Roma Guy, January 8, 2014, San Francisco, California.

Jessica Halem, May 4, 2014, May 6, 2014, June 4, 2014, Chapel Hill, North Carolina, to Providence, Rhode Island, by Skype.

Heidi Hartmann, June 2, 2018, Chapel Hill, North Carolina, to Washington, DC, by Skype.

Giselle Hass, November 12, 2014, Durham, North Carolina, to Bethesda, Maryland, by Skype.

Kathleen Hendrix, June 2, 2014, Chapel Hill, North Carolina, to Canandaigua, New York, by Skype.

Daisy Hernandez, October 16, 2016, Chapel Hill, North Carolina, to Cincinnati, Ohio, by Skype.

Leila Hessini, April 16, 2014, Chapel Hill, North Carolina.

Pat Hussain, April 19, 2017, Atlanta, Georgia.

Lisa Jervis, March 23, 2017, Greensboro, North Carolina, to Oakland, California, by Skype.

Sujatha Jesudason, October 11, 2017, Chapel Hill, North Carolina, to Brooklyn, New York, by Skype.

Paula Kamen, February 15, 2017, Chapel Hill, North Carolina, to Evanston, Illinois, by Skype.

Musimbi Kanyoro, December 19, 2013, Chapel Hill, North Carolina, to Toronto, Ontario, by Skype.

Marlene Kim, May 27, 2016, Chapel Hill, North Carolina, to Boston, Massachusetts, by Skype.

Frances Kissling, June 10, 2014, Washington, DC.

Sharon Kotuk, July 16, 2014, Chapel Hill, North Carolina, to Arlington, Virginia, by telephone.

Judy Kramer, May 2, 2012, Palo Alto, California.

Cindy Lewis, October 20, 2014, Chapel Hill, North Carolina, to Oakland, California, by Skype.

Jean Lin, February 6, 2015, Durham, North Carolina, to Berkeley, California, by Skype.

Andrea Mitchell, June 10, 2014, Washington, DC.

Susan Mooney, March 21, 2014, Chapel Hill, North Carolina, to New York City, by Skype.

Julie Moss, June 26, 2014, Tahlequah, Oklahoma, to Chapel Hill, North Carolina, by Skype.

Anne Firth Murray, November 24, 2014, Durham, North Carolina, to Menlo Park, California, by Skype.

Nadine Naber, October 5, 2016, Chapel Hill, North Carolina, to Chicago, Illinois, by Skype.

Premilla Nadasen, April 13, 2017, Chapel Hill, North Carolina, to New York City, by Skype.

Anita Nayar, New York City, August 10, 2015.

elmira Nazome, April 30, 2015, Chapel Hill, North Carolina, to Highland Park, New Jersey, by Skype.

Helen Neuborne, August 28, 2014, Chapel Hill, North Carolina, to New York City, by Skype.

Barbara O'Leary, February 26, 2014, March 5, 2014, March 14, 2014, March 19, 2014, by Facebook.

Julia Chinyere Oparah, February 3, 2017, Chapel Hill, North Carolina, to Oakland, California, by Skype.

Roxanne Dunbar Ortiz, January 8, 2014, San Francisco, California.

Corbett O'Toole, January 29, 2015, Durham, North Carolina, to Richmond, California, by Skype.

Rosalind Petchesky, June 6, 2013, New York City.

Suzanne Pharr, January 17, 2017, Chapel Hill, North Carolina, to Little Rock, Arkansas, by Skype.

Ai-Jen Poo, October 11, 2016, Chapel Hill, North Carolina, to Chicago, Illinois, by Skype.

Jennifer L. Pozner, September 26, 2017, Chapel Hill, North Carolina, to Brooklyn, New York, by Skype.

Margaret Prescod, October 14, 2014 Los Angeles, California, January 10, 2018, Chapel Hill, North Carolina, to Los Angeles, California, by Skype.

Amy Richards, September 10, 2014, New York City.

Kathleen Richards, January 7, 2014, Oakland, California.

Mari Riddle, June 30, 2016, Chapel Hill, North Carolina, to Los Angeles, California, by Skype.

Maria Riley, July 22, 2014, Chapel Hill, North Carolina, to Adrian, Michigan, by telephone.

Beth Ritchie, January 29, 2018, Chapel Hill, North Carolina, to Chicago, Illinois, by telephone.

Sharon Rogers, October 28, 2014, Durham, North Carolina, to Washington, DC, November 8, 2017, Chapel Hill, North Carolina, to Washington, DC, by telephone.

Rachel Rosenbloom, April 29, 2014, Chapel Hill, North Carolina, to Boston, Massachusetts, by Skype.

Patricia Rosenfield, June 16, 2013, Chapel Hill, North Carolina, to New York City, by Skype.

Loretta Ross, February 23, 2013, Chapel Hill, North Carolina; April 20, 2013, Greensboro, North Carolina; August 9, 2017, Atlanta, Georgia.

Cynthia Rothschild, October 21, 2015, Chapel Hill, North Carolina, to Brooklyn, New York, by Skype.

Joanne Sandler, May 2, 2014, Chapel Hill, North Carolina, to New York City, by Skype.

Jill Savitt, April 9, 2014, Chapel Hill, North Carolina, to Brooklyn, New York, by Skype.

Dylan Scholinski, September 6, 2014, Chapel Hill, North Carolina, to Denver, Colorado, by Skype.

Mab Segrest, March 9, 2018, Durham, North Carolina.

Vicki Semler, January 8, 2013, Brooklyn, New York.

Rinku Sen, September 10, 2014, New York City.

Donna Shalala, May 19, 2014, Greensboro, North Carolina, to Miami, Florida, by Skype.

Ritu Sharma, November 21, 2014, Durham, North Carolina, to Annapolis, Maryland, by Skype.

Eveline Shen, November 11, 2014, Durham, North Carolina, to Oakland, California, by Skype.

Aliza Sherman, September 27, 2017, Chapel Hill, North Carolina, to Anchorage, Alaska, by Skype.

Jael Siliman, April 30, 2013, Chapel Hill, North Carolina, to Kolkata, India, by Skype.

Leni Silverstein, May 20, 2014, Chapel Hill, North Carolina, to New York City, by Skype.

Melissa Silverstein, May 1, 2014, Chapel Hill, North Carolina, to Brooklyn, New York, by Skype.

Monica Simpson, August 9, 2017, Atlanta, Georgia.

Alice Skenandore, April 25, 2017, Chapel Hill, North Carolina, to Green Bay, Wisconsin, by Skype.

Eleanor Smeal, May 31, 2017, Chapel Hill, North Carolina, to Arlington, Virginia, by Skype.

Andrea Smith, January 15, 2017, Chapel Hill, North Carolina, to Long Beach, California, by Skype.

Pamela Sparr, August 27, 2014, and October 17, 2014, Chapel Hill, North Carolina, to Cambridge, Massachusetts, by Skype.

Susan Sygall, December 29, 2014, Chapel Hill, North Carolina, to Eugene, Oregon, by Skype.

Linda Tarr Whelan, September 23, 2014, Durham, North Carolina, to Burlington, Vermont, by Skype.

Vicky Tauli-Corpuz, September 7, 2013, Chapel Hill, North Carolina, to Washington, DC, by Skype.

Elena Mary Costello Tzintzún, October 18, 2017, Chapel Hill, North Carolina, to Columbus, Ohio, by Skype.

Urvashi Vaid, July 23, 2014, Chapel Hill, North Carolina, to Provincetown, Massachusetts, by Skype.

Carmen Delgado Votaw, January 3, 2014, Washington, DC.

Anne Walker, February 18, 2013, Greensboro, North Carolina, to Melbourne, Australia, by Skype.

Michaela Walsh, January 6, 2015, Chapel Hill, North Carolina, to New York City, by Skype.

Ara Wilson, October 13, 2014, Durham, North Carolina.

Marie Wilson, March 20, 2014, New York City.

Andi Zeisler, March 10, 2017, Chapel Hill, North Carolina, to Portland, Oregon, by Skype.

ORAL INTERVIEWS BY VOICES OF FEMINISM ORAL HISTORY PROJECT, SOPHIA SMITH COLLECTION

Katherine Acey, interview by Kelly Anderson, July 19, 20, and 29, 2007.

Charon Asetoyer, interview by Joyce Follet, September 1–2, 2005.

Byllye Y. Avery, interview by Loretta Ross, July 21–22, 2005.

Linda Burnham, interview by Loretta J. Ross, March 18, 2015.
Marlene Fried, interview by Joyce Follett, August 14–15, 2007.
Sara K. Gould, interview by Kelly Anderson, November 16, 2007.
Mary Chung Hayashi, interview by Loretta J. Ross, December 15, 2006.
Marian Kramer, interview by Loretta Ross, February 1–2, 2014.
Luz Alvarez Martinez, interview by Loretta J. Ross, December 6–7, 2004.
Suzanne Pharr, interview by Kelly Anderson, June 28–29, 2005.
Luz Rodriguez, interview by Joyce Follet, June 16–17, 2006.
Loretta Ross, interview by Joyce Follet, November 3–5, 2004, December 1–3, 2004, February 4, 2005.
Peggy Saika, interview by Loretta Ross, February 20, 2006.

OTHER ORAL HISTORIES

Rabab Abdulhadi, interview by Nadine Naber, April 2, 2004. Global Feminisms: Comparative Case Studies of Women's Activism and Scholarship, University of Michigan.
Charlotte Bunch, interview by Katy Morris and Kayla Ginsburg, June 10, 2011. Women and Social Movements International, Alexander Street, A Proquest Company.
Mandy Carter, interview by Rose Norman, March 26, 2013. Sinister Wisdom '93/Southern Lesbian-Feminist Oral History Supplement.
Pat Hussain, interview by Lorraine Fontana, May 6, 2013. Sinister Wisdom '93/Southern Lesbian-Feminist Oral History Supplement.
Pam McMichael, interview by Rose Norman, April 3, 2013. Sinister Wisdom '93/Southern Lesbian-Feminist Oral History Supplement.
Corbett O'Toole, interview by Denise Sherer Jacobson, 1998. Disability Rights and Independent Living Movement Oral History Series, Regional Oral History Office, Bancroft Library, University of California, Berkeley.
Suzanne Pharr, interview by Rose Norman, March 28, 2013. Sinister Wisdom '93/Southern Lesbian-Feminist Oral History Supplement.
Andrea Smith, interview by Maria Cotera, June 24, 2003. Global Feminisms: Comparative Case Studies of Women's Activism and Scholarship, University of Michigan.

SELECTED BLOGS/ZINES/WEBSITES

"A Labor of Love: Black Mama's Bailout Action + Reflection." *Southerners on New Ground*. May 16, 2017. https://southernersonnewground .org/a-labor-of-love/.
"About the Global Grrrl Zine Network." *Grrrl Zine Network*. 2000–2008. www.grrrlzines.net/about.htm.
Berger, Melody, ed. "Loretta Ross." *The F-Word: A Feminist Handbook for the Revolution* 3 (2008): 8–9.

"Black Women on the Net." *Women'space* 3, no. 3 (Spring 1998). www
.collectionscanada.gc.ca/eppp-archive/100/202/300/womenspace
/back1/vol33e.html.

Feminist Newswire. "Hundreds March for Marissa Alexander in Jacksonville." *Feminist Daily Newswire*. July 29, 2014. https://feminist
.org/blog/index.php/2014/07/29/hundreds-march-for-marissa
-alexander-in-jacksonville/.

"Free Marissa Alexander." *Free Marissa Now.* www.freemarissanow.org/.

Freedman, Jenna. "Zines Are Not Blogs: A Not Unbiased Analysis." *Lower
East Side Librarian*. 2006. http://lowereastsidelibrarian.info/articles
/zinesarenotblogs.

Freeman, Jo. "The Tyranny of Structurelessness." www.jofreeman.com
/joreen/tyranny.htm.

"French and Italian Zines and Resources." *Grrrl Zine Network*. www
.grrrlzines.net/zines/french_italian.htm.

Gagliardi, Jennifer. "Beijing95-L." *Women'space* 3, no. 3 (Spring 1998).

Guest Contributor. "No Climate Justice Without Gender Justice: Women at the
Forefront of the People's Climate March." *Feminist Wire*. September
29, 2014. https://thefeministwire.com/2014/09/climate-justice
-without-gender-justice-women-forefront-peoples-climate-march/.

Landsbaum, Claire. "The Women's March on Washington Platform Calls
for Reform on Every Level." *The Cut*. January 13, 2017. www.thecut
.com/2017/01/the-womens-march-on-washington-platform-calls
-for-reform-on-every-level.html.

Magik, Marisa. "The Grrrl Zine Network, an Interview with Elke." *Grrrl
Zine Network*. December 2001. www.grrrlzines.net/interviews
/grrrlzinenetwork.htm.

O'Leary, Barbara Ann. "Virtual Sisterhood." *Women'space*. Summer 1996.
www.collectionscanada.gc.ca/eppp-archive/100/202/300/womens
pace/back1/vol21a.html.

"Reproductive Justice and Marissa Alexander." *Free Marissa Now*. www
.freemarissanow.org/fact-sheet-on-reproductive-justice--marissa
-alexander.html.

Richards, Cecile. "A Response to an Open Letter on Reproductive Justice and 'Choice.'" *Rewire.News*. August 5, 2014. https://rewire
.news/article/2014/08/05/response-open-letter-reproductive
-justice-choice/.

Sarkeesian, Anita. "Link Round Up: Feminist Critiques of SlutWalk."
Feminist Frequency. May 16, 2011. https://feministfrequency
.com/2011/05/16/link-round-up-feminist-critiques-of-slutwalk/.

Simpson, Monica. "Reproductive Justice and 'Choice': An Open Letter to
Planned Parenthood." *Rewire.News*. August 5, 2014. https://rewire
.news/article/2014/08/05/reproductive-justice-choice-open-letter
-planned-parenthood/.

Stanek, Jill. "How Planned Parenthood Used Social Media to Crush Komen." LifeSite. February 6, 2012. www.lifesitenews.com/opinion/how -planned-parenthood-used-social-media-to-crush-komen.

Zobl, Elke. "Digress Magazine and Queer Zinesters Have Lives Too, an Interview with Annie Knight." *Grrrl Zine Network*. June 2005. www .grrrlzines.net/interviews/digress.htm.

———. "Living in a Place of Contradictions: Creating a Place to Exist." *Grrrl Zine Network*. February 2003. www.grrrlzines.net/interviews /soldier.htm.

Audiovisual

Disabled Women: Visions and Voices from the 4th World Conference on Women. Directed by Suzanne C. Levine and Patricia Chadwick. Wide Vision Productions, 1996.

Passionate Politics: The Life and Work of Charlotte Bunch. Directed by Tami Gold. New York: New Day Films, 2011.

"United Nations Conference on Women." C-SPAN. August 21, 1995. www .c-span.org/video/?66799-1/united-nations-conference-women.

Newspapers, Periodicals, and News Websites

Chicago Tribune
CNN
Dallas Morning News
Ebony
Forum '95
Huffington Post
Los Angeles Times
Ms.
NBC News
New America Weekly
New York Times
People's Tribune

Reuters
Rolling Stone
The Atlantic
The Guardian
The Nation
Time
USA Today
Vanderbilt Magazine
Vox
Wall Street Journal
Washington Post

Published Works

Agnihotri, Indu. "Evolving a Women's Agenda: Report from Beijing." *Economic and Political Weekly* 30, no. 50 (December 16, 1994): 3195–3198.

Alt-WID. "Free Trade's Impact on Women." *Breaking Boundaries: Women, Free Trade and Economic Integration.* Washington, DC: Alt-WID, 1993.

———. *Reaganomics and Women: Structural Adjustment U.S. Style, 1980– 1992.* Washington, DC: Alt-WID, 1992.

Anand, Anita, with Gouri Salvi. *Beijing! UN Fourth World Conference on Women.* New Delhi: Women's Feature Service, 1998.

Asian Communities for Reproductive Justice. *A New Vision for Advancing Our Movement for Reproductive Rights and Reproductive Justice.* Oakland, CA: Asian Communities for Reproductive Justice, 2005.

Avenoso, Karen. "Feminism's Newest Foot Soldiers." *Elle*, March 1993, 114–118.

Banks, Karen, Sally Burch, Irene Leon, Sonja Boezak, and Liz Probert. *Networking for Change: The APC WNSP's First 8 Years.* The Philippines: APC Women's Networking and Support Programme, 2000.

Brail, Stephanie. "Take Back the Net." *On the Issues*, Winter 1994, 39–42.

"Bringing Together Feminist Theory and Practice: A Collective Interview." *Signs* 21, no. 4 (Summer 1996): 917–951.

Bunch, Charlotte. *Passionate Politics, Essays, 1968–1986: Feminist Theory in Action.* New York: St. Martin's Press, 1987.

Bunch, Charlotte, and Claudia Hinojosa. *Lesbians Travel the Roads of Feminism Globally.* New Brunswick, NJ: Center for Women's Global Leadership, 2000.

Bunch, Charlotte, and Niamh Reilly. *Demanding Accountability: The Global Campaign and Vienna Tribunal for Women's Human Rights.* New York: Center for Women's Global Leadership and United Nations Development Fund for Women, 1994.

Burnham, Linda. "Beijing and Beyond." *CrossRoads: Contemporary Political Analysis & Left Dialogue* 59 (March 1996): 15–18.

———. "Racism in US Welfare Policy: A Human Rights Issue." Working Paper Series, 2. Oakland, CA: Women of Color Resource Center, 2002.

———. "Welfare Reform, Family Hardship, and Women of Color." In *Lost Ground: Welfare Reform, Poverty, and Beyond*, edited by Randy Albelda and Ann Withorn, 43–56. Cambridge, MA: South End Press, 2002.

Chamberlain, Christopher H. *A Citizens' Guide to Gender and the World Bank.* Washington, DC: Bank Information Center, 1996.

Cherny, Lynn, and Elizabeth Reba Weise, eds. *Wired Women: Gender and New Realities in Cyberspace.* Seattle, WA: Seal Press, 1996.

Combahee River Collective. "Combahee River Collective Statement." In *Home Girls: A Black Feminist Anthology*, edited by Barbara Smith, 264–274. New York: Kitchen Table Press, 1983; reprint, New Brunswick, NJ: Rutgers University Press, 2000.

Commission for Racial Justice. *United Church of Christ, Toxic Wastes and Race in the United States: A National Report of the Racial and Socio-Economic Characteristics of Communities with Hazardous Waste Sites.* New York: United Church of Christ Commission for Racial Justice, 1987.

Crenshaw, Kimberlé Williams. "Demarginalizing the Intersection of Race and Sex: A Black Feminist Critique of Antidiscrimination Doctrine, Feminist Theory and Antiracist Politics." *University of Chicago Legal Forum* (1989): 139–167.

———. "Mapping the Margins: Intersectionality, Identity Politics, and Violence against Women of Color." *Stanford Law Review* 43, no. 6 (1991): 1241–1299.

Dutt, Mallika. "Some Reflections on U.S. Women of Color and the United Nations World Conference on Women and NGO Forum in Beijing, China." *Feminist Studies* 22, no. 3 (Autumn 1996): 519–528.

Edgcomb, Elaine, Joyce Klein, and Peggy Clark. *The Practice of Microenterprise in the U.S.* Washington, DC: The Aspen Institute, 1996.

Faludi, Susan. *Backlash: The Undeclared War on American Women.* New York: Crown, 1991.

Findlen, Barbara. *Listen Up: Voices from the Next Feminist Generation.* Seattle: Seal Press, 1995.

Foundation Center and Women's Funding Network. *Accelerating Change for Women and Girls: The Role of Women's Funds.* New York: Foundation Center, 2009.

"Fourth World Conference on Women." *Off Our Backs* 25, no. 10 (November 1995): 1, 4–5.

Freeman, Jo. "The Real Story of Beijing." *Off Our Backs* 26 (March 1996): 1, 8–11, 22–27.

Freire, Paulo. *Pedagogy of the Oppressed.* New York: Seabury Press, 1968.

Friedlander, Eva, ed. *Look at the World Through Women's Eyes: Plenary Speeches from the NGO Forum on Women, Beijing, '95.* Huai-jou hsien, China: Women Ink, 1995.

Gittler, Alice Mastrangelo. "Mapping Women's Global Communications and Networking." In *Women@Internet: Creating New Cultures in Cyberspace*, edited by Wendy Harcourt, 91–101. London: Zed Books, 1999.

Grewal, Inderpal. "'Women's Rights as Human Rights': Feminist Practices, Global Feminism, and Human Rights Regimes in Transnationality." *Citizenship Studies* 3, no. 3 (1999): 337–354.

Hernandez, Daisy, and S. Bushra Rehman. *Colonize This! Young Women of Color on Today's Feminism.* New York: Seal Press, 2002.

Hershey, Laura. "Pursuing an Agenda Beyond Barriers: Women with Disabilities." *Women's Studies Quarterly* 24, nos. 1/2 (1996): 60–63.

Hinojosa, Claudia, and Susana T. Fried. *Bringing Women's Human Rights Home: Report of the 1996 Women's Global Leadership Institute.* New Brunswick, NJ: Center for Women's Global Leadership, 1996.

hooks, bell. *Feminist Theory: From Margin to Center.* Boston: South End Press, 1984.

Hosken, Fran. "Toward a Definition of Women's Human Rights." *Human Rights Quarterly*, Spring 1981, 1–10.

Huemann, Emily, and Jean Wiley. *The Challenge of Microenterprise: The CWED Story.* Edited by Jan Breidenbach and Mari Riddle. Oakland, CA: National Economic Development & Law Center and the Coalition for Women's Economic Development, 1999.

Hull, Gloria T., Patricia Bell Scott, and Barbara Smith, eds. *All the Women Are White, All the Blacks Are Men, But Some of Us Are Brave: Black Women's Studies.* New York: Feminist Press at CUNY, 1993.

Huntemann, Nina B. "Creating Safe Cyberspace: Feminist Political Discourse on the Internet." Master's thesis, University of Massachusetts Amherst, 1997.

Jain, Devaki. "Building Alliances: A Southern Perspective." *Focus on Gender* 2 (October 1994): 15–19.

Kamen, Paula. *Feminist Fatale: Voices from the 'Twentysomething' Generation Explore the Future of the 'Women's Movement.'* New York: Donald I. Fine, 1991.

Kole, Ellen S. "Myths and Realities in Internet Discourse: Using Computer Networks for Data Collection and the Beijing World Conference on Women." *Gazette: The International Journal for Communication Studies* 60, no. 4 (August 1998): 343–360.

"Lesbians Take On the UN." *Trouble and Strife* 33 (Summer 1996): 35–43.

López, Mercedes. "Discussing Economics on the Border." *Corresponencia*, Winter/Spring 1991–1992, 15–17.

Losa, Susana. "Hashtag Feminism, #SolidarityIsForWhiteWomen, and the Other #FemFuture." *Ada: A Journal of Gender, New Media, and Technology* 5 (2014). https://adanewmedia.org/2014/07/issue5-loza.

Louie, Miriam Ching, with Linda Burnham. *WEdGE: Women's Education in the Global Economy.* Berkeley, CA: Women of Color Resource Center, 2000.

Martinez, Elizabeth. "Caramba, Our Anglo Sisters Just Didn't Get It." *Network News* 17, no. 6 (November–December 1992): 1, 4–5.

———. *De Colores Means All of Us: Latina Views for a Multi-Colored Century.* Cambridge, MA: South End Press, 1998.

———. "Where Was the Color in Seattle? Looking for Reasons Why the Great Battle Was So White." *Monthly Review* 52, no. 3 (July 2000): 141–148.

Morrison, Toni. *Race-ing Justice, Engendering Power: Essays on Anita Hill, Clarence Thomas, and the Construction of Social Reality.* New York: Pantheon Books, 1992.

Murray, Pauli. "Women's Rights Are a Part of Human Rights." In *The American Women's Movement, 1945–2000: A Brief History with Documents*, edited by Nancy MacLean, 69–71. Boston: Bedford/St. Martin's, 2009.

Nadasen, Premilla. "Black Feminism Will Save Us All." *In These Times*, September 11, 2018, http://inthesetimes.com/article/21429/black-feminism-intersectional-donald-trump-class race.

Penn, Shana. *The Women's Guide to the Wired World: A User-Friendly Handbook and Resource Directory.* New York: Feminist Press at CUNY, 1997.

Pfister, Bonnie. "Communiques from the Front: Young Activists Chart Feminism's Third Wave," *On the Issues*, Summer 1993, 23–26.

Raheim, S., and Jason J. Friedman. "Microenterprise Development in the Heartland: Self-Employment as a Self-Sufficiency Strategy for TANF Recipients in Iowa 1993–1998." *Journal of Microfinance* 1, no. 1 (1999): 1.

Reichert, Elisabeth. "'Keep on Moving Forward': NGO Forum on Women, Beijing, China." *Social Development Issues* 18, no. 1 (1996): 61–71.

Reilly, Niamh, ed. *Without Reservation: The Beijing Tribunal on Accountability for Women's Human Rights.* New Brunswick, NJ: Center for Women's Global Leadership, 1996.

Roberts, Dorothy. *Killing the Black Body: Race, Reproduction, and the Meaning of Liberty.* New York: Pantheon, 1997.

Romany, Celina. "On Surrendering Privilege: Diversity in a Feminist Redefinition of Human Rights Law." In *From Basic Needs to Basic Rights: Women's Claim to Human Rights,* edited by Margaret Schuler, 543–553. Washington, DC: Women, Law, and Development International, 1995.

Ross, Loretta. "When Funding Hurts" (mimeograph), originally published in *Collective Voices* 1, no. 3 (September 2005).

Schechter, Susan. *Women and Male Violence: The Visions and Struggles of the Battered Women's Movement.* Cambridge, MA: South End Press, 1982.

Segrest, Mab. *Born to Belonging: Writings on Spirit and Justice.* New Brunswick, NJ: Rutgers University Press, 2002.

———. *Memoir of a Race Traitor.* Boston: South End Press, 1994.

Sen, Rinku. *We Are the Ones We Are Waiting For: Women of Color Organizing for Transformation.* Durham, NC: US Urban Rural Mission, 1995.

Sherman, Aliza. *cybergrrl!: A Woman's Guide to the World Wide Web.* New York: Ballantine Books, 1998.

Sinclair, Carla. *Net Chick: A Smart-Girl Guide to the Wired World.* New York: Holt, 1996.

Sorenson, Inga. "A Lesbian Presence." *Synapse* 34 (Winter Solstice 1995).

Southwest Organizing Project. *Intel Inside New Mexico: A Case Study of Environmental and Economic Injustice.* Albuquerque, NM: Southwest Organizing Project, 1995.

———. *Report on the Interfaith Hearings on Toxic Poisoning in Communities of Color.* Albuquerque, NM: Southwest Organizing Project, 1993.

Sparr, Pamela. *United Methodist Study Guide on Global Economics—Seeking a Christian Ethic.* Prepared for the Women's Division by the Mission Education and Cultivation Program Department, General Board of Global Ministries, The United Methodist Church, 1993.

Spivak, Gayatri Chakravorty. "'Woman' as Theatre: United Nations Conference on Women, Beijing 1995." *Radical Philosophy* 75 (January/February 1996): 2–4.

Stanley Foundation. *Building on Beijing: United States NGOs Shape a Women's National Agenda.* Muscatine, IA: Stanley Foundation, 1996.

Unitarian Universalist Service Committee. *Is It Reform?: The 1998 Report of the Welfare and Human Rights Monitoring Project*. Cambridge, MA: Unitarian Universalist Service Committee, 1998.

Unity '99. *Report from Beijing: The 1995 U.N. Fourth World Conference on Women and the Non-Governmental Organizations Forum as Seen by U.S. Journalists of Color*. Edited by Helen Zia. Kirkland, WA: Unity '99, 1996.

Walker, Rebecca. *To Be Real: Telling the Truth and Changing the Face of Feminism*. New York: Anchor Books, 1995.

Williams, Lydia. "Gender Equity and the World Bank Group: A Post-Beijing Assessment." *Women's International Network News* 24, no. 1 (Winter 1998): 7.

———. "Women's Eyes on the World Bank." *Agenda* 13, no. 34 (1997): 103–108.

Wilson, Ara. "Lesbian Visibility and Sexual Rights at Beijing." *Signs* 22, no. 1 (Autumn 1996): 214–218.

Women's Environment and Development Organization. *Mapping Progress: Assessing Implementation of the Beijing Platform*. New York: Women's Environmental and Development Organization, 1998.

Wood, Peregrine. *Putting Beijing Online: Women Working in Information and Communication Technologies: Experiences from the APC Women's Networking Support Programme*. Philippines: Association for Progressive Communications Women's Networking Support Programme, 2000.

SECONDARY SOURCES

Abramovitz, Mimi. *Under Attack, Fighting Back: Women and Welfare in the United States*. New York: Monthly Review Press, 2000.

Adams, Kate. "Built Out of Books: Lesbian Energy and Feminist Ideology in Alternative Publishing." *Journal of Homosexuality* 34, nos. 3–4 (1998): 113–141.

Allen, Robert L. *Black Awakening in Capitalist America: An Analytic History*. Garden City, NY: Doubleday, 1969.

Alvarez, Sonia E. "Beyond NGO-ization? Reflections from Latin America." *Development* 52, no. 2 (2009): 175–184.

———. "Latin American Feminisms 'Go Global': Trends of the 1990s and Challenges for the New Millennium." In *Cultures of Politics, Politics of Cultures: Re-Visioning Latin American Social Movements*, edited by Evelina Dagnino, Sonia E. Alvarez, Arturo Escobar, 114–122. Boulder, CO: Westview Press, 1998.

Alvarez, Sonia E., Elisabeth Jay Friedman, Ericka Beckman, Maylei Blackwell, Norma Stoltz Chinchilla, Nathalie Lebon, Marysa Navarro, and Marcela Ríos Tobar. "Encountering Latin American and Caribbean Feminisms." *Signs* 28, no. 2 (Winter 2003): 537–579.

Anderson, Bonnie S. *Joyous Greetings: The First International Women's Movement, 1830–1860*. New York: Oxford University Press, 2000.

Anderson, Carol. *Eyes Off the Prize: The United Nations and the African American Struggle for Human Rights, 1944–1955*. New York: Cambridge University Press, 2003.

Anheier, Helmut K., and Diana Leat. *Creative Philanthropy: Toward a New Philanthropy for the Twenty-First Century*. New Brunswick, NJ: Routledge, 2006.

Antrobus, Peggy. *The Global Women's Movement: Origins, Issues and Strategies*. London: Zed Books, 2004.

Arnove, Robert F. *Philanthropy and Cultural Imperialism: The Foundations at Home and Abroad*, 1st Midland Book ed. Bloomington: Indiana University Press, 1982.

Arreola, Veronica. "Back to the #FemFuture." *Viva La Feminista*, 2013, www.vivalafeminista.com/2013/04/back-to-femfuture.html.

Bahar, Saba. "Human Rights Are Women's Right: Amnesty International and the Family." In *Global Feminisms Since 1945: Rewriting Histories*, edited by Bonnie G. Smith, 265–289. New York: Routledge, 2000.

Bao, Xiaolan. *Holding Up More Than Half the Sky: Chinese Garment Workers in New York City, 1948–92*. Urbana: University of Illinois Press, 2001.

Basu, Amrita. *The Challenge of Local Feminisms: Women's Movements in Global Perspective*. Boulder, CO: Westview Press, 1995.

———. "Globalization of the Local/Localization of the Global: Mapping Transnational Women's Movements." *Meridians* 1 (Autumn 2000): 68–84.

Baumgardner, Jennifer, and Amy Richards. *Manifesta: Young Women, Feminism, and the Future*. New York: D and M Publishers, 2000.

Beins, Agatha. *Liberation in Print: Feminist Periodicals and Social Movement Identity*. Athens: University of Georgia Press, 2017.

Bernal, Victoria, and Inderpal Grewal. *Theorizing NGOs: States, Feminisms, and Neoliberalism*. Durham, NC: Duke University Press, 2014.

Bhatt, Ela R. *We Are Poor but So Many: The Story of Self-Employed Women in India*. New York: Oxford University Press, 2006.

Blain, Keisha N. *Set the World on Fire: Black Nationalist Women and the Global Struggle for Freedom*. Philadelphia: University of Pennsylvania Press, 2018.

Bolt, Christine. *Sisterhood Questioned: Race, Class and Internationalism in the American and British Women's Movements, c. 1880s–1970s*. London: Routledge, 2004.

Boris, Eileen. "Consumers of the World Unite! Campaigns Against Sweating, Past and Present." In *Sweatshop USA: The American Sweatshop in Historical and Global Perspective*, edited by Daniel E. Bender and Richard A. Greenwald, 203–224. New York: Routledge, 2003.

Boris, Eileen, and Jennifer Klein. *Caring for America: Home Health Workers in the Shadow of the Welfare State.* New York: Oxford University Press, 2012.

Boris, Eileen, and Premilla Nadasen. "Domestic Workers Organize!" *Working USA: The Journal of Labor and Society* 11 (December 2008): 413–424.

Boris, Elizabeth T. "The Nonprofit Sector in the 1990s." In *Philanthropy and the Nonprofit Sector in a Changing America*, edited by Charles T. Clotfelter and Thomas Ehrlich, 1–33. Bloomington: Indiana University Press, 1999.

Bricker-Jenkins, Mary, Carrie Young, and Cheri Honkala. "Using Economic Human Rights in the Movement to End Poverty." In *Challenges in Human Rights: A Social Work Perspective*, edited by Elisabeth Reichert, 122–137. New York: Columbia University Press, 2007.

Bumiller, Kristin. *In an Abusive State: How Neoliberalism Appropriated the Feminist Movement Against Sexual Violence.* Durham, NC: Duke University Press, 2008.

Bunch, Charlotte. "How Women's Rights Became Recognized as Human Rights." In *The Unfinished Revolution: Voices from the Global Fight for Women's Rights*, edited by Minky Worden, 29–39. New York: Seven Stories Press, 2012.

———. "Opening Doors for Feminism: UN World Conferences on Women." *Journal of Women's History* 24, no. 4 (Winter 2012): 213–221.

Bunster-Burotto, Ximena. "Surviving Beyond Fear: Women and Torture in Latin America." In *Women and Change in Latin America*, edited by June Nash and Helen Safa, 297–335. New York: Bergin & Garvey, 1986.

Cabezas, Amalia, Ellen Reese, and Marguerite Waller. *The Wages of Empire: Neoliberal Policies, Repression and Women's Resistance.* New York: Routledge, 2007.

Campbell, W. Joseph. *1995: The Year the Future Began.* Oakland: University of California Press, 2015.

Canaday, Margot. *The Straight State: Sexuality and Citizenship in Twentieth-Century America.* Princeton, NJ: Princeton University Press, 2009.

Carroll, Tamar W. *Mobilizing New York: AIDS, Antipoverty, and Feminist Activism.* Chapel Hill: University of North Carolina Press, 2015.

Castledine, Jacqueline L. *Cold War Progressives: Women's Interracial Organizing for Peace and Freedom.* Urbana: University of Illinois Press, 2012.

Chappell, Marisa. *The War on Welfare: Family, Poverty, and Politics in Modern America.* Philadelphia: University of Pennsylvania Press, 2010.

Chateauvert, Melinda. *Sex Workers Unite: A History of the Movement from Stonewall to SlutWalk.* Boston: Beacon Press, 2013.

Chen, Martha Alter. "Engendering World Conferences: The International Women's Movement and the UN." In *NGOs, the UN, and Global Governance*, edited by Thomas G. Weiss and Leon Gordenker, 139–155. Boulder, CO: Lynne Rienner Publishers, 1996.

Cho, Sumi, Kimberlé Williams Crenshaw, and Leslie McCall. "Toward a Field of Intersectionality Studies: Theory, Applications, and Praxis." *Signs* 38, no. 4 (2013): 786–810.

Chowdhury, Elora Halim. *Transnationalism Reversed: Women Organizing Against Gendered Violence in Bangladesh*. Albany: State University of New York Press, 2011.

Clark, Ann Marie, Elisabeth J. Friedman, and Kathryn Hochstetler. "The Sovereign Limits of Global Civil Society: A Comparison of NGO Participation in UN World Conferences on the Environment, Human Rights, and Women." *World Politics* 51, no. 1 (1998): 1–35.

Cobble, Dorothy Sue. "A Higher 'Standard of Life' for the World: U.S. Labor Women's Reform Internationalism and the Legacies of 1919." *Journal of American History* 100, no. 4 (March 2014): 1052–1085.

———. "International Women's Trade Unionism and Education." *International Labor and Working-Class History* 90 (Fall 2016): 153–163.

———. *The Other Women's Movement: Workplace Justice and Social Rights in Modern America*. Princeton, NJ: Princeton University Press, 2004.

———. *The Sex of Class: Women Transforming American Labor*. Ithaca, NY: Cornell University Press, 2007.

Cobble, Dorothy Sue, Linda Gordon, and Astrid Henry. *Feminism Unfinished: A Short, Surprising History of American Women's Movements*. New York: Liveright Publishing, 2015.

Cohen, Helen Scheuer. "How Far Can Credit Travel? A Comparative Study of the Grameen Bank in Bangladesh and the Women's Self-Employment Project in Chicago." Master's thesis, Massachusetts Institute of Technology, 1989.

Cole, Jennifer, Jason Nolan, Yukari Seko, Katherine Mancuso, and Alejandra Ospina. "GimpGirl Grows Up: Women with Disabilities Rethinking, Redefining, and Reclaiming Community." *New Media and Society* 13, no. 7 (2011): 1161–1179.

Cooper, Brittney. *Beyond Respectability: The Intellectual Thought of Race Women*. Urbana: University of Illinois Press, 2017.

Cooper, Hannah L. F. "War on Drugs Policing and Police Brutality." *Substance Use & Misuse* 50, nos. 8–9 (2015): 1188–1194.

Córdova, Teresa. "Grassroots Mobilizations in the Southwest for Environmental and Economic Justice." *International Journal of Public Administration* 25, nos. 2–3 (2002): 333–349.

Counts, Alex. *Small Loans, Big Dreams: How Nobel Prize Winner Muhammad Yunus and Microfinance Are Changing the World*. Hoboken, NJ: John Wiley & Sons, 2008.

Davis, Kathy. *The Making of Our Bodies, Ourselves: How Feminism Travels Across Borders*. Durham, NC: Duke University Press, 2007.

Devaki, Jain. *Women, Development, and the UN: A Sixty-Year Quest for Equality and Justice*. Bloomington: Indiana University Press, 2005.

Dicker, Rory Cooke, and Alison Peipmeier. *Catching a Wave: Reclaiming Feminism for the 21st Century*. Boston: Northeastern University Press, 2003.

Dow, Bonnie J. *Watching Women's Liberation, 1970: Feminism's Pivotal Year on the Network News*. Urbana: University of Illinois Press, 2014.

Eckel, Jan, and Samuel Moyn, eds. *The Breakthrough: Human Rights in the 1970s*. Philadelphia: University of Pennsylvania Press, 2014.

Ehrenreich, Barbara, and Arlie Russell Hochschild. *Global Woman: Nannies, Maids, and Sex Workers in the New Economy*. New York: Metropolitan Books, 2003.

Eichorn, Kate. *The Archival Turn in Feminism: Outrage in Order*. Philadelphia: Temple University Press, 2013.

Elkins, Julie, and Shareen Hertel. "Sweatshirts and Sweatshops: Labor Rights, Student Activism, and the Challenges of Collegiate Apparel Manufacturing." In *Human Rights in Our Own Backyard: Injustice and Resistance in the United States*, edited by William T. Armaline, Davita Silfen Gasberg, and Bandana Purkayastha, 9–21. Philadelphia: University of Pennsylvania Press, 2011.

Engler, Mark, and Paul Engler. *This Is an Uprising: How Nonviolent Revolt Is Shaping the 21st Century*. New York: Bold Type Books, 2016.

Enke, Finn. *Finding the Movement: Sexuality, Contested Space, and Feminist Activism*. Durham, NC: Duke University Press, 2007.

———. "Taking Over Domestic Space: The Battered Women's Movement and Public Protest." In *The World the Sixties Made: Politics and Culture in Recent America*, edited by Van Gosse and Richard Moser, 162–190. Philadelphia: Temple University Press, 2003.

Enloe, Cynthia. *Bananas, Beaches, and Bases: Making Feminist Sense of International Politics*. Berkeley: University of California, 2000.

Eschle, Catherine. "'Skeleton Women': Feminism and the Anti-Globalization Movement." *Signs* 30, no. 3 (Spring 2005): 1741–1769.

Evans, Sara M. *Journeys That Opened Up the World: Women, Student Christian Movements, and Social Justice, 1955–1975*. New Brunswick, NJ: Rutgers University Press, 2003.

Everett, Anna. *Digital Diaspora: A Race for Cyberspace*. Albany: State University of New York Press, 2009.

Farrell, Amy. *Yours in Sisterhood: Ms. Magazine and the Promise of Popular Feminism*. Chapel Hill: University of North Carolina Press, 1998.

Ferguson, Karen. *Top Down: The Ford Foundation, Black Power, and the Reinvention of Racial Liberalism*. Philadelphia: University of Pennsylvania Press, 2013.

Ferree, Myra Max, and Aili Mari Tripp, eds. *Global Feminism: Transnational Women's Activism, Organizing and Human Rights*. New York: New York University Press, 2006.

Fine, Janice. *Worker Centers: Organizing Communities at the Edge of the Dream*. Ithaca, NY: Cornell University Press, 2006.

Francis, Megan Ming. "The Price of Civil Rights: Black Lives, White Funding, and Movement Capture." *Law & Society Review* 53, no. 1 (March 2019): 275–309.

Francisco-Menchavez, Valerie. *The Labor of Care: Filipina Migrants and Transnational Families in the Digital Age*. Urbana: University of Illinois Press, 2018.

Fraser, Arvonne S., and Irene Tinker, eds. *Developing Power: How Women Transformed International Development*. New York: Feminist Press at CUNY, 2004.

Fraser, Nancy. *Fortunes of Feminism: From State-Managed Capitalism to Neoliberal Crisis*. Brooklyn, NY: Verso Books, 2013.

Frederickson, Mary. "Citizens for Democracy: The Industrial Programs of the YWCA." In *Sisterhood and Solidarity: Workers' Education for Women, 1914–1984*, edited by Joyce L. Kornbluh and Mary Frederickson, 75–106. Philadelphia: Temple University Press, 1984.

Freedman, Estelle B. *No Turning Back: The History of Feminism and the Future of Women*. New York: Ballantine Books, 2002.

Friedman, Elisabeth Jay. "Gendering the Agenda: The Impact of the Transnational Women's Rights Movement at the UN Conferences of the 1990s." *Women's Studies International Forum* 26 (July–August 2003): 313–331.

———. "The Reality of Virtual Reality: The Internet and Gender Equality Advocacy in Latin America." *Latin American Politics and Society* 43, no. 3 (2005): 1–34.

———. "Women's Human Rights: The Emergence of a Movement." In *Women's Rights, Human Rights: International Feminist Perspectives*, edited by Julie Peters and Andrea Wolper, 18–35. New York: Routledge, 1995.

Garner, Karen. *Gender and Foreign Policy in the Clinton Administration*. Boulder, CO: First Forum Press, 2013.

———. *Shaping a Global Women's Agenda: Women's NGOs and Global Governance, 1925–1985*. Manchester, England: Manchester University Press, 2010.

Geary, Daniel. *Beyond Civil Rights: The Moynihan Report and Its Legacy*. Philadelphia: University of Pennsylvania Press, 2015.

Gelb, Joyce, and Vivien Hart. "Feminist Politics in a Hostile Environment: Obstacles and Opportunities." In *How Social Movements Matter*, edited by Marco Giugni, Doug McAdam, and Charles Tilly, 149–181. Minneapolis: University of Minnesota Press, 1999.

Gillis, Stacie, Gillian Howie, and Rebecca Munford. *Third Wave Feminism: A Critical Exploration*. New York: Palgrave Macmillan, 2004.

Gilmore, Stephanie, ed. *Feminist Coalitions: Historical Perspectives on Second-Wave Feminism in the United States*. Urbana: University of Illinois Press, 2008.

———. *Groundswell: Grassroots Feminist Activism in Postwar America*. New York: Routledge, 2013.

Giridharadas, Anand. *Winners Take All: The Elite Charade of Changing the World*. New York: Alfred A. Knopf, 2018.

Giroux, Henry. "The Terror of Neoliberalism: Rethinking the Significance of Cultural Politics." *College Literature* 32, no. 1 (2005): 1–19.

Gordon, Jennifer. *Suburban Sweatshops: The Fight for Immigrant Rights*. Cambridge, MA: Belknap Press of Harvard University Press, 2005.

Gordon, Linda. *Pitied but Not Entitled: Single Mothers and the History of Welfare, 1890–1935*. Cambridge, MA: Harvard University Press, 1994.

Gore, Dayo F. *Radicalism at the Crossroads: African American Women Activists in the Cold War*. New York: New York University Press, 2011.

Gottlieb, Robert. *Forcing the Spring: The Transformation of the American Environmental Movement*, rev. ed. Washington, DC: Island Press, 2005.

Gottschalk, Marie. *The Prison and the Gallows: The Politics of Mass Incarceration in America*. New York: Cambridge University Press, 2006.

Greene, Christina. *Our Separate Ways: Women and the Black Freedom Movement in Durham, North Carolina*. Chapel Hill: University of North Carolina Press, 2005.

Grover, William F., and Joseph G. Peschek. *The Unsustainable Presidency: Clinton, Bush, Obama, and Beyond*. New York: Palgrave Macmillan, 2014.

Guest Editors. "The History of Critical Resistance." *Social Justice* 27, no. 3 (2000): 6–10.

Gutiérrez, Elena R. *Fertile Matters: The Politics of Mexican-Origin Women's Reproduction*. Austin: University of Texas Press, 2008.

Hall, Jacquelyn Dowd. *Sisters and Rebels: A Struggle for the Soul of America*. New York: W. W. Norton & Company, 2019.

Hammer, Zoe. "Critical Resistance and the Prison Abolitionist Movement." In *Human Rights in Our Own Backyard: Injustice and Resistance in the United States*, edited by William T. Armaline, Davita Silfen Glasberg, and Bandana Purkayastha, 244–250. Philadelphia: University of Pennsylvania Press, 2011.

Hartmann, Susan. *The Other Feminists: Activists in the Liberal Establishment*. New Haven, CT: Yale University Press, 1998.

Hawkesworth, Mary. "Engendering Globalization." In *Globalization and Feminist Activism*, edited by Mary Hawkesworth, 1–28. New York: Rowman & Littlefield, 2006.

Hawthorne, Susan, and Renate Klein, eds. *Cyberfeminism: Connectivity, Critique, and Creativity*. North Melbourne, Australia: Spinifex Press, 1999.

Henry, Astrid. *Not My Mother's Sister: Generational Conflict and Third-Wave Feminism*. Bloomington: Indiana University Press, 2004.

Henry, David. "Neoliberalism as Creative Destruction." *Annals of the American Academy of Political and Social Science* 610, no. 1 (2007): 21–44.

Hewitt, Nancy, ed. *No Permanent Waves: Recasting Histories of U.S. Feminism*. New Brunswick, NJ: Rutgers University Press, 2010.

Higashida, Cheryl. *Black Internationalist Feminism: Women Writers of the Black Left, 1945–1999*. Urbana: Illinois University Press, 2013.

Hobson, Emily K. *Lavender and Red: Liberation and Solidarity in the Gay and Lesbian Left*. Oakland: University of California Press, 2016.

Hoffman, Donna L., and Thomas P. Novak. "Bridging the Racial Divide on the Internet." *Science* 280, no. 5362 (April 1998): 390–391.

Hogan, Kristen. *The Feminist Bookstore Movement: Lesbian Antiracism and Feminist Accountability*. Durham, NC: Duke University Press, 2016.

Hogan, Wesley C. *On the Freedom Side: How Five Decades of Youth Activism Have Remixed American History*. Chapel Hill: University of North Carolina Press, 2019.

Hondagneu-Sotelo, Pierrette. *Doméstica: Immigrant Workers Cleaning and Caring in the Shadows of Affluence*, 2nd ed. Berkeley: University of California Press, 2007.

Howard, John, ed. *Carryin' On in the Lesbian and Gay South*. New York: New York University Press, 1997.

———. *Men Like That: A Southern Queer History*. Chicago: University of Chicago Press, 2000.

Hunter, Tera. *To 'Joy My Freedom: Southern Black Women's Lives and Labors After the Civil War*. Cambridge, MA: Harvard University Press, 1997.

INCITE! Women of Color Against Violence, ed. *The Revolution Will Not Be Funded: Beyond the Non-Profit Industrial Complex*. Cambridge, MA: South End Press, 2007.

Jain, Devaki. *Women, Development, and the UN: A Sixty-Year Quest for Equality and Justice*. Bloomington: Indiana University Press, 2005.

Joachim, Jutta M. *Agenda Setting, the UN, and NGOs: Gender Violence and Reproductive Rights*. Washington, DC: Georgetown University Press, 2007.

Johnson, Jessica M. "#FemFuture, History, and Loving Each Other Harder." Diaspora Hypertext (blog), April 12, 2013. https://dh.jmjafrx.com/2013/04/12/femfuture-history-loving-each-other-harder/.

Johnson, Joan Marie. *Funding Feminism: Monied Women, Philanthropy, and the Women's Movement, 1870–1967*. Chapel Hill: University of North Carolina Press, 2017.

Jones, Feminista. *Reclaiming Our Space: How Black Feminists are Changing the World from the Tweets to the Streets*. Boston: Beacon Press, 2019.

Jurik, Nancy C. *Bootstrap Dreams: U.S. Microenterprise Development in an Era of Welfare Reform*. Ithaca, NY: ILR Press, 2005.

Katzenstein, Mary Fainsod. *Faithful and Fearless: Moving Feminist Protest Inside the Church and Military*. Princeton, NJ: Princeton University Press, 1998.

———. "Feminism within American Institutions: Unobtrusive Mobilization in the 1980s." *Signs* 16, no. 1 (Autumn 1990): 27–54.

Kauffman, L. A. *How to Read a Protest: The Art of Organizing and Resistance*. Oakland: University of California Press, 2018.

Kelleher, David, and Manjima Bhattacharjya. *The Amnesty International Journey: Women and Human Rights*. Brighton, England: BRIDGE Cutting Edge Programme on Gender and Social Movements, 2013.

Keshen, Michael. "Whatever Happened to Webrings." Hover (blog), July 7, 2015. www.hover.com/blog/what-ever-happened-to-webrings/.

Kim, E. Tammy. "Organizing the Unorganizable." *Dissent*, Spring 2015, 59–64.

King, Seon M. "Evaluations of Women-Centered U.S. Microenterprise Development Programs." *Affilia: Journal of Women and Social Work* 27, no. 1 (2012): 71–83.

Korey, William. *Taking on the World's Repressive Regimes: The Ford Foundation's International Human Rights Policies and Practices*. New York: Palgrave Macmillan, 2007.

Kornbluh, Felicia. *The Battle for Welfare Rights: Politics and Poverty in Modern America*. Philadelphia: University of Pennsylvania Press, 2007.

Kornbluh, Felicia, and Gwendolyn Mink. *Ensuring Poverty: Welfare Reform in Feminist Perspective*. Philadelphia: University of Pennsylvania Press, 2018.

Kuiper, Edith, and Drucilla K. Barker. *Feminist Economics and the World Bank: History, Theory, and Policy*. London: Routledge, 2005.

Kunzel, Regina. *Criminal Intimacy: Prison and the Uneven History of Modern American Sexuality*. Chicago: University of Chicago Press, 2010.

Lang, Sabine. "The NGOization of Feminism." In *Transitions, Environments, Translations: Feminisms in International Politics*, edited by Joan Wallach Scott, Cora Kaplan, and Debra Keates, 101–120. New York: Routledge, 1997.

Laughlin, Kathleen A., Julie Gallagher, Dorothy Sue Cobble, Eileen Boris, Premilla Nadasen, Stephanie Gilmore, and Leandra Zarnow. "Is It Time to Jump Ship? Historians Rethink the Waves Metaphor." *Feminist Formations* 22 (Spring 2010): 76–135.

Levenstein, Lisa. "Faxing Feminism: The Global Women's Movement and the 1995 Controversy over Huairou." *Global Social Policy* 14, no. 2 (August 2014): 228–243.

———. "From 'Innocent Children' to Unwanted Migrants and Unwed Moms: Two Chapters in the Discourse on Welfare in the United States, 1960–1961." *Journal of Women's History* 11, no. 4 (Winter 2000): 10–33.

———. "A Social Movement for a Global Age: US Feminists and the Beijing Women's Conference of 1995." *Journal of American History* 105, no. 2 (September 2018): 336–365.

Liebowitz, Debra J. "Constructing Cooperation: Feminist Activism and NAFTA." In *Feminist Locations: Global and Local, Theory and Practice*, edited by Marianne DeKoven, 176–184. New Brunswick, NJ: Rutgers University Press, 2001.

———. "Gender and Identity in an Era of Globalization: Transnational Political Organizing in North America." PhD diss., Rutgers University, 2000.

———. "Gendering (Trans)National Advocacy." *International Feminist Journal of Politics* 4, no. 2 (2002): 173–196.

———. "Governing Globalization: Feminist Engagements with International Trade Policy." In *Global Governance: Feminist Perspectives*, edited by Shirin Rai and Georgina Waylen, 207–233. New York: Palgrave MacMillan, 2008.

Link, William A. *Righteous Warrior: Jesse Helms and the Rise of Modern Conservatism*. New York: St. Martin's Press, 2008.

Louie, Miriam Ching Yoon. *Sweatshop Warriors: Immigrant Women Workers Take on the Global Factory*. Cambridge, MA: South End Press, 2001.

MacLean, Nancy. *Freedom Is Not Enough: The Opening of the American Workplace*. Boston: Harvard University Press, 2006.

Mananzala, Rickke, and Dean Spade. "The Nonprofit Industrial Complex and Trans Resistance." *Sexuality Research and Social Policy* 5, no. 1 (March 2008): 53–71.

Marcus, Sara. *Girls to the Front: The True Story of the Riot Grrrl Revolution*. New York: Harper Perennial, 2010.

Marino, Katherine M. *Feminism for the Americas: The Making of an International Human Rights Movement*. Chapel Hill: University of North Carolina Press, 2019.

Martin, Courtney E., and Vanessa Valenti. "#FemFuture: Online Revolution." *New Feminist Solutions* 8 (2013). http://bcrw.barnard.edu/publications/femfuture-online-revolution/.

Materson, Lisa G. "African American Women's Global Journeys and the Construction of Cross-Ethnic Racial Identity." *Women's Studies International Forum* 32 (January–February 2009): 224–239.

Matthews, Nancy. "Feminist Clashes with the State: Tactical Choices by State-Funded Rape Crisis Centers." In *Feminist Organizations: Harvest of the New Women's Movement*, edited by Myra Marx Ferree and

Patricia Yancey Martin, 291–305. Philadelphia: Temple University Press, 1995.

McDuffie, Erik S. *Sojourning for Freedom: Black Women, American Communism, and the Making of Black Left Feminism.* Durham, NC: Duke University Press, 2011.

McGuire, Danielle L. *At the Dark End of the Street: Black Women, Rape, and Resistance: A New History of the Civil Rights Movement from Rosa Parks to the Rise of Black Power.* New York: Alfred A. Knopf, 2010.

Miller, Elizabeth B. A. "Moving to the Head of the River: The Early Years of the U.S. Battered Women's Movement." PhD diss., University of Kansas, 2010.

Mink, Gwendolyn. "Feminists, Welfare Reform, and Justice." *Social Justice* 25, no. 1 (Spring 1998): 146–157.

———. *The Wages of Motherhood: Inequality in the Welfare State, 1917–1942.* Ithaca, NY: Cornell University Press, 1995.

———, ed. *Whose Welfare?* Ithaca, NY: Cornell University Press, 1999.

Moghadam, Valentine M. *Globalization and Social Movements: Islamism, Feminism, and the Global Justice Movement.* New York: Rowman & Littlefield, 2013.

———. *Globalizing Women: Transnational Feminist Networks.* Baltimore: Johns Hopkins University Press, 2005.

Mogul, Joey L., Andrea J. Richie, and Kay Whitlock. *Queer (In)Justice: The Criminalization of LGBT People in the United States.* Boston: Beacon Press, 2011.

Mohanty, Chandra Talpade. "Under Western Eyes: Feminist Scholarship and Colonial Discourses." *Boundary* 2, nos. 12–13 (1984): 333–358.

———. "'Under Western Eyes' Revisited: Feminist Solidarity through Anticapitalist Struggles." *Signs* 28, no. 2 (Winter 2003): 499–535.

Moore, Monika Z. "Hazards of Inequality: Comparing Two Neighborhoods in San Francisco in the 1989 Loma Prieta Earthquake." Master's thesis, Oregon State University, 2007.

Morgen, Sandra. *Into Our Own Hands: The Women's Health Movement in the United States, 1969–1990.* New Brunswick, NJ: Rutgers University Press, 2002.

Morris, Tiyi M. *Womanpower Unlimited and the Black Freedom Struggle in Mississippi.* Athens: University of Georgia Press, 2015.

Murphy, Tim. "A New Way to Look at Race." *Brown Alumni Magazine,* July/August 2017. www.brownalumnimagazine.com/articles /2017-06-30/a-new-way-to-look-at-race.

Nadasen, Premilla. "Expanding the Boundaries of the Women's Movement: Black Feminism and the Struggle for Welfare Rights," *Feminist Studies* 28, no. 2 (2002): 271–301.

———. *Household Workers Unite: The Untold History of African American Women Who Built a Movement.* Boston: Beacon Press, 2015.

———. *Welfare Warriors: The Welfare Rights Movement in the United States.* New York: Routledge, 2004.

Nelson, Jennifer. *More than Medicine: A History of the Feminist Women's Health Movement.* New York: New York University Press, 2015.

———. *Women of Color and the Reproductive Rights Movement.* New York: New York University Press, 2003.

Nicholson, Linda. "Feminism in 'Waves': Useful Metaphor or Not?" *New Politics* 12, no. 4 (Winter 2010): 34–39.

Olcott, Jocelyn. "Empires of Information: Media Strategies for the 1975 International Women's Year." *Journal of Women's History* 24, no. 4 (2012): 24–48.

———. *International Women's Year: The Greatest Consciousness-Raising Event in History.* New York: Oxford University Press, 2017.

Orleck, Annelise. *Rethinking American Women's Activism.* New York: Routledge, 2014.

———. *Storming Caesar's Palace: How Black Mothers Fought Their Own War on Poverty.* Boston: Beacon Press, 2005.

———. *"We Are All Fast Food Workers": The Global Uprising Against Poverty Wages.* Boston: Beacon Press, 2018.

Parmar, Inderjeet. *Foundations of the American Century: The Ford, Carnegie, and Rockefeller Foundations in the Rise of American Power.* New York: Columbia University Press, 2012.

Payne, Charles. *I've Got the Light of Freedom: The Organizing Tradition and the Mississippi Freedom Struggle.* Berkeley: University of California Press, 1995.

Petchesky, Rosalind Pollack. *Global Prescriptions: Gendering Health and Human Rights.* London: Zed Books, 2003.

———. "From Population Control to Reproductive Rights." *Reproductive Health Matters* 6 (November 1995): 152–161.

Piepmeier, Alison. *Girl Zines: Making Media, Doing Feminism.* New York: New York University Press, 2009.

Poo, Ai-Jen. "A Twenty-First Century Organizing Model: Lessons from the New York Domestic Workers Bill of Rights Campaign." *New Labor Forum*, January 2011, 51–55.

Ramaswamy, Ramya. "Mandy Carter: Activism During the 1990 and 1996 Helms-Gantt Campaigns." *OutHistory*, n.d. http://outhistory.org/exhibits/show/nc-lgbt/party-politics/mandy-carter.

Ransby, Barbara. *Ella Baker and the Black Freedom Movement: A Radical Democratic Vision.* Chapel Hill: University of North Carolina Press, 2005.

———. *Making All Black Lives Matter: Reimagining Freedom in the 21st Century.* Berkeley: University of California Press, 2018.

Reger, Jo. *Different Wavelengths: Studies of the Contemporary Women's Movement.* New York: Routledge, 2005.

———, ed. *Everywhere and Nowhere: Contemporary Feminism in the United States*. New York: Oxford University Press, 2012.

Reilly, Niamh. *Women's Human Rights: Seeking Gender Justice in a Globalizing Age*. Cambridge, England: Polity Press, 2009.

Reinelt, Claire. "Moving onto the Terrain of the State: The Battered Women's Movement and the Politics of Engagement." In *Feminist Organizations: Harvest of the New Women's Movement*, edited by Myra Marx Ferree and Patricia Yancey Martin, 84–104. Philadelphia: Temple University Press, 1995.

Richards, Amy, and Marianne Schnall. "Cyberfeminism: Networking the Net." In *Sisterhood Is Forever: The Women's Anthology for a New Millennium*, edited by Robin Morgan, 517–525. New York: Washington Square Press, 2003.

Richie, Beth. *Arrested Justice: Black Women, Violence, and America's Prison Nation*. New York: New York University Press, 2012.

———. *Compelled to Crime: The Gender Entrapment of Battered Black Women*. New York: Routledge, 1996.

Rodgers, Daniel T. *Age of Fracture*. Cambridge, MA: Belknap Press of Harvard University Press, 2011.

Roelofs, Joan. *Foundations and Public Policy: The Mask of Pluralism*. Albany: State University of New York Press, 2003.

Ross, Loretta J. "The Color of Choice: White Supremacy and Reproductive Justice." In *Color of Violence: The INCITE! Anthology*, edited by INCITE!, 53–65. Durham, NC: Duke University Press, 2016.

Ross, Loretta, Lynn Roberts, Erika Derkas, Whitney Peoples, and Pamela Bridgewater Toure, eds. *Radical Reproductive Justice: Foundations, Theory, Practice, Critique*. New York: Feminist Press at CUNY, 2017.

Ross, Loretta J., and Rickie Solinger. *Reproductive Justice: An Introduction*. Oakland: University of California Press, 2017.

Roth, Benita. *Separate Roads to Feminism: Black, Chicana and White Feminist Movements in America's Second Wave*. New York: Cambridge University Press, 2004.

Rothschild, Cynthia. *Written Out: How Sexuality is Used to Attack Women's Organizing*. New York: International Gay and Lesbian Human Rights Commission and Center for Women's Global Leadership, 2005.

Rupp, Leila J. "The Persistence of Transnational Organizing: The Case of the Homophile Movement." *American Historical Review* 116, no. 4 (2011): 1014–1039.

———. *Worlds of Women: The Making of an International Women's Movement*. Princeton, NJ: Princeton University Press, 1997.

Rupp, Leila, and Verta Taylor. "Forging Feminist Identity in an International Movement: A Collective Identity Approach to Feminism." *Signs* 24 no. 2 (Winter 1999): 363–386.

————. *Survival in the Doldrums: The American Women's Rights Movement, 1945 to the 1960s.* Oxford, England: Oxford University Press, 1987.

Russo, Anahi. *An Activist's Life: A Companion Discussion Guide to the Film* Passionate Politics: The Life and Work of Charlotte Bunch. New Brunswick, NJ: Center for Women's Global Leadership, 2013.

Russo, Ann. "The Feminist Majority Foundation's Campaign to Stop Gender Apartheid." *International Feminist Journal of Politics* 8, no. 4 (December 2006): 557–580.

Seidman, Rachel. *Speaking of Feminism: Today's Activists on the Past, Present and Future of the US Women's Movement.* Chapel Hill: University of North Carolina Press, 2019.

Sen, Rinku. *Stir It Up: Lessons in Community Organizing and Advocacy.* San Francisco: John Wiley & Sons, 2003.

Shade, Leslie Regan. *Gender & Community in the Social Construction of the Internet.* New York: Peter Lang, 2002.

Shevinsky, Elissa, ed. *Lean Out: The Struggle for Gender Equality in Tech and Startup Culture.* New York: OR Books, 2015.

Shirk, Martha, and Anna S. Wadia. *Kitchen Table Entrepreneurs: How Eleven Women Escaped Poverty and Became Their Own Bosses.* Boulder: Westview Press, 2004.

Silliman, Jael, Marlene Gerber Fried, Loretta Ross, and Elena Gutiérrez. *Undivided Rights: Women of Color Organize for Reproductive Justice.* Cambridge, MA: South End Press, 2004.

Sklar, Kathryn Kish. "Human Rights Discourse in Women's Rights Conventions in the United States, 1848–70." In *Revisiting the Origins of Human Rights*, edited by Pamela Slotte and Miia Halme, 163–188. Cambridge: Cambridge University Press, 2015.

Smith, Nat, and Eric Stanley. *Captive Genders: Trans Embodiment and the Prison Industrial Complex.* Oakland, CA: AK Press, 2011.

Snyder, R. Claire. "What Is Third-Wave Feminism? A New Directions Essay." *Signs* 34, no. 1 (Autumn 2008): 175–196.

Spalter-Roth, Roberta, and Ronnee Schreiber. "Outsider Issues and Insider Tactics: Strategic Tensions in the Women's Policy Network during the 1980s." In *Feminist Organizations: Harvest of the New Women's Movement*, edited by Myra Marx Ferree and Patricia Yancey Martin, 105–127. Philadelphia: Temple University Press, 1995.

Strohmer, Therese M. "Soldiers, Not WACs: How Women's Integration Transformed the Army, 1964–1994." PhD diss., University of North Carolina Greensboro, 2016.

Stryker, Susan. *Transgender History.* New York: Seal Press, 2008.

Sullivan, Richard, and Kimi Lee. "Lessons from the Los Angeles Garment Worker Center." *Signs* 33, no. 3 (Spring 2008): 527–532.

Sussman, Max. "INCITE! Women of Color Against Violence: An Interview with Co-founders Nadine Naber and Andrea Smith." *Critical Moment* 22 (2007).

Swinth, Kristen. *Feminism's Forgotten Fight: The Unfinished Struggle for Work and Family*. Cambridge, MA: Harvard University Press, 2008.

Tait, Vanessa. *Poor Workers' Unions: Rebuilding Labor from Below*. Cambridge, MA: South End Press, 2005.

Tambe, Ashwini, Alissa D. Trotz, and Gita Sen. "Historical Reflections on DAWN: An Interview with Gita Sen." *Comparative Studies of South Asia, Africa and the Middle East* 30, no. 2 (2010): 214–217.

Taylor, Keeanga-Yamahtta. *How We Got Free: Black Feminism and the Combahee River Collective*. Chicago: Haymarket Books, 2017.

Tetrault, Lisa. "The Incorporation of American Feminism: Suffragists and the Postbellum Lyceum." *Journal of American History* 96, no. 4 (March 2010): 1027–1056.

———. *The Myth of Seneca Falls: Memory and the Women's Suffrage Movement, 1848–1898*. Chapel Hill: University of North Carolina Press, 2014.

Thompson, Becky. "Multiracial Feminism: Recasting the Chronology of Second Wave Feminism." *Feminist Studies* 28, no. 2 (Summer 2002): 337–360.

Thompson, Brock. *The Un-natural State: Arkansas and the Queer South*. Fayetteville: University of Arkansas Press, 2010.

Threlkeld, Megan. *Pan American Women: U.S. Internationalists and Revolutionary Mexico*. Philadelphia: University of Pennsylvania Press, 2014.

Thuma, Emily L. *All Our Trials: Prisons, Policing, and the Feminist Fight to End Violence*. Urbana: University of Illinois Press, 2019.

Valk, Anne M. "Living a Feminist Lifestyle: The Intersection of Theory and Action in a Lesbian Feminist Collective." *Feminist Studies* 28, no. 2 (Summer, 2002): 303–332.

———. *Radical Sisters: Second-Wave Feminism and Black Liberation in Washington, D.C*. Urbana: University of Illinois Press, 2010.

Van Eck, Clara A. "Changing the Message: Battered Women's Advocates and Their Fight Against Domestic Violence at the Local, State, and Federal Level, 1970s–1990s." Master's thesis, Old Dominion University, 2017.

Villanueva, Edgar. *Decolonizing Wealth: Indigenous Wisdom to Heal Divides and Restore Balance*. Oakland, CA: Berrett-Koehler Publishers, 2018.

Wamsley, E. Sue. "Constructing Feminism Across Borders: The Pan-American Women's Movement and the Founding of the Inter-American Commission on Women." In *Crossing Boundaries: Women's Organizing in Europe and the Americas, 1880s–1940s*, edited by Pernilla Jonsson, Silke Neunsinger, and Joan Sangster, 51–71. Uppsala, Sweden: Uppsala University Press, 2007.

Wei, Tingting. "A Look at the Beijing Conference through Lesbian Eyes." *Asian Journal of Women's Studies* 21, no. 3 (2015): 316–325.

Weldon, S. Laurel. "Inclusion, Solidarity, and Social Movements: The Global Movement Against Gender Violence." *Perspectives on Politics* 4, no. 1 (2006): 55–74.

Wessinger, Catherine, ed. *Religious Institutions and Women's Leadership: New Roles Inside the Mainstream.* Columbia: University of South Carolina Press, 1996.

West, Jessamyn. "Life in the Trenches of Print and Web Publishing: An Interview with Jenna Freedman, Curator of the Barnard Zine Collection." *Serials Review* 32, no. 4 (2006): 298–302.

White, Deborah Gray. *Lost in the USA: American Identity from the Promise Keepers to the Million Mom March.* Urbana: University of Illinois Press, 2017.

Wilkerson, Jessica. *To Live Here, You Have to Fight: How Women Led Appalachian Struggles for Social Justice.* Urbana: University of Illinois Press, 2019.

Willetts, Peter. *Non-Governmental Organizations in World Politics: The Construction of Global Governance.* New York: Routledge, 2011.

Williams, Mariama. "A Perspective on Feminist International Organizing from the Ground Up." In *Feminist Strategies in International Governance*, edited by Gülay Caglar, Elisabeth Prügl, and Susanne Zwingel, 92–108. New York: Routledge, 2012.

Witham, Nick. "US Feminists and Central America in the 'Age of Reagan': The Overlapping Contexts of Activism, Intellectual Culture and Documentary Filmmaking." *Journal of American Studies* 48, no. 1 (February 2014): 199–221.

Women's March Organizers and Condé Nast. *Together We Rise: Behind the Scenes at the Protest Heard Around the World.* New York: HarperCollins, 2018.

Wu, Judy Tzu-Chun. *Radicals on the Road: Internationalism, Orientalism, and Feminism During the Vietnam Era.* Ithaca, NY: Cornell University Press, 2013.

Yarrow, Allison. *90s Bitch: Media, Culture, and the Failed Promise of Gender Equality.* New York: Harper Perennial, 2018.

Zeisler, Andi. *We Were Feminists Once: From Riot Grrrl to CoverGirl, the Buying and Selling of a Political Movement.* New York: PublicAffairs, 2016.

Zugman, Karen. "Political Consciousness and New Social Movement Theory: The Case of Fuerza Unida." *Social Justice* 30, no. 1 (Spring 2003): 153–176.

NOTES

INTRODUCTION

1. Sarah Frostenson, "The Women's Marches May Have Been the Largest Demonstration in US History," *Vox*, January 31, 2017, www.vox .com/2017/1/22/14350808/womens-marches-largest-demonstration-us -history-map; Nina Agrawal, "How the Women's March Came into Being," *Los Angeles Times*, January 21, 2017, www.latimes.com/nation/la-na-pol -womens-march-live-how-the-women-s-march-came-into-1484865755 -htmlstory.html; Alanna Vagianos and Damon Dahlen, "89 Badass Feminist Signs from the Women's March on Washington," *Huffington Post*, January 21, 2017, www.huffingtonpost.com/entry/89-badass-feminist-signs-from -the-womens-march-on-washington_us_5883ea28e4b070d8cad310cd; Lyndsey Matthews, "Here's the Full Transcript of Angela Davis's Women's March Speech," January 21, 2017, www.elle.com/culture/career-politics/ a42337/angela-davis-womens-march-speech-full-transcript/. On the march, see also Women's March Organizers and Condé Nast, *Together We Rise: Behind the Scenes at the Protest Heard Around the World* (New York: HarperCollins, 2018); L. A. Kauffman, *How to Read a Protest: The Art of Organizing and Resistance* (Oakland: University of California Press, 2018).

2. Heidi M. Przybyla and Fredreka Schouten, "At 2.6 Million Strong, Women's Marches Crush Expectations," *USA Today*, January 21, 2017, updated January 22, 2017, www.usatoday.com/story/news/politics/2017/01/21 /womens-march-aims-start-movement-trump-inauguration/96864158/.

3. "Women of color" is the term those activists most frequently used to describe themselves in the nineties and so I employ it here.

4. Jo Reger, *Everywhere and Nowhere: Contemporary Feminism in the United States* (New York: Oxford University Press, 2012).

5. Gina Bellafante, "Feminism: It's All About Me!" *Time*, June 29, 1998, 54–62.

6. For examples of other forms of activism, see Benita Roth, *Separate Roads to Feminism: Black, Chicana and White Feminist Movements in America's Second Wave* (New York: Cambridge University Press, 2004); Stephanie Gilmore, ed., *Feminist Coalitions: Historical Perspectives on Second-Wave Feminism in the United States* (Urbana: University of Illinois Press, 2008); Premilla Nadasen, "Expanding the Boundaries of the Women's Movement: Black Feminism and the Struggle for Welfare Rights," *Feminist Studies* 28, no. 2 (2002): 271–301; Anne M. Valk, *Radical Sisters: Second-Wave Feminism and Black Liberation in Washington, D.C.* (Urbana: University of Illinois Press, 2010); Jessica Wilkerson, *To Live Here, You Have to Fight: How Women Led Appalachian Struggles for Social Justice* (Urbana: University of Illinois Press, 2019).

7. Combahee River Collective, "Combahee River Collective Statement," 1977, http://circuitous.org/scraps/combahee.html; Keeanga-Yamahtta Taylor, *How We Got Free: Black Feminism and the Combahee River Collective* (Chicago: Haymarket Books, 2017).

8. Explorations of the history of US feminists' global activism include Keisha N. Blain, *Set the World on Fire: Black Nationalist Women and the Global Struggle for Freedom* (Philadelphia: University of Pennsylvania Press, 2018); Judy Tzu-Chun Wu, *Radicals on the Road: Internationalism, Orientalism, and Feminism During the Vietnam Era* (Ithaca, NY: Cornell University Press, 2013); Kathy Davis, *The Making of Our Bodies, Ourselves: How Feminism Travels Across Borders* (Durham, NC: Duke University Press, 2007); Karen Garner, *Shaping a Global Women's Agenda: Women's NGOs and Global Governance, 1925–85* (Manchester, England: Manchester University Press, 2010); Tiyi M. Morris, *Womanpower Unlimited and the Black Freedom Struggle in Mississippi* (Athens: University of Georgia Press, 2015), 85–111; Bonnie S. Anderson, *Joyous Greetings: The First International Women's Movement, 1830–1860* (New York: Oxford University Press, 2000); Lisa G. Materson, "African American Women's Global Journeys and the Construction of Cross-Ethnic Racial Identity," *Women's Studies International Forum* 32 (January–February 2009): 35–42; Erik S. McDuffie, *Sojourning for Freedom: Black Women, American Communism, and the Making of Black Left Feminism* (Durham, NC: Duke University Press, 2011); Leila J. Rupp, *Worlds of Women: The Making of an International Women's Movement* (Princeton, NJ: Princeton University Press, 1997); Megan Threlkeld, *Pan American Women: U.S. Internationalists and Revolutionary Mexico* (Philadelphia: University of Pennsylvania Press, 2014); Dorothy Sue Cobble, "A Higher 'Standard of Life' for the World: U.S. Labor Women's Reform Internationalism and the Legacies of 1919," *Journal of American History* 100, no. 4 (March 2014): 1052–1085; E. Sue Wamsley, "Constructing Feminism Across Borders: The Pan-American Women's Movement and the Founding of the Inter-American Commission on Women," in *Crossing Boundaries: Women's Organizing in Europe and the Americas, 1880s–1940s*, ed. Pernilla Jonsson, Silke Neunsinger, and Joan

Sangster (Uppsala, Sweden: Uppsala University Press, 2007), 51–71; Dayo F. Gore, *Radicalism at the Crossroads: African American Women Activists in the Cold War* (New York: New York University Press, 2011); Cheryl Higashida, *Black Internationalist Feminism: Women Writers of the Black Left, 1945–1999* (Urbana: University of Illinois Press, 2013); Christine Bolt, *Sisterhood Questioned: Race, Class and Internationalism in the American and British Women's Movements, c. 1880s–1970s* (London: Routledge, 2004); Jacqueline L. Castledine, *Cold War Progressives: Women's Interracial Organizing for Peace and Freedom* (Urbana: University of Illinois Press, 2012); Katherine M. Marino, *Feminism for the Americas: The Making of an International Human Rights Movement* (Chapel Hill: University of North Carolina Press, 2019); Estelle B. Freedman, *No Turning Back: The History of Feminism and the Future of Women* (New York: Ballantine Books, 2002); Nick Witham, "US Feminists and Central America in the 'Age of Reagan': The Overlapping Contexts of Activism, Intellectual Culture and Documentary Filmmaking," *Journal of American Studies* 48, no. 1 (February 2014): 199–221; Jocelyn Olcott, *International Women's Year: The Greatest Consciousness-Raising Event in History* (New York: Oxford University Press, 2017).

9. Premilla Nadasen, "How Did Feminism Come to Include Everything from Environmentalism to Palestinian Rights?" *Washington Post*, February 1, 2019, www.washingtonpost.com/outlook/2019/02/01/how-did -feminism-come-include-everything-environmentalism-palestinian -rights/?utm_term=.355896ca8bb3.

10. Melody Berger, ed., "Loretta Ross," *The F-Word: A Feminist Handbook for the Revolution* 3 (2008): 9.

11. Henry Giroux, "The Terror of Neoliberalism: Rethinking the Significance of Cultural Politics," *College Literature* 32, no. 1 (2005): 1, 8; David Henry, "Neoliberalism as Creative Destruction," *Annals of the American Academy of Political and Social Science* 610, no. 1 (2007): 28.

12. The Sentencing Project, "Incarcerated Women and Girls, 1980–2016," www.sentencingproject.org/publications/incarcerated-women-and-girls/; The Sentencing Project, "Criminal Justice Facts," www.sentencingproject .org/criminal-justice-facts/.

13. Eva Friedlander, ed., *Look at the World Through Women's Eyes: Plenary Speeches from the NGO Forum on Women, Beijing, '95* (Huai-jou hsien, China: Women Ink, 1995), 24–26.

14. Henry, "Neoliberalism as Creative Destruction," 23.

15. Andi Zeisler, *We Were Feminists Once: From Riot Grrrl to CoverGirl, the Buying and Selling of a Political Movement* (New York: PublicAffairs, 2016), Kindle locations 2814–2418; "Women Now Empowered by Everything a Woman Does," *The Onion*, February 19, 2003, www.theonion.com/women -now-empowered-by-everything-a-woman-does-1819566746. See also Allison Yarrow, *90s Bitch: Media, Culture, and the Failed Promise of Gender Equality* (New York: Harper Perennial, 2018).

16. Henry, "Neoliberalism as Creative Destruction," 24–25. For a feminist critique, see Alt-WID, *Reaganomics and Women: Structural Adjustment U.S. Style, 1980–1992* (Washington, DC: Alt-WID, 1992).

17. William F. Grover and Joseph G. Peschek, *The Unsustainable Presidency: Clinton, Bush, Obama, and Beyond* (New York: Palgrave Macmillan, 2014), 35–70.

18. Linda Burnham, "Beijing and Beyond," *Crossroads: Contemporary Political Analysis & Left Dialogue* 59 (March 1996): 18.

19. Loretta Ross, interview with author, August 9, 2017. Important historical studies of the personal dimensions of civil rights struggles include Barbara Ransby, *Ella Baker and the Black Freedom Movement: A Radical Democratic Vision* (Chapel Hill: University of North Carolina Press, 2005); and Charles Payne, *I've Got the Light of Freedom: The Organizing Tradition and the Mississippi Freedom Struggle* (Berkeley: University of California Press, 1995).

20. Many of the welfare rights, environmental justice, and labor activists did not publicly describe themselves as feminists, but I found them taking feminist positions, networking with feminist organizations, and participating in feminist gatherings. Examples of scholars emphasizing the need to paint a full portrait of feminist history by including women of color and working-class women who did not publicly describe themselves as feminists include Premilla Nadasen, "Expanding the Boundaries of the Women's Movement: Black Feminism and the Struggle for Welfare Rights," *Feminist Studies* 28, no. 2 (2002): 270–301; Erik S. McDuffie, *Sojourning for Freedom: Black Women, American Communism, and the Making of Black Left Feminism* (Durham, NC: Duke University Press, 2011), 3–5; Kathleen A. Laughlin, Julie Gallagher, Dorothy Sue Cobble, Eileen Boris, Premilla Nadasen, Stephanie Gilmore, and Leandra Zarnow, "Is It Time to Jump Ship? Historians Rethink the Waves Metaphor," *Feminist Formations* 22 (Spring 2010): 103; Emily L. Thuma, *All Our Trials: Prisons, Policing, and the Feminist Fight to End Violence* (Urbana: University of Illinois Press, 2019), 8–9; Finn Enke, *Finding the Movement: Sexuality, Contested Space, and Feminist Activism* (Durham, NC: Duke University Press, 2007), 4–5.

21. Sara Marcus, *Girls to the Front: The True Story of the Riot Grrrl Revolution* (New York: Harper Perennial, 2010); Annelise Orleck, *Rethinking American Women's Activism* (New York: Routledge, 2014); Dorothy Sue Cobble, Linda Gordon, and Astrid Henry, *Feminism Unfinished: A Short, Surprising History of American Women's Movements* (New York: Liveright Publishing, 2015); Dorothy Sue Cobble, *The Sex of Class: Women Transforming American Labor* (Ithaca, NY: Cornell University Press, 2007); Melinda Chateauvert, *Sex Workers Unite: A History of the Movement from Stonewall to SlutWalk* (Boston: Beacon Press, 2013); Tamar W. Carroll, *Mobilizing New York: AIDS, Antipoverty, and Feminist Activism* (Chapel Hill: University of North Carolina Press, 2015); Kate Eichorn, *The Archival Turn in Feminism: Outrage in Order* (Philadelphia: Temple University Press, 2013).

22. Zeisler, *We Were Feminists Once*; Premilla Nadasen, "Black Feminism Will Save Us All," *In These Times*, September 11, 2018, http://inthesetimes .com/article/21429/black-feminism-intersectional-donald-trump-class-race.

23. On feminist praxis, the intersection between theory and practice, see Ransby, *Ella Baker and the Black Freedom Movement*, 271, 370, 410.

24. Historians and activists have criticized the "wave" metaphor for reducing feminism to a "first wave" of early-twentieth-century suffragists, a "second wave" of 1960s and 1970s primarily white women's liberationists, and a third wave of 1990s multicultural activists. The metaphor is often used in narratives that foreground white women's activism and often mistakenly suggest that feminism in each period coalesced around a single set of tactics and ideas. Commentary on the wave model includes Linda Nicholson, "Feminism in 'Waves': Useful Metaphor or Not?" *New Politics* 12, no. 4 (Winter 2010), 34–39; Becky Thompson, "Multiracial Feminism: Recasting the Chronology of Second Wave Feminism," *Feminist Studies* 28 (Summer 2002), 337–360; Laughlin et al., "Is It Time to Jump Ship?," 76–135.

25. On the "third wave," see Cobble, Gordon, and Henry, *Feminism Unfinished*, 147–225; Jennifer Baumgardner and Amy Richards, *Manifesta: Young Women, Feminism, and the Future* (New York: D and M Publishers, 2000); Rory Cooke Dicker and Alison Peipmeier, *Catching a Wave: Reclaiming Feminism for the 21st Century* (Boston: Northeastern University Press, 2003); Daisy Hernandez and S. Bushra Rehman, *Colonize This! Young Women of Color on Today's Feminism* (New York: Seal Press, 2002); Barbara Findlen, ed., *Listen Up: Voices from the Next Feminist Generation* (Seattle: Seal Press, 1995); Rebecca Walker, ed., *To Be Real: Telling the Truth and Changing the Face of Feminism* (New York: Anchor Books, 1995); Leandra Zarnow, "From Sisterhood to Girlie Culture: Closing the Great Divide Between Second and Third Wave Popular Feminism," in *No Permanent Waves: Recasting Histories of U.S. Feminism*, ed. Nancy Hewitt (New Brunswick, NJ: Rutgers University Press, 2010), 273–302; Ednie Kaeh Garrison, "U.S. Feminism-Grrrl Style! Youth (Sub)cultures and the Technologics of the Third Wave," in *No Permanent Waves*, ed. Hewitt, 379–402; Stacie Gillis, Gillian Howie, and Rebecca Munford, *Third Wave Feminism: A Critical Exploration* (New York: Palgrave Macmillan, 2004); R. Claire Synder, "What Is Third-Wave Feminism? A New Directions Essay," *Signs* 34 (Autumn 2008): 175–196; Alison Piepmeier, *Girl Zines: Making Media, Doing Feminism* (New York: New York University Press, 2009); Marcus, *Girls to the Front*; Jo Reger, ed., *Different Wavelengths: Studies of the Contemporary Women's Movement* (New York: Routledge, 2005); Reger, *Everywhere and Nowhere*; Astrid Henry, *Not My Mother's Sister: Generational Conflict and Third-Wave Feminism* (Bloomington: Indiana University Press, 2004); Eichorn, *Archival Turn in Feminism*.

26. Suzanne Pharr, interview with author, January 17, 2017; Eichorn, *Archival Turn in Feminism*.

CHAPTER ONE: A MOVEMENT WITHOUT A CENTER

1. Susan Sygall, interview with author, December 29, 2014; Corbett O'Toole, interview with author, January 29, 2015.

2. Paula Kamen, *Feminist Fatale: Voices from the "Twentysomething" Generation Explore the Future of the "Women's Movement"* (New York: Donald I. Fine, 1991), 1.

3. Joyce Gelb and Vivien Hart, "Feminist Politics in a Hostile Environment: Obstacles and Opportunities," in *How Social Movements Matter*, ed. Marco Giugni, Doug McAdam, and Charles Tilly (Minneapolis: University of Minnesota Press, 1999), 152–155, 177.

4. Kamen, *Feminist Fatale*, 17, 263–264, 276–277. On intersectionality, see Sumi Cho, Kimberlé Williams Crenshaw, and Leslie McCall, "Toward a Field of Intersectionality Studies: Theory, Applications, and Praxis," *Signs* 38, no. 4 (2013): 786–810; Kimberlé Williams Crenshaw, "Demarginalizing the Intersection of Race and Sex: A Black Feminist Critique of Antidiscrimination Doctrine, Feminist Theory and Antiracist Politics," *University of Chicago Legal Forum* 1989, no. 1 (1989): 139–167; Kimberlé Williams Crenshaw, "Mapping the Margins: Intersectionality, Identity Politics, and Violence against Women of Color," *Stanford Law Review* 43, no. 6 (1991): 1241–1299.

5. William F. Grover and Joseph G. Peschek, *The Unsustainable Presidency: Clinton, Bush, Obama, and Beyond* (New York: Palgrave Macmillan, 2014), 35–70.

6. Susan Faludi, *Backlash: The Undeclared War on American Women* (New York: Crown, 1991).

7. Ms. Foundation for Women, *Statement of Support, Revenue and Expenses and Changes in Fund Balances for the Year Ending June 30, 1990*; Marie Wilson, interview with author, March 20, 2014; Judith Stone, "Phenomenal Woman: Coming to a White House Near You," Oprah.com, www.oprah .com/spirit/phenomenal-woman-marie-c-wilson#ixzz4mocQkyWn; Charles Euchner, "The Unsinkable Marie Collins Wilson," *Vanderbilt*, Spring 2007, 52–53; Helmut K. Anheier and Diana Leat, *Creative Philanthropy: Toward a New Philanthropy for the Twenty-First Century* (New York: Routledge, 2006), 53.

8. Wilson, interview with author, March 20, 2014; Stone, "Phenomenal Woman"; Euchner, "The Unsinkable Marie Collins Wilson"; Olivia B. Waxman, "The Inside Story of Why Take Your Daughter to Work Day Exists," *Time*, April 27, 2017.

9. Faludi, *Backlash*.

10. Kamen, *Feminist Fatale*, 99.

11. Wilson, interview with author, March 20, 2014; "Beijing and Beyond: Putting Meat on the Bones," box 69 unprocessed, Ms. Foundation for Women Records, Acc 07S-63, Sophia Smith Collection, Smith College, Northampton, Massachusetts [hereafter cited as MFW].

12. Bonnie Pfister, "Communiques from the Front: Young Activists Chart Feminism's Third Wave," *On the Issues*, Summer 1993, 23–25; Shea Dean, "Great

Expectations: The Women's Action Coalition," Found SF, www.foundsf.org /index.php?title=Great_Expectations:_The_Women%27s_Action_Coalition.

13. Idelisse Malavé to Marcia A. Smith, January 9, 1994, Grant 09390010, R-7668, Ford Foundation Records, Rockefeller Center Archives, Sleepy Hollow, New York [hereafter cited as FFR].

14. Idelisse Malavé and Kalima Rose to Ms. Foundation Beijing and Beyond Participants, October 12, 1995, box 73 unprocessed, MFW; Report, Donors Meeting, The Ford Foundation/Women & Philanthropy, February 15, 1995, box 7, folder US Preps, Kristen Timothy Papers, Department of Rare Books and Special Collections, Princeton University Library, Princeton, New Jersey [hereafter cited as Timothy Papers]; Ms. Foundation, "A Report to the Ford Foundation on the United Nations Fourth World Conference on Women, Held in Beijing, China," circa 1997, Grant 94360, R-7336, FFR. In the leadup to the conference, Eleanor Smeal of the Feminist Majority Foundation and Sarah Moten of the National Council of Negro Women established what they called the US Network for the Fourth World Conference on Women and Beyond. Smeal and Moten were cochairs of this group, which was primarily made up of established middle-class and professional organizations. On this network, see documents in box 75 unprocessed, MFW.

15. Jill Savitt to Beijing and Beyond Media Group, August 11, 1995, box 71 unprocessed, MFW.

16. Jill Savitt to Beijing and Beyond Media Group, August 11, 1995, box 71 unprocessed, MFW; "United Nations Conference on Women," C-SPAN, August 21, 1995, www.c-span.org/video/?66799-1/united-nations -conference-women.

17. Jo Freeman, "The Tyranny of Structurelessness," www.jofreeman. com/joreen/tyranny.htm.

18. Helen Neuborne, interview with author, August 28, 2014; Roberta Spalter-Roth and Ronnee Schreiber, "Outsider Issues and Insider Tactics: Strategic Tensions in the Women's Policy Network during the 1980s," in *Feminist Organizations: Harvest of the New Women's Movement*, ed. Myra Marx Ferree and Patricia Yancey Martin (Philadelphia: Temple University Press, 1995), 121–122.

19. Charon Asetoyer, interview with Joyce Follet, September 1–2, 2005, Voices of Feminism Oral History Project, 1990–2014, Sophia Smith Collection, Smith College, Northampton, Massachusetts [hereafter cited as VOF].

20. Ms. Foundation for Women, "Beijing and Beyond," Proposal and Concept Paper for the Ford Foundation, February 7, 1995, box 4 Beijing, folder Ms. Foundation, Center for Women's Global Leadership Records, Special Collections and University Archives, Rutgers University, New Brunswick, New Jersey; Grant 950–0537, R-7336, FFR.

21. "Beijing and Beyond: Putting Meat on the Bones," box 69 unprocessed, MFW.

22. "Ms Foundation Grassroots Delegation to Beijing," box 74 unprocessed, MFW. For a list of all of the activists, donors, and "fella travelers"

included in the delegation, see "Ms Foundation Delegation to Beijing," box 49, folder Beijing, 1995, Mab Segrest Papers, David M. Rubenstein Rare Book and Manuscript Library, Duke University, Durham, North Carolina [hereafter cited as Duke Archives].

23. "Ms Foundation for Women, Beijing Delegation," press release, n.d. circa 1995, box 71 unprocessed, MFW; "Facts About the Ms. Foundation Delegation," June 19, 1995, box 71 unprocessed, MFW; Sara Gould to author, January 9, 2019.

24. Pamela Chiang, interview with author, October 9, 2018; Chiang, interview with author, December 3, 2014.

25. Ellen Bravo, interview with author, May 27, 2014; Lisa Genasci, "She Learned About the 9-to-5 Grind the Hard Way," *Los Angeles Times*, June 1, 1995, www.latimes.com/archives/la-xpm-1995-06-01-fi-8401-story.html.

26. Rinku Sen, interview with author, September 10, 2014; Tim Murphy, "A New Way to Look at Race," *Brown Alumni Magazine*, July/August 2017, 23; Rinku Sen, *We Are the Ones We Are Waiting For: Women of Color Organizing for Transformation* (Durham, NC: US Urban Rural Mission, 1995), 55.

27. Bradley, interview with author, April 6, 2015; Sen, interview with author, September 10, 2014; Chiang, interview with author, December 3, 2014.

28. Melissa Wilson, interview with author, March 20, 2014.

29. Sara Gould, interview with author, July 17, 2014.

30. Bradley, interview with author, April 6, 2015.

31. Melissa Bradley, interview with author, April 6, 2015; Bravo, interview with author, May 27, 2014; "Evaluation of Beijing Trip," box 73 unprocessed, MFW.

32. Jill Savitt, interview with author, April 9, 2014.

33. Sen, interview with author, September 10, 2014; Connie Evans, interview with author, July 16, 2014.

34. Sen, interview with author, September 10, 2014.

35. Gould, interview with author, July 17, 2014; Joanne Sandler, interview with author, May 2, 2014.

36. Upon returning to the United States, the foundation sent a letter to participants raising the possibility of them forming an "independent network" that was not "the Ms. Foundation Network." It also convened a follow-up meeting for a smaller group and had the activists design and facilitate the sessions. The participants in that meeting still did not decide to form a national network. See Idelisse Malavé and Kalima Rose to Ms Foundation Beijing and Beyond Participants, October 12, 1995, box 73 unprocessed, MFW; Ms. Foundation for Women, Beyond Beijing Networking Meeting Report, box 29, folder Beijing Follow-Up Fall '95, Clinton Presidential Records, Women's Initiatives and Outreach, 2006–1098–F (segment 4), William J. Clinton Presidential Library Archives, Little Rock, Arkansas [hereafter cited as Clinton Archives].

CHAPTER TWO: "WE HAD FAR LESS
TO TEACH THAN TO LEARN"

1. Mab Segrest, *Born to Belonging: Writings on Spirit and Justice* (New Brunswick, NJ: Rutgers University Press, 2002), 56; Tingting Wei, "A Look at the Beijing Conference through Lesbian Eyes," *Asian Journal of Women's Studies* 21, no. 3 (2015): 319; Urvashi Vaid, interview with author, July 23, 2014; Jessica Halem, interview with author, May 7, 2014.

2. Jo Freeman, "The Real Story of Beijing," *off our backs* 26 (March 1996): 1, 8–11, 22–27.

3. Freeman, "The Real Story of Beijing."

4. Freeman, "The Real Story of Beijing"; Jennifer Gagliardi to beijing95–l@netcom.com, August 28, 1995, in author's possession.

5. Elisabeth Reichert, "'Keep on Moving Forward': NGO Forum on Women, Beijing, China," *Social Development Issues* 18, no. 1 (1996): 90; *NGO Forum on Women Beijing '95: Schedule of Activities* (1995); Freeman, "The Real Story of Beijing"; Robin Morgan, "Dispatch from Beijing," *Ms.*, January/February 1996, 12–21.

6. Elisabeth Reichert, "'Keep on Moving Forward,'" 90; *NGO Forum on Women Beijing '95: Schedule of Activities*; Freeman, "The Real Story of Beijing"; Morgan, "Dispatch from Beijing."

7. Roxanne Dunbar-Ortiz, interview with author, January 8, 2014; "Update on UN Conference on Women—NGO Forum," August 1, 1995, box 1, folder Pre-Going to China, Acc. #97-062, Papers Relating to the United Nations 4th World Conference on Women, Beijing, 1992–2001, Department of Special Collections and University Archives, Stanford Libraries, Stanford, California [hereafter cited as UN4WCW Papers]; Winona LaDuke, "I Fight Like a Woman," *Unity '99: Report from Beijing* (1996): 33.

8. Mandalit del Barco, "China Latina: From the Barrios to Beijing," *Unity '99: Report from Beijing* (1996): 19.

9. Vaid, interview with author, July 23, 2014; Rinku Sen, interview with author, September 10, 2014. See also Karen Avenoso, "Feminism's Newest Foot Soldiers," *Elle*, March 1993, 116; Ellen Bravo, interview with author, May 27, 2014.

10. del Barco, "China Latina," 19. There were also some US Latinas who felt comfortable in the tent.

11. Mallika Dutt, "Some Reflections on U.S. Women of Color and the United Nations World Conference on Women and NGO Forum in Beijing, China," *Feminist Studies* 22, no. 3 (1996): 523; Bravo, interview with author, May 27, 2014.

12. Lora Jo Foo, interview with author, January 8, 2014; Peggy Saika, interview with Loretta Ross, February 20, 2006, VOF.

13. Lora Jo Foo, interview with author, January 8, 2014.

14. Foo, interview with author, January 8, 2014; Saika, interview with Ross, February 20, 2006.

15. Dutt, "Some Reflections," 525.

16. Foo, interview with author, January 8, 2014; Saika, interview with Ross, February 20, 2006; Dutt, "Some Reflections," 525; Foo to author, December 27, 2018.

17. Loretta Ross, interview with author, April 20, 2013; Connie Evans, interview with author, July 16, 2014.

18. Eveline Shen, interview with author, November 11, 2014; Dutt, "Some Reflections," 520–521; Linda Burnham, interview with author, July 11, 2013; Linda Burnham, "Beijing and Beyond," *Crosssroads: Contemporary Political Analysis & Left Politics* 59 (March 1996): 18; Jenny Knauss, "Beijing Report," 1995, box 74 unprocessed, MFW; Judy Kramer, interview with author, May 2, 2012.

19. Pamela Chiang, interview with author, December 3, 2014.

20. Shen, interview with author, November 11, 2014.

21. Corbett O'Toole, interview with author, January 29, 2015.

22. Black Women of the Diaspora Taskforce, "Statement of Black Women of the Diaspora Taskforce," n.d., box 1, folder International Network of Women of Color, Accession 97-275, UN4WCW Papers; "10 Years After Nairobi—Ethnic and Racial Women Impact the Global Women's Agenda," statement prepared for the 29th Session of the Commission on the Status of Women in Preparation for the UN 4th World Conference on Women, March 16, 1995, box 1, folder Strategic Planning Sessions for Women of Color Activists, Accession 97-063, UN4WCW Papers; "U.S. Latinas Attending the Fourth World Conference on Women and Other Women's Advocates in the U.S.," sent to listserv by Maria_Alvarez@instinet.com, August 24, 1995, www.un.org/esa/gopher-data/conf/fwcw/fwcw/v02.n062.

23. Roma Guy, interview with author, January 8, 2014.

24. O'Toole, interview with author, January 29, 2015; Corbett O'Toole, interview with Denise Sherer Jacobson, 1998, Disability Rights and Independent Living Movement Oral History Series, Regional Oral History Office, Bancroft Library, University of California, Berkeley.

25. O'Toole, interview with author, January 29, 2015.

26. Susan Sygall, interview with author, December 29, 2014.

27. O'Toole, interview with author, January 29, 2015.

28. O'Toole, interview with author, January 29, 2015; O'Toole, interview with Jacobson, 1998.

29. O'Toole, interview with author, January 29, 2015; Cindy Lewis, interview with author, October 20, 2014.

30. Rina Jimenez David, "Disabled at the Forum: Marginalized as Always," *Forum '95*, September 2, 1995, 13; O'Toole, interview with author, January 29, 2015; Lewis, interview with author, October 20, 2014; Dunbar-Ortiz, interview with author, January 8, 2014.

31. Laura Hershey, "Pursuing an Agenda Beyond Barriers: Women with Disabilities," *Women's Studies Quarterly* 24, nos. 1–2 (1996): 60; Sygall, interview with author, December 29, 2014; O'Toole, interview with author, January 29, 2015.

32. O'Toole, interview with author, January 29, 2015.

33. O'Toole, interview with author, January 29, 2015; Harilyn Rousso, "Bringing Beijing Home," box 73 unprocessed, MFW.

34. Lewis, interview with author, October 20, 2014; *Disabled Women: Visions and Voices from the 4th World Conference on Women*, dir. Suzanne C. Levine and Patricia Chadwick (Wide Vision Productions, 1996); Sygall, interview with author, December 29, 2014; O'Toole, interview with author, January 29, 2015.

35. On earlier roots of transnational gay organizing, see Leila J. Rupp, "The Persistence of Transnational Organizing: The Case of the Homophile Movement," *American Historical Review* 116, no. 4 (2011): 1014–1039.

36. Julie Dorf, interview with author, May 6, 2014.

37. Rachel Rosenbloom, interview with author, April 29, 2014; Dorf, interview with author, May 6, 2014.

38. Eliza Byard, interview with author, June 13, 2014.

39. Charlotte Bunch and Claudia Hinojosa, *Lesbians Travel the Roads of Feminism Globally* (New Brunswick, NJ: Center for Women's Global Leadership, 2000), 14; Byard, interview with author, June 13, 2014; Dylan Scholinski, interview with author, September 6, 2014.

40. "Lesbians Take on the UN," *Trouble and Strife*, no. 33 (Summer 1996), www.troubleandstrife.org/articles/issue-33/lesbians-take-on-the-un/; Tingting Wei, "A Look at the Beijing Conference through Lesbian Eyes," *Asian Journal of Women's Studies* 21, no. 3 (2015): 317; Bunch and Hinojosa, *Lesbians Travel the Roads*, 15.

41. Inga Sorenson, "A Lesbian Presence," *Synapse* 34 (Winter Solstice 1995); "Harassment of Lesbian Sisters Is Harassment of All Women," flyer, box overflow Beijing Conference 1995, folder Beijing Conference 4, Lesbian Herstory Archives, Brooklyn, New York.

42. Scholinski, interview with author, September 6, 2014.

43. "Fourth World Conference on Women," *off our backs* 25, no. 10 (November 1995): 1; Lynne O'Donnell, Huairou, China, September 5 (Reuters), box 1, folder UN Conference/Beijing 1995, Robin Morgan Papers, 1940–2014, Duke Archives; Rosenbloom, interview with author, April 29, 2014.

44. Rosenbloom, interview with author, April 29, 2014; Halem, interview with author, May 7, 2014; Dorf, interview with author, May 6, 2014; Charlotte Bunch, "Opening Doors for Feminism: UN World Conferences on Women," *Journal of Women's History* 24, no. 4 (Winter 2012): 219; Cynthia Rothschild, *Written Out: How Sexuality Is Used to Attack Women's Organizing* (New York: International Gay and Lesbian Human Rights Commission and Center for Women's Global Leadership, 2005), 84–97.

45. Rosenbloom, interview with author, April 29, 2014; Halem, interview with author, May 7, 2014; Dorf, interview with author, May 6, 2014; Bunch, "Opening Doors for Feminism," 219.

46. Rosenbloom, interview with author, April 29, 2014; Halem, interview with author, May 7, 2014; Dorf, interview with author, May 6, 2014;

"Statement Delivered by Palesa Beverley Ditsie of South Africa," United Nations Fourth World Conference on Women Beijing, China, September 13, 1995, www.un.org/esa/gopher-data/conf/fwcw/conf/ngo/13123944.txt; Rothschild, *Written Out*, 84–97.

47. Rosalind Pollack Petchesky, *Global Prescriptions: Gendering Health and Human Rights* (London: Zed Books, 2003), 31–39; Bunch and Hinojosa, *Lesbians Travel the Roads*, 14–15; Ara Wilson, "Lesbian Visibility and Sexual Rights at Beijing," *Signs* 22, no. 1 (Autumn 1996): 214–218.

48. Sen, interview with author, September 10, 2014.

49. Sen, interview with author, September 10, 2014; Byard, interview with author, June 13, 2014; Vaid, interview with author, July 23, 2014. See also Bradley, interview with author, April 6, 2015; Bravo, interview with author, May 27, 2014; Amy Richards, interview with author, September 10, 2014.

CHAPTER THREE: THE WORLDWIDE
DEBUT OF ONLINE ACTIVISM

1. Edie Farwell, interview with author, April 15, 2014; Edie Farwell to author, January 8, 2019.

2. Farwell, interview with author, April 15, 2014; Farwell to author, January 8, 2019.

3. W. Joseph Campbell, *1995: The Year the Future Began* (Oakland: University of California Press, 2015), 21–22; Todd Copilevitz, "In 1995 Everyone Became Caught in the Same Web," *Dallas Morning News*, December 29, 1995, 37A.

4. Campbell, *1995*, 21–22; Aliza Sherman, *cybergrrl!: A Woman's Guide to the World Wide Web* (New York: Ballantine Books, 1998), 21.

5. Barbara O'Leary, interview with author, September 8, 2017.

6. O'Leary, interview with author, September 8, 2017.

7. Relevant literature includes Peregrine Wood, *Putting Beijing Online: Women Working in Information and Communication Technologies: Experiences from the APC Women's Networking Support Programme* (n.p.: Association for Progressive Communications Women's Networking Support Programme, 2000), 13–14; Leslie Regan Shade, *Gender & Community in the Social Construction of the Internet* (New York: Peter Lang, 2002), 37; Bonnie J. Dow, *Watching Women's Liberation, 1970: Feminism's Pivotal Year on the Network News* (Urbana: University of Illinois Press, 2014); Kristen Hogan, *The Feminist Bookstore Movement: Lesbian Antiracism and Feminist Accountability* (Durham, NC: Duke University Press, 2016); Agatha Beins, *Liberation in Print: Feminist Periodicals and Social Movement Identity* (Athens: University of Georgia Press, 2017); Jocelyn Olcott, "Empires of Information: Media Strategies for the 1975 International Women's Year," *Journal of Women's History* 24, no. 4 (2012): 24–48; Leandra Zarnow, "From Sisterhood to Girlie Culture: Closing the Great Divide Between Second and Third Wave Popular Feminism," in *No Permanent Waves: Recasting Histories of U.S. Feminism*, ed. Nancy Hewitt (New Brunswick, NJ: Rutgers University Press, 2010),

273–302; Alison Piepmeier, *Girl Zines: Making Media, Doing Feminism* (New York: New York University Press, 2009); Sara Marcus, *Girls to the Front: The True Story of the Riot Grrrl Revolution* (New York: HarperPerennial, 2010); Kristen Schilt, "'The Punk White Privilege Scene': Riot Grrrl, White Privilege, and Zines," in *Different Wavelengths: Studies of the Contemporary Women's Movement*, ed. Jo Reger (New York: Routledge, 2005), 39–56; Dawn Bates and Maureen C. McHugh, "Zines: Voices of Third Wave Feminists," in *Different Wavelengths*, ed. Reger, 179–194; Kate Adams, "Built Out of Books: Lesbian Energy and Feminist Ideology in Alternative Publishing," *Journal of Homosexuality* 34, nos. 3–4 (1998): 113–141; Kathy Davis, *The Making of Our Bodies, Ourselves: How Feminism Travels Across Borders* (Durham, NC: Duke University Press, 2007); Amy Farrell, *Yours in Sisterhood: Ms. Magazine and the Promise of Popular Feminism* (Chapel Hill: University of North Carolina Press, 1998).

8. Elissa Shevinsky, ed., *Lean Out: The Struggle for Gender Equality in Tech and Startup Culture* (New York: OR Books, 2015); Wood, *Putting Beijing Online*, 8.

9. Environmentalists, feminists, and peace activists were the earliest adopters; see Peter Willetts, *Non-Governmental Organizations in World Politics: The Construction of Global Governance* (New York: Routledge, 2011), 93, 113.

10. "Women, the Information Revolution and the Beijing Conference," *Women2000*, 1 (October 1996): 2, box 3, folder Internet Strategy and Internet Availability in China, Timothy Papers; Oliva Acosta and Malcolm Chapman, "Report on the Internet/World Wide Web Activities for the Fourth World Conference on Women," October 15, 1995, New York, box 3, folder Internet Strategy and Internet Availability in China, Timothy Papers; Wood, *Putting Beijing Online*; Barbara O'Leary, interview with author, February 26, 2014, March 5, 2014, March 14, 2014, March 19, 2014; Sally Burch, interview with author, March 23, 2014. On communications efforts at the first UN conference on women in 1975, see Olcott, "Empires of Information."

11. Edie Farwell, "Internet Links Huairou to the World and Beyond . . . ," *Forum '95*, September 4, 1995, 6; Karen Banks, "Information and Communication Technologies: *A Women's Agenda*," March 17, 1999, www.aworc.org/bpfa/pub/sec_j/com00004.html.

12. O'Leary, interview with author, September 8, 2017.

13. O'Leary, interview with author, February 26, 2014, September 8, 2017.

14. O'Leary, interview with author, February 26, 2014, September 8, 2017.

15. O'Leary, interview with author, February 26, 2014.

16. O'Leary, interview with author, September 8, 2017.

17. O'Leary, interview with author, March 14, 2014; Susan Mooney, interview with author, March 21, 2014; FWCW Secretariat/Division for the Advancement of Women, "Women, the Information Revolution and the Beijing

Conference," www.womenaid.org/press/info/cyberpioneers/inforevnet.html; World Association for Christian Communication, ISI International, International Women's Tribune Center, *Women Empowering Communication Conference and Registration Form* (1994), Grant 09390010, R-7666, FFR. For another international gathering, see "Meeting Summary, Information of 1995: Brainstorming Session I Strategies and Possibilities for Using E-mail," box 3, folder Internet Strategy and Internet Availability in China, Timothy Papers. For examples of post-Beijing international gatherings, see Susan Hawthorne and Renate Klein, eds., *Cyberfeminism: Connectivity, Critique, and Creativity* (North Melbourne, Australia: Spinifex Press, 1999), v.

18. Barbara O'Leary, interview with author, March 5, 2014.

19. Sarah Collins, "Women of the World Build a Future in Cyberspace," *Chicago Tribune*, May 19, 1996; Shana Penn, *The Women's Guide to the Wired World: A User-Friendly Handbook and Resource Directory* (New York: Feminist Press at CUNY, 1997), 136.

20. jennifer@wcw.apc.org to list, September 13, 1995, www.geocities archive.org/arclc/w/e/wellesley/8984/sept03.html#; Sally Burch, "An Experience in Promoting Women's Use of Electronic Networking," paper presented at Empowering Information Tools for Grassroots Women, Global Knowledge Conference, Toronto, 1997.

21. Susan Mooney, interview with author, March 21, 2014; Farwell, interview with author, April 15, 2014; Sally Burch, interview with author, March 23, 2014; O'Leary interview with author, February 26, 2014.

22. Mooney, interview with author, March 21, 2014; O'Leary, interview with author, February 26, 2014, May 14, 2014.

23. O'Leary, interview with author, February 26, 2014, March 5, 2014.

24. O'Leary, interview with author, March 19, 2014; Mooney, interview with author, March 21, 2014.

25. Jennifer Gagliardi, "Beijing95-L," *Women'space* 3, no. 3 (Spring 1998), www.collectionscanada.gc.ca/eppp-archive/100/202/300/womenspace /back1/vol33d.html; Alice Mastrengelo Gittler, "Taking Hold of Electronic Communications: Women Making a Difference," *Journal of International Communication* 3, no. 1 (1996): 89–90.

26. Gittler, "Taking Hold of Electronic Communications," 89–90; Gagliardi, "Beijing95-L"; Shade, *Gender & Community in the Social Construction of the Internet*, 38–39; Nina B. Huntemann, "Creating Safe Cyberspace: Feminist Political Discourse on the Internet" (Master's thesis, University of Massachusetts Amherst, 1997); Collins, "Women of the World Build a Future in Cyberspace."

27. Burch, interview with author, March 23, 2014.

28. Farwell, interview with author, April 15, 2014.

29. Wood, *Putting Beijing Online*, 21.

30. Karen Banks, Sally Burch, Irene Leon, Sonja Boezak, and Liz Probert, *Networking for Change: The APC WNSP's First 8 Years* (The Philippines:

APC Women's Networking and Support Programme, 2000), 26; Wood, *Putting Beijing Online*, 3.

31. "Women, the Information Revolution and the Beijing Conference," https://web.archive.org/web/20190703222022/www.un.org/womenwatch /daw/public/w2intro.htm; Acosta and Chapman, "Report on the Internet/ World Wide Web"; Wood, *Putting Beijing Online*; Collins, "Women of the World Build a Future in Cyberspace." It seems likely that over half of these users were from the United States. See Ellen S. Kole, "Myths and Realities in Internet Discourse: Using Computer Networks for Data Collection and the Beijing World Conference on Women," *Gazette* 6, no. 4 (1998): 351.

32. Wood, *Putting Beijing Online*, 50–52.

33. By this time, O'Leary had started an organization called Virtual Sisterhood to help feminist organizations establish themselves online and integrate digital tools into their work. O'Leary, interview with author, March 5, 2014; "APC Women's Networking Support Program WCW Online Info Update," July 1995, http://web.archive.org/web/20010713043308/www.igc.org /beijing/ngo/apc/bul4.html.

34. "Women, the Information Revolution and the Beijing Conference," https://web.archive.org/web/20190703222022/www.un.org/womenwatch /daw/public/w2intro.htm; Alice Mastrangelo Gittler, "Mapping Women's Global Communications and Networking," in *Women@Internet: Creating New Cultures in Cyberspace*, ed. Wendy Harcourt (London: Zed Books, 1999), 95. On the roots of this activism in the early 1990s, see Anita Anand with Gouri Salvi, *Beijing! UN Fourth World Conference on Women* (New Delhi: Women's Feature Service, 1998), 101; O'Leary, interview with author, March 5, 2014.

35. Gagliardi, "BEIJING95-L"; O'Leary, interview with author, March 5, 2014; "APC Women's Networking Support Program WCW Online Info Update."

36. "If a Woman's Conference Falls in the Forest. . . ?" *Body Politic* 5, no. 10 (October/November 1995): 2.

37. "Complaint Culture," *Forum '95*, September 7, 1995, 2; Shade, *Gender & Community in the Social Construction of the Internet*, 39; Kole,"Myths and Realities in Internet Discourse," 351; Gisele-Audrey Mills, "Cyberspace Is Womenspace," *CrossRoads* 59 (March 1996): 26.

38. O'Leary, interview with author, March 19, 2014.

39. Wood, *Putting Beijing Online*, front matter, no page number; Jeffrey Parker, Reuters news article, no title, clipping, September 5, 1995, box 1, folder Beijing Conf. '95, Robin Morgan Papers, Duke Archives; Gittler, "Mapping Women's Global Communications," 95.

40. Penn, *The Women's Guide to the Wired World*, esp. 136; Alice Mastrangelo Gittler, "Learning from IT: IWTC's Experience with Information Technologies," *AIWIDNews* 10, no. 2 (1996): 6; Gittler, "Taking Hold of Electronic Communications."

CHAPTER FOUR: HOW FEMINISM WENT VIRAL

1. Sharon Rogers, interview with author, October 28, 2014.

2. One of the most publicized accounts of the emergence of online feminism has been criticized for overlooking the importance of women of color: Courtney E. Martin and Vanessa Valenti, "#FemFuture: Online Revolution," *New Feminist Solutions* 8 (2013), http://bcrw.barnard.edu/publica tions/femfuture-online-revolution/. Such critiques include Veronica Arreola, "Back to the #FemFuture," *Viva La Feminista* (2013), www.vivalafeminista .com/2013/04/back-to-femfuture.html; Jessica M. Johnson, "#FemFuture, History, and Loving Each Other Harder," Postcolonial Digital Human- ities (blog), 2013, http://dhpoco.org/blog/2013/03/18/femfuture-history -loving-each-other-harder/; Susana Losa, "Hashtag Feminism, #Solidarity IsForWhiteWomen, and the Other #FemFuture," *Ada: A Journal of Gender, New Media, and Technology* 5 (2014), https://adanewmedia.org/2014/07 /issue5-loza/. For a recent account of Black women's influence on social media, see Feminista Jones, *Reclaiming Our Space: How Black Feminists are Changing the World from the Tweets to the Streets* (Boston: Beacon Press, 2019).

3. On the origins of the term "digital divide," see Elisabeth Jay Friedman, "The Reality of Virtual Reality: The Internet and Gender Equality Advocacy in Latin America," *Latin American Politics and Society* 43, no. 3 (2005): 28.

4. Michelle Singletary, "Revving Up Their Computer Power; Now Black Americans Are Outpacing Whites on Online Services," *Washington Post*, September 29, 1997, accessed through Proquest. See also Dana Canedy, "Vir- tual Community for African-Americans," *New York Times*, October 8, 1998, G10; Donna L. Hoffman and Thomas P. Novak, "Bridging the Racial Divide on the Internet," *Science* 280, no. 5362 (April 1998): 391; Anna Everett, *Dig- ital Diaspora: A Race for Cyberspace* (Albany: State University of New York Press, 2009), 10.

5. Hoffman and Novak "Bridging the Racial Divide on the Internet," 391.

6. Amy Richards and Marianne Schnall, "Cyberfeminism: Networking the Net," in *Sisterhood Is Forever: The Women's Anthology for a New Millen- nium*, ed. Robin Morgan (New York: Washington Square Press, 2003), 518.

7. Rogers, interview with author, October 28, 2014.

8. Rogers, interview with author, October 28, 2014.

9. Rogers, interview with author, October 28, 2014.

10. Rogers, interview with author, October 28, 2014; Karen Banks, "In- formation and Communication Technologies: *A Women's Agenda*," March 17, 1999, www.aworc.org/bpfa/pub/sec_j/com00004.html; Judy Kramer, in- terview with author, May 2, 2012.

11. Kim Gandy, interview with author, May 28, 2017.

12. Laila Al-Marayati, interview with author, August 22, 2014.

13. Al-Marayati, interview with author, August 22, 2014.

14. Al-Marayati, interview with author, August 22, 2014.

15. Al-Marayati, interview with author, August 22, 2014.

16. Al-Marayati, interview with author, August 22, 2014. See also Nadine Naber, interview with author, October 5, 2016.

17. Shana Penn, *The Women's Guide to the Wired World: A User-Friendly Handbook and Resource Directory* (New York: Feminist Press, 1997); My Sistah's Room, https://web.archive.org/web/19980213201930/www.ourspace.com:80/sistah/. See also Meanderings, https://web.archive.org/web/19970505051608/www.newsavanna.com:80/meanderings/; Everett, *Digital Diaspora*, 20; "Black Women on the Net," *Women'space* 3, no. 3 (Spring 1998), www.collectionscanada.gc.ca/eppp-archive/100/202/300/womenspace/back1/vol33e.html; Carla Sinclair, *Net Chick: A Smart-Girl Guide to the Wired World* (New York: Henry Holt, 1996), 199–200.

18. Kate Eichorn, *The Archival Turn in Feminism: Outrage in Order* (Philadelphia: Temple University Press, 2013), 71–72; Alison Piepmeier, *Girl Zines: Making Media, Doing Feminism* (New York: New York University Press, 2009).

19. Aliza Sherman, "Estronet.com—Next Wave Zine Web Collective," *Ms.*, September/October 1998, 41; gURL Palace, https://web.archive.org/web/19980504195617/http://gurl.com:80/connection/palace/; chickclick, https://web.archive.org/web/20001109070300/www.chickclick.com:80/. For a comparison of zines and blogs, see Jenna Freedman, "Zines Are Not Blogs: A Not Unbiased Analysis," Lower East Side Librarian (blog), 2006, http://lowereastsidelibrarian.info/articles/zinesarenotblogs, and Jessamyn West, "Life in the Trenches of Print and Web Publishing: An Interview with Jenna Freedman, Curator of the Barnard Zine Collection," *Serials Review* 32, no. 4 (2006): 268.

20. Elena Mary Costello Tzintzún, interview with author, October 18, 2017; "Blogtitlan Reunion," elenamary.com (blog), October 25, 2014, http://elenamary.com/2011/10/blogtitlan-reunion/; "Constant Blog Change," elenamary.com (blog), July 18, 2007, http://elenamary.com/2007/07/constant-blog-change/.

21. Jennifer Cole, Jason Nolan, Yukari Seko, Katherine Mancuso, and Alejandra Ospina, "GimpGirl Grows Up: Women with Disabilities Rethinking, Redefining, and Reclaiming Community," *New Media and Society* 13, no. 7 (2011): 1161–1179; GimpGirl Community, https://web.archive.org/web/20010723121431/www.gimpgirl.com/cripculture/express/results.html.

22. Cole et al., "GimpGirl Grows Up," 168–169.

23. Leslie Regan Shade, *Gender & Community in the Social Construction of the Internet* (New York: Peter Lang, 2002), 34.

24. "Welcome to FAVNET," www.oocities.org/Wellesley/8984/favnet-info.html.

25. Veronica Arreola, interview with author, September 8, 2017.

26. Arreola, interview with author, September 8, 2017.

27. Arreola, interview with author, September 8, 2017.

28. Arreola, interview with author, September 8, 2017; Jennifer Pozner, interview with author, September 26, 2017.

29. Arreola, interview with author, September 8, 2017.

30. Arreola, interview with author, September 8, 2017. On the campaign, see Ann Russo, "The Feminist Majority Foundation's Campaign to Stop Gender Apartheid," *International Feminist Journal of Politics* 8, no. 4 (December 2006): 557–580.

31. Arreola, interview with author, September 8, 2017; Wade Goodwyn, "20 Years Later Jonesboro Shooting Survivors Conflicted over Parkland," National Public Radio, March 23, 2018, www.npr.org/2018/03/23/596103091/20 -years-later-jonesboro-shooting-survivors-conflicted-over-parkland; "Columbine High School Shootings Fast Facts," CNN, May 1, 2019, www.cnn .com/2013/09/18/us/columbine-high-school-shootings-fast-facts/index .html.

32. Arreola, interview with author, September 8, 2017; Michael Keshen, "Whatever Happened to Webrings?," Hover (blog), July 7, 2015, www.hover .com/blog/what-ever-happened-to-webrings/.

33. Arreola, interview with author, September 8, 2017; Keshen, "Whatever Happened to Webrings?"

34. EstroClick, https://web.archive.org/web/20000304012908/http:// estroclick.chickclick.com:80/. For these and other similar sites, see Jennifer Baumgardner and Amy Richards, *Manifesta: Young Women, Feminism, and the Future* (New York: D and M Publishers, 2000), 359–361. See also Carla Sinclair, *Net Chicks: A Smart-Girl Guide to the Wired World* (New York: Henry Holt, 1996).

35. On this process, see Andi Zeisler, *We Were Feminists Once: From Riot Grrrl to CoverGirl, the Buying and Selling of a Political Movement* (New York: PublicAffairs, 2016); Andi Zeisler, interview with author, March 10, 2017.

36. Zeisler, interview with author, March 10, 2017. See also Zeisler, *We Were Feminists Once*.

37. Robin Frost, "Women On-line: Cybergrrl Aims to Show the Way," *Wall Street Journal*, May 30, 1996, B8; Malia Zoghlin, "Cybergrrl Web Site Creates a Community for Women," *Chicago Tribune*, February 11, 1998, 1.

38. Stephanie Brail, "The Price of Admission: Harassment and Free Speech in the Wild, Wild West," in *Wired Women: Gender and New Realities in Cyberspace*, ed. Lynn Cherny and Elizabeth Reba Weise (Seattle: Seal Press, 1996), 143–146; Stephanie Brail, "Take Back the Net," *On the Issues*, Winter 1994, 39–42. See also Penn, *The Women's Guide to the Wired World*, 46–52; Judy Anderson "ydu.J," "Not for the Faint of Heart: Contemplations on Usenet," in *Wired Women*, 127.

39. "Don't Become an Online Victim," https://web.archive.org/web/ 20190227091826/http://haltabuse.org/onlinesafety.PDF; WHO@: Working to Halt Online Abuse, https://web.archive.org/web/20181118102608/www .haltabuse.org/about/about.shtml.

40. "About WHOA," www.mit.edu/activities/safe/tofile/whoa/about .html; Penn, *The Women's Guide to the Wired World*, 48–52. For a slightly different reference to a funhouse mirror, see Amanda Hess, "When Online Procrastination Is Your Job," *New York Times*, July 24, 2019, www

.nytimes.com/2019/07/24/technology/personaltech/internet-culture.html ?smid=nytcore-ios-share.

41. Grrrl Zine Network, "About," www.grrrlzines.net/about.htm; Elke Zobl, "Living in a Place of Contradictions: Creating a Place to Exist," Grrrl Zine Network, February 2003, www.grrrlzines.net/interviews/soldier .htm; Marisa, "The Grrrl Zine Network: An Interview with Elke," Grrrl Zine Network, December 2001, www.grrrlzines.net/interviews/grrrlzinenetwork .htm; Elke Zobl, "*Digress Magazine* and *Queer Zinesters Have Lives Too*: An Interview with Annie Knight," Grrrl Zine Network, June 2005, www.grrrlzines. net/interviews/digress.htm; "French and Italian: Zines and Resources," Grrrl Zine Network, https://web.archive.org/web/20020203130708/http:// grrrlzines.net/zines/french_italian.htm.

42. Kimberlé Williams Crenshaw, "Black Women Still in Defense of Ourselves," *The Nation*, October 24, 2011, www.thenation.com/article/black -women-still-defense-ourselves/; Premilla Nadasen, interview with author, April 13, 2017.

43. Toni M. Bond to Marva Collins, letter, August 5, 1994, box 1, folder Women of African Descent for Reproductive Justice (1994–1995), Sister-Song Women of Color Reproductive Justice Collective Records, 1996–2010, Acc #105-44, Sophia Smith Collection, Smith College, Northampton, Massachusetts [hereafter cited as SisterSong Records]; Draft Advertisement— Washington Post August 12, 1994, box 1, folder Women of African Descent for Reproductive Justice (1994–1995), SisterSong Records; "Black Women on Health Care Reform," August 16, 1994, box 1, folder Women of African Descent for Reproductive Justice (1994–1995), SisterSong Records.

44. Cynthia Tornquist and Reuters, "Million Woman March Fills Philadelphia Streets," October 25, 1997, CNN.com, www.cnn.com/US/9710/25 /million.woman.march2/.

45. Everett, *Digital Diaspora*, 49, 58, 65.

46. Everett, *Digital Diaspora*, 49, 59–60, 71–78; Tornquist and Reuters, "Million Woman March Fills Philadelphia Streets." On participants' experiences of the march, see Deborah Gray White, *Lost in the USA: American Identity from the Promise Keepers to the Million Mom March* (Urbana: University of Illinois Press, 2017), 99–108.

47. On uncompensated labor, see Martin and Valenti, "#FemFuture," http://bcrw.barnard.edu/publications/femfuture-online-revolution/.

CHAPTER FIVE: MAKING A LIVING FROM SOCIAL CHANGE

1. INCITE! Women of Color Against Violence, Conference Summary, *Color of Violence: Violence Against Women of Color*, UC Santa Cruz, 2000, in author's possession; Heidi Hartmann, Ellen Bravo, Charlotte Bunch, Nancy Hartsock, Roberta Spalter-Roth, Linda Williams, and Maria Blanco, "Bringing Together Feminist Theory and Practice: A Collective Interview," *Signs* 21, no. 4 (Summer 1996): 917–951, esp. 925, 931.

2. Lisa Tetrault, "The Incorporation of American Feminism: Suffragists and the Postbellum Lyceum," *Journal of American History* 96 (March 2010):

1027–1056; Joan Marie Johnson, *Funding Feminism: Monied Women, Philanthropy, and the Women's Movement, 1870–1967* (Chapel Hill: University of North Carolina Press, 2017).

3. Megan Ming Francis, "The Price of Civil Rights: Black Lives, White Funding, and Movement Capture," *Law & Society Review* 53, no. 1 (March 2019): 275–309.

4. Mary Fainsod Katzenstein. *Faithful and Fearless: Moving Feminist Protest Inside the Church and Military* (Princeton, NJ: Princeton University Press, 1998); Mary Fainsod Katzenstein, "Feminism within American Institutions: Unobtrusive Mobilization in the 1980s," *Signs* 16, no. 1 (Autumn 1990): 27–54; Therese M. Strohmer, "Soldiers, Not WACs: How Women's Integration Transformed the Army, 1964–1994" (PhD diss., University of North Carolina Greensboro, 2016). For one of the studies of the historical roots of feminist organizing within male-dominated institutions, see Susan Hartmann, *The Other Feminists: Activists in the Liberal Establishment* (New Haven, CT: Yale University Press, 1998). For specific examples of activism among academics, see Rabab Abdulhadi, interview with Nadine Naber, April 2, 2004, Global Feminisms: Comparative Case Studies of Women's Activism and Scholarship, University of Michigan; Andrea Smith, interview with Maria Cotera, June 23, 2003, Global Feminisms: Comparative Case Studies of Women's Activism and Scholarship, University of Michigan; Premilla Nadasen, interview with author, April 13, 2017.

5. Katzenstein. *Faithful and Fearless*, ix–x, xi, 10, 12; Katzenstein, "Feminism within American Institutions," 27–28.

6. Linda Burnham, interview with author, July 11, 2013.

7. Linda Burnham, interview with Loretta J. Ross, March 18, 2015, VOF; Burnham, interview with author, July 11, 2013; Daisy Hernandez, interview with author, October 16, 2016.

8. Burnham, interview with Ross, March 18, 2015; Burnham, interview with author, July 11, 2013.

9. Burnham, interview with Ross, March 18, 2015; Burnham, interview with author, July 11, 2013.

10. Ross, interview with Follet, November 3–5, 2004, December 1–3, 2004, February 4, 2005; Saika, interview with Ross, February 20, 2006; Mandy Carter, interview with author, September 9, 2017.

11. Nicholas Lemann, "Citizen 501(c)(3)," *The Atlantic*, February 1997, www .theatlantic.com/magazine/archive/1997/02/citizen-501c3/376777/.

12. The Foundation Center and Women's Funding Network, *Accelerating Change for Women and Girls: The Role of Women's Funds* (New York: The Foundation Center, 2009).

13. This figure ("doubling") is adjusted for inflation. See "Philanthropic Giving By and For Women Rises, Study Finds" (press release), June 23, 2009, http://foundationcenter.org/about-us/press-room/archive /philanthropic-giving-by-and-for-women-on-the-rise-study-finds.

14. Helen Neuborne, interview with author, August 28, 2014; Rinku Sen, *Stir It Up: Lessons in Community Organizing and Advocacy* (San Francisco: John Wiley & Sons, 2003); *Ms. Foundation for Women Annual Report 2000*; The Foundation Center and Women's Funding Network, *Accelerating Change for Women and Girls*; Katherine Acey, interview with Kelly Anderson, July 19, 20, and 29, 2007, VOF; "Astraea at 40," www.astraeafoundation.org /about-us/astraea-at-40/.

15. Hartmann, *The Other Feminists*, 132–175; Susan Berresford, interview with author, March 8, 2016. On the Ford Foundation more generally, see Karen Ferguson, *Top Down: The Ford Foundation, Black Power, and the Reinvention of Racial Liberalism* (Philadelphia: University of Pennsylvania Press, 2013); William Korey, *Taking on the World's Repressive Regimes: The Ford Foundation's International Human Rights Policies and Practices* (New York: Palgrave Macmillan, 2007); Inderjeet Paramar, *Foundations of the American Century: The Ford, Carnegie, and Rockefeller Foundations in the Rise of American Power* (New York: Columbia University Press, 2012).

16. Neuborne, interview with author, August 28, 2014; Alison Bernstein, interview with author, March 29, 2016. Though Black women formed their own pressure group within Ford and some groups run by minorities had received funding earlier, their numbers were very small. See Hartmann, *The Other Feminists*, 142–143, 168.

17. "Donors Meeting, the Ford Foundation/Women & Philanthropy, UN 1995 World Conference on Women/NGO Forum," 1995, box 7, folder US Preps, Timothy Papers; Amrita Basu, "Globalization of the Local/Localization of the Global: Mapping Transnational Women's Movements," *Meridians* 1 (Autumn 2000): 74; Marcia Smith, Elizabeth Campbell, and Steve Zwerling, "Women's Program Forum Report on Foundation Activities in Connection with the United Nations Fourth World Conference on Women and NGO Forum on Women," September 12, 1996, grant 94360, reel 7336, FFR.

18. Ross, interview with author, April 20, 2013; Neuborne, interview with author, August 28, 2014.

19. Loretta Ross, "When Funding Hurts" (mimeograph), originally published in *Collective Voices* 1, no. 3 (September 2005); Byllye Avery, interview with author, May 16, 2017.

20. Ross, "When Funding Hurts"; Amy Richards, interview with author, September 10, 2014.

21. Ross, interview with Follet, November 3–5, 2004, December 1–3, 2004, February 4, 2005; Luz Alvarez Martinez, interview with Loretta J. Ross, December 6–7, 2004, VOF; Charon Asetoyer, interview with Joyce Follet, September 1–2, 2005, VOF.

22. Ross, interview with author, August 9, 2017; Ross, interview with Follet, November 3–5, 2004, December 1–3, 2004, February 4, 2005; Luz Rodriguez, interview with Joyce Follet, June 16–17, 2006, VOF. On SisterSong's origins, see also Rachel Strickler and Monica Simpson, "A Brief Herstory of

SisterSong," in *Radical Reproductive Justice: Foundations, Theory, Practice, Critique*, ed. Loretta Ross, Lynn Roberts, Erika Derkas, Whitney Peoples, and Pamela Bridgewater Toure (New York: Feminist Press at CUNY, 2017), Kindle locations 852–998.

23. Jael Silliman, Marlene Gerber Fried, Loretta Ross, and Elena Gutiérrez, *Undivided Rights: Women of Color Organize for Reproductive Justice* (Cambridge, MA: South End Press, 2004).

24. Loretta Ross, Lynn Roberts, Erika Derkas, Whitney Peoples, and Pamela Bridgewater Toure, eds., *Radical Reproductive Justice: Foundations, Theory, Practice, Critique* (New York: Feminist Press at CUNY, 2017).

25. Rodriguez, interview with Follet, June 16–17, 2006; Avery, interview with author, May 16, 2017; Ross, interview with Follet, November 3–5, 2004, December 1–3, 2004, February 4, 2005.

26. Ross, interview with Follet, November 3–5, 2004, December 1–3, 2004, February 4, 2005.

27. Ross, interview with Follet, November 3–5, 2004, December 1–3, 2004, February 4, 2005; Rodriguez, interview with Follet, June 16–17, 2006; Avery, interview with author, May 16, 2017.

28. Rodriguez, interview with Follet, June 16–17, 2006; Dázon Dixon Diallo, interview with author, April 11, 2017; Ross, interview with author, August 9, 2017.

29. Alice Skenandore, interview with author, April 24, 2017.

30. Rodriguez, interview with Follet, June 16–17, 2006; Skenandore, interview with author, April 24, 2017.

31. Ross, interview with Follet, November 3–5, 2004, December 1–3, 2004, February 4, 2005; Ross, interview with author, August 9, 2017.

32. Suzanne Pharr, interview with author, January 17, 2017; Pharr to author, June 20, 2019; Finn Enke, "Taking Over Domestic Space: The Battered Women's Movement and Public Protest," in *The World the Sixties Made: Politics and Culture in Recent America*, ed. Van Gosse and Richard Moser (Philadelphia: Temple University Press, 2003), 162–190; Elizabeth B. A. Miller, "Moving to the Head of the River: The Early Years of the U.S. Battered Women's Movement" (PhD diss., University of Kansas, 2010).

33. Pharr, Notes for Funding the Revolution Speech, INCITE! Conference, Santa Barbara, April 30, 2004, in author's possession.

34. Pharr, interview with author, January 17, 2017; Susan Schechter, *Women and Male Violence: The Visions and Struggles of the Battered Women's Movement* (Cambridge, MA: South End Press, 1982); INCITE!, ed., *The Revolution Will Not Be Funded: Beyond the Non-Profit Industrial Complex* (Cambridge, MA: South End Press, 2007), 11.

35. Pharr, interview with author, January 17, 2017; Pharr, Notes for Funding the Revolution Speech; Suzanne Pharr, interview with Kelly Anderson, June 28 and 29, 2005, VOF; Andrea Smith, interview with author, January 13, 2017; Nancy Matthews, "Feminist Clashes with the State: Tactical Choices by State-Funded Rape Crisis Centers," in *Feminist Organizations: Harvest*

of the New Women's Movement, ed. Myra Marx Ferree and Patricia Yancey Martin (Philadelphia: Temple University Press, 1995), 304; Claire Reinelt, "Moving Onto the Terrain of the State: The Battered Women's Movement and the Politics of Engagement," in *Feminist Organizations*, 101; Elizabeth T. Boris, "The Nonprofit Sector in the 1990s," in *Philanthropy and the Nonprofit Sector in a Changing America*, ed. Charles T. Clotfelter and Thomas Ehrlich (Bloomington: Indiana University Press, 1999), 2–3; Nancy Fraser, *Fortunes of Feminism: From State-Managed Capitalism to Neoliberal Crisis* (Brooklyn, NY: Verso Books, 2013), 221–223; Ruth Wilson Gilmore, "In the Shadow of the Shadow State," in *The Revolution Will Not Be Funded*, 44–47.

36. Pharr, interview with Anderson, June 28 and 29, 2005; Pharr, interview with author, January 17, 2017; Suzanne Pharr, interview with Rose Norman, March 28, 2013, Sinister Wisdom '93/Southern Lesbian-Feminist Oral History Supplement. An exception was Black Women's Health Project founder Byllye Avery, who was known for sending sympathetic program officers to help jumpstart initiatives representing other racial ethnic groups. See Byllye Y. Avery, interview with Loretta Ross, July 21–22, 2005, VOF; Luz Alvarez Martinez, interview with Loretta J. Ross, December 6–7, 2004; Luz Alvarez Martinez, interview with author, January 7, 2014; Mary Chung Hayashi, interview with Loretta J. Ross, December 15, 2006, VOF.

37. Pharr, interview with Anderson, June 28 and 29, 2005; Roberta Spalter-Roth and Ronnee Schreiber, "Outsider Issues and Insider Tactics: Strategic Tensions in the Women's Policy Network during the 1980s," in *Feminist Organizations*, 120–121.

38. Ross, interview with author, April 20, 2013; Eleanor Smeal, interview with author, May 31, 2017.

39. Charlotte Bunch, interview with author, March 20, 2013.

40. On *Ms.* magazine's approach to running advertisements in the 1970s and 1980s, see Amy Erdman Farrell, *Yours in Sisterhood: Ms. Magazine and the Promise of Popular Feminism* (Chapel Hill: University of North Carolina Press, 1998).

41. Andi Zeisler, interview with author, March 10, 2017; Lisa Jervis, interview with author, March 23, 2017.

42. Zeisler, interview with author, March 10, 2017.

43. Kim Gandy, interview with author, May 28, 2017; NOW Foundation Board Meeting, April 29, 2001, unapproved minutes, box 414, folder 9, National Organization for Women, Additional Records, 1970–2011, Arthur and Elizabeth Schlesinger Library on the History of Women in America, Radcliffe College, Cambridge, Massachusetts [hereafter cited as Schlesinger Library]; "National Organization for Women, Inc 2016 Budget—DRAFT," https://now.org/wp-content/uploads/2015/10/2016-NOW-Inc-Budget-Draft-.pdf; Max Sussman, "INCITE! Women of Color Against Violence: An Interview with Co-founders Nadine Naber and Andrea Smith," *Critical Moment* 22 (2007).

44. INCITE!, *The Revolution Will Not Be Funded*, 8–9.

45. Elements of their critique had been aired by activists as early as the 1960s and were later given theoretical expression in scholarship that explored "NGOization" in developing countries. During the early twenty-first century, US women of color and their white allies developed and spread their own analyses. Victoria Bernal and Inderpal Grewal, *Theorizing NGOs: States, Feminisms, and Neoliberalism* (Durham, NC: Duke University Press, 2014); Robert L. Allen, *Black Awakening in Capitalist America: An Analytic History* (Garden City, NY: Doubleday, 1969); Sonia E. Alvarez, "Latin American Feminisms 'Go Global': Trends of the 1990s and Challenges for the New Millennium," in *Cultures of Politics, Politics of Cultures: Re-Visioning Latin American Social Movements*, ed. Evelina Dagnino, Sonia E. Alvarez, and Arturo Escobar (Boulder, CO: Westview Press, 1998), 114–122; Sonia E. Alvarez, "Beyond NGO-ization? Reflections from Latin America," *Development* 52, no. 2 (2009): 175–184; Ferguson, *Top Down*; Joan Roelofs, *Foundations and Public Policy: The Mask of Pluralism* (Albany: State University of New York Press, 2003); Robert F. Arnove, *Philanthropy and Cultural Imperialism: The Foundations at Home and Abroad*, 1st Midland Book ed. (Bloomington: Indiana University Press, 1982); Sabine Lang, "The NGOization of Feminism," in *Transitions, Environments, Translations: Feminisms in International Politics*, ed. Joan Wallach Scott, Cora Kaplan, and Debra Keates (New York: Routledge, 1997), 101–120; Marlene Fried, interview with Joyce Follett, August 14 and 15, 2007, VOF.

46. Andrea Smith, interview with author, January 13, 2017; Andrea Smith, interview with Maria Cotera, June 24, 2003; INCITE! Women of Color Against Violence, "Color of Violence: Violence Against Women of Color UC Santa Cruz, April 28–29, 2000, Conference Summary"; Sussman, "INCITE! Women of Color Against Violence"; INCITE!, *The Revolution Will Not Be Funded*, 11. For a related academic critique of the relationship between the feminist campaign against violence and the state, see Kristin Bumiller, *In an Abusive State: How Neoliberalism Appropriated the Feminist Movement Against Sexual Violence* (Durham, NC: Duke University Press, 2008).

47. *Ms. Foundation for Women Annual Report 2000*, 15.

48. INCITE!, *The Revolution Will Not Be Funded*, i–ii. Susan Berresford to author, February 14, 2019; *Ford Foundation Annual Report 2004*.

49. Suzanne Pharr, Notes for Funding the Revolution Speech; Rickke Mananzala and Dean Spade, "The Nonprofit Industrial Complex and Trans Resistance," *Sexuality Research and Social Policy* 5, no. 1 (March 2008): 59.

50. Pharr, Notes for Funding the Revolution Speech; Sujatha Jesudason, interview with author, October 11, 2017. INCITE!, *The Revolution Will Not Be Funded*, cites Robert F. Arnove, *Philanthropy and Cultural Imperialism: The Foundations at Home and Abroad* (Boston: G. K. Hall, 1980), as an early influence. Contemporary critiques include Anand Giridharadas, *Winners Take All: The Elite Charade of Changing the World* (New York: Alfred A. Knopf, 2018); Edgar Villanueva, *Decolonizing Wealth: Indigenous Wisdom to*

Heal Divides and Restore Balance (Oakland, CA: Berrett-Koehler Publishers, 2018).

51. Smith, interview with author, January 13, 2017.

52. Smith, interview with author, January 13, 2017; Reinelt, "Moving Onto the Terrain of the State," 101.

CHAPTER SIX: "WOMEN'S RIGHTS ARE HUMAN RIGHTS"

1. Susan Davis, interview with author, June 7, 2013.

2. Valentine M. Moghadam, *Globalizing Women: Transnational Feminist Networks* (Baltimore: Johns Hopkins University Press, 2005), 6–8; Peggy Antrobus, *The Global Women's Movement: Origins, Issues and Strategies* (London: Zed Books, 2004), 18–19; Elisabeth Jay Friedman, "Gendering the Agenda: The Impact of the Transnational Womens Rights Movement at the UN Conferences of the 1990s," *Women's Studies International Forum* 26 (July–August 2003): 318–319; Amrita Basu, "Globalization of the Local/Localization of the Global: Mapping Transnational Women's Movements," *Meridians* 1, no. 1 (Autumn 2000): 70–72. For a more pessimistic assessment of North–South relations that did not foreclose the possibility of productive future alliances, see Devaki Jain, "Building Alliances: A Southern Perspective," *Focus on Gender* 2 (October 1994): 15–19. Explorations of women of color's transnational activism include Keisha N. Blain, *Set the World on Fire: Black Nationalist Women and the Global Struggle for Freedom* (Philadelphia: Temple University Press, 2018); Cheryl Higashida, *Black Internationalist Feminism: Women Writers of the Black Left, 1945–1999* (Urbana: University of Illinois Press, 2013); Judy Tzu-Chun Wu, *Radicals on the Road: Internationalism, Orientalism, and Feminism During the Vietnam Era* (Ithaca, NY: Cornell University Press, 2013); Erik S. McDuffie, *Sojourning for Freedom: Black Women, American Communism, and the Making of Black Left Feminism* (Durham, NC: Duke University Press, 2011); Dayo F. Gore, *Radicalism at the Crossroads: African American Women Activists in the Cold War* (New York: New York University Press, 2011).

3. Friedman, "Gendering the Agenda."

4. Charlotte Bunch, interview with author, March 20, 2013; S. Laurel Weldon, "Inclusion, Solidarity, and Social Movements: The Global Movement Against Gender Violence," *Perspectives on Politics* 4, no. 1 (2006): 60–61.

5. Anahi Russo, *An Activist's Life: A Companion Discussion Guide to the Film* Passionate Politics: The Life and Work of Charlotte Bunch (New Brunswick, NJ: Center for Women's Global Leadership, 2013), 5–6, 9–10; Tami Gold, producer, *Passionate Politics: The Life and Work of Charlotte Bunch* (2011); Charlotte Bunch, *Passionate Politics, Essays, 1968–1986: Feminist Theory in Action* (New York: St. Martin's Press, 1987), 6–9.

6. On The Furies, see Anne M. Valk, "Living a Feminist Lifestyle: The Intersection of Theory and Action in a Lesbian Feminist Collective," *Feminist Studies* 28, no. 2 (Summer, 2002): 303–332; Anne M. Valk, *Radical Sisters:*

Second-Wave Feminism and Black Liberation in Washington, D.C. (Urbana: University of Illinois Press, 2008), 135–157.

7. Russo, *An Activist's Life*, 9–12.

8. Bunch, *Passionate Politics*, 17–18; Gold, *Passionate Politics*.

9. Studies of such activism include Blain, *Set the World on Fire*; Higashida, *Black Internationalist Feminism*; Wu, *Radicals on the Road*; McDuffie, *Sojourning for Freedom*; Gore, *Radicalism at the Crossroads*; Emily K. Hobson, *Lavender and Red: Liberation and Solidarity in the Gay and Lesbian Left* (Oakland: University of California Press, 2016); Nick Witham, "US Feminists and Central America in the 'Age of Reagan': The Overlapping Contexts of Activism, Intellectual Culture and Documentary Filmmaking," *Journal of American Studies* 48, no. 1 (2014): 199–221.

10. Bunch, interview with author, March 20, 2013; Bunch to author, January 14, 2019; Joanne Sandler, interview with author, May 2, 2014.

11. Moghadam, *Globalizing Women*, 8–11; Antrobus, *The Global Women's Movement*, 18–20; Ashwini Tambe, Alissa D. Trotz, and Gita Sen, "Historical Reflections on DAWN: An Interview with Gita Sen," *Comparative Studies of South Asia, Africa and the Middle East* 30, no. 2 (2010): 214–217; Sonia E. Alvarez, Elisabeth Jay Friedman, Ericka Beckman, Maylei Blackwell, Norma Stoltz Chinchilla, Nathalie Lebon, Marysa Navarro, and Marcela Ríos Tobar, "Encountering Latin American and Caribbean Feminisms," *Signs* 28, no. 2 (Winter 2003): 537–579.

12. Bunch, interview with author, January 5, 2015; Charlotte Bunch, "How Women's Rights Became Recognized as Human Rights," in *The Unfinished Revolution: Voices from the Global Fight for Women's Rights*, ed. Minky Worden (New York: Seven Stories Press, 2012), 31.

13. Weldon, "Inclusion, Solidarity, and Social Movements," 60–67; Niamh Reilly, *Women's Human Rights: Seeking Gender Justice in a Globalizing Age* (Cambridge: Polity Press, 2009), 71.

14. Weldon, "Inclusion, Solidarity, and Social Movements," 63–67.

15. Charlotte Bunch, interview with Katy Morris and Kayla Ginsburg, June 10, 2011, Women and Social Movements International, Alexander Street, A Proquest Company ; Charlotte Bunch to author, August 12, 2019.

16. Bunch, interview with Morris and Ginsburg, June 10, 2011. For similar approaches, see Julie Dorf, interview with author, May 6, 2014; Cynthia Rothschild, interview with author, October 21, 2015.

17. Bunch to author, August 12, 2019.

18. Bunch, interview with author, January 5, 2015; Bunch to author, January 15, 2019.

19. For examples of earlier efforts of US feminists and civil rights activists to advocate for human rights, see Kathryn Kish Sklar, "Human Rights Discourse in Women's Rights Conventions in the United States, 1848–70," in *Revisiting the Origins of Human Rights*, ed. Pamela Slotte and Miia Halme (Cambridge: Cambridge University Press, 2015), 163–188; Pauli Murray, "Women's Rights Are a Part of Human Rights," in *The American Women's*

Movement, 1945–2000: A Brief History with Documents, ed. Nancy MacLean (Boston: Bedford/St Martin's, 2009), 69–71; Carol Anderson, *Eyes Off the Prize: The United Nations and the African American Struggle for Human Rights, 1944–1955* (Cambridge: Cambridge University Press, 2003).

20. Katherine M. Marino, *American Feminism: The History of a Hemispheric Movement* (Chapel Hill: University of North Carolina Press, 2018).

21. On the flourishing of international human rights movements in the 1970s, see Jan Eckel and Samuel Moyn, eds., *The Breakthrough: Human Rights in the 1970s* (Philadelphia: University of Pennsylvania Press, 2014).

22. Fran Hosken, "Toward a Definition of Women's Human Rights," *Human Rights Quarterly*, Spring 1981, 1–10.

23. Elisabeth Friedman, "Women's Human Rights: The Emergence of a Movement," in *Women's Rights, Human Rights: International Feminist Perspectives*, ed. Julie Peters and Andrea Wolper (New York: Routledge, 1995), 22–23; Ximena Bunster-Burotto, "Surviving Beyond Fear: Women and Torture in Latin America," in *Women and Change in Latin America*, ed. June Nash and Helen Safa (New York: Bergin & Garvey, 1986), 297–335; Bunch, "How Women's Rights Became Recognized as Human Rights," 31; Bunch, interview with author, March 20, 2013.

24. Bunch, "How Women's Rights Became Recognized as Human Rights," 29–31. See also Bunch, interview with author, March 20, 2013.

25. Friedman, "Women's Human Rights," 25–27; Reilly, *Women's Human Rights*, 69–70. Saba Bahar, "Human Rights Are Women's Right: Amnesty International and the Family," in *Global Feminisms Since 1945: Rewriting Histories*, ed. Bonnie G. Smith (New York: Routledge, 2000), 265–289. Over the next decade, influenced by feminists' success on the international stage, Amnesty waged a Stop Violence Against Women campaign, which in six years produced sixty-four reports and involved all sectors of its operations. On resistance to women's human rights within Amnesty International, see David Kelleher and Manjima Bhattacharjya, "The Amnesty International Journey: Women and Human Rights" (Brighton, England: BRIDGE Cutting Edge Programme on Gender and Social Movements, 2013).

26. Bunch, interview with author, March 20, 2013; Bunch, "How Women's Rights Became Recognized as Human Rights."

27. Bunch, interview with author, March 20, 2013; Bunch, "How Women's Rights Became Recognized as Human Rights."

28. Grant 9500656, Reel 7088, FFR.

29. Bunch, interview with author, January 5, 2015; Bunch, interview with Morris and Ginsburg, June 10, 2011.

30. Anita Nayar, interview with author, August 10, 2015; Jael Silliman, interview with author, April 30, 2013; "Donors Meeting, The Ford Foundation/Women & Philanthropy, UN 1995 World Conference on Women/NGO Forum," 1995, box 7, folder US Preps, Timothy Papers; Basu, "Globalization of the Local/Localization of the Global: Mapping Transnational Women's Movements," 74; Marcia Smith, Elizabeth Campbell, and Steve Zwerling,

"Women's Program Forum Report on Foundation Activities in Connection with the United Nations Fourth World Conference on Women and NGO Forum on Women," September 12, 1996, grant 94360, reel 7336, FFR; Cynthia Eyakuse, interview with author, August 29, 2014; Bunch, interview with author, March 20, 2013; Bunch, interview with author, January 5, 2015.

31. Liz Abzug, interview with author, June 6, 2012; Joan Frankson, interview with author, May 21, 2013; Davis, interview with author, June 7, 2013.

32. Jessica Halem, interview with author, May 7, 2014; Nayar, interview with author, August 10, 2015; Frankson, interview with author, May 21, 2013; Eyakuze, interview with author, August 29, 2014.

33. Bunch, interview with Morris and Ginsburg, June 10, 2011; Bunch interview with author, January 5, 2015; Russo, *An Activist's Life*, 2, 22–24; Mallika Dutt, interview with author, February 11, 2014. On organized sex workers' adoption of human rights frameworks, see Melinda Chateauvert, *Sex Workers Unite: A History of the Movement from Stonewall to SlutWalk* (Boston: Beacon Press, 2013).

34. Bunch, "How Women's Rights Became Recognized as Human Rights," 30; Charlotte Bunch and Niamh Reilly, *Demanding Accountability: The Global Campaign and Vienna Tribunal for Women's Human Rights* (New York: Center for Women's Global Leadership and United Nations Development Fund for Women, 1994), 4–5.

35. Friedman, "Gendering the Agenda," 319–320.

36. Friedman, "Gendering the Agenda," 320. On earlier uses of a women's caucus at the UN, see Ann Marie Clark, Elisabeth J. Friedman, and Kathryn Hochstetler, "The Sovereign Limits of Global Civil Society: A Comparison of NGO Participation in UN World Conferences on the Environment, Human Rights, and Women," *World Politics*, 51, no. 1 (1998): 24.

37. Radhika Balakrishnan, interview with author, June 18, 2015.

38. Davis, interview with author, June 7, 2013; Balakrishnan, interview with author, June 18, 2015; Ritu Sharma, interview with author, November 21, 2014.

39. Sharma, interview with author, November 21, 2014.

40. Anita Nayar, interview with author, August 10, 2015.

41. Davis, interview with author, June 7, 2013; Nayar, interview with author, August 10, 2015.

42. Balakrishnan, interview with author, June 18, 2015; Nayar, interview with author, August 10, 2015; Sharma, interview with author, November 21, 2014; Elisabeth Freidman, interview with author, June 11, 2014; Ara Wilson, "Lesbian Visibility and Sexual Rights in Beijing," *Signs* 22, no. 1 (Autumn 1996): 216.

43. Friedman, interview with author, June 11, 2014; Adrienne Germain, interview with author, January 7, 2015.

44. Leni Silverstein, interview with author, May 20, 2014.

45. Ara Wilson, interview with author, October 13, 2014; Ara Wilson to author, June 20, 2019.

46. Bunch, "How Women's Rights Became Recognized as Human Rights," 30; Bunch and Reilly, *Demanding Accountability*, 4–5.

47. Bunch and Reilly, *Demanding Accountability*, 103–104.

48. Martha Alter Chen, "Engendering World Conferences: The International Women's Movement and the UN," in *NGOs, the UN, and Global Governance*, ed. Thomas G. Weiss and Leon Gordenker (Boulder, CO: Lynne Rienner Publishers, 1996), 144; Friedman, "Gendering the Agenda," 320.

49. Bunch and Reilly, *Demanding Accountability*, 104–106; Reilly, "Women's Human Rights," 73; Friedman, "Gendering the Agenda," 322.

50. Friedman, "Gendering the Agenda," 322–323; Rosalind Pollack Petchesky, "From Population Control to Reproductive Rights," *Reproductive Health Matters* 6 (November 1995): 152–161; Adrienne Germain, interview with author, January 7, 2015; Chen, "Engendering World Conferences."

51. Freidman, "Gendering the Agenda," 324–325; Anita Anand with Gouri Salvi, *Beijing! UN Fourth World Conference on Women* (New Delhi: Women's Feature Service, 1998).

52. Pamela Sparr, "Briefing for Congressional Staff on Economic Policy Implications of the Beijing 'Platform for Action,'" October 5, 1995, in author's possession; Devaki Jain, *Women, Development, and the UN: A Sixty-Year Quest for Equality and Justice* (Bloomington: Indiana University Press, 2005), 127; Gayatri Chakravorty Spivak, "'Woman' as Theatre: United Nations Conference on Women, Beijing 1995," *Radical Philosophy* 75 (January/February 1996): 2–4; Nayar, interview with author, August 10, 2015. Critiques of human rights discourses include Celina Romany, "On Surrendering Privilege: Diversity in a Feminist Redefinition of Human Rights Law," in *From Basic Needs to Basic Rights: Women's Claim to Human Rights*, ed. Margaret Schuler (Washington, DC: Women, Law, and Development International, 1995), 543–553; Inderpal Grewal, "'Women's Rights as Human Rights': Feminist Practices, Global Feminism, and Human Rights Regimes in Transnationality," *Citizenship Studies* 3, no. 3 (1999): 337–354. For a more recent example, see Elora Halim Chowdhury, *Transnationalism Reversed: Women Organizing Against Gendered Violence in Bangladesh* (Albany: State University of New York Press, 2011). The women's human rights network responded to critiques by giving increasing airtime to testimony about violations of economic rights at their tribunals. See Bunch and Reilly, *Demanding Accountability*, 109–110; Niamh Reilly, ed., *Without Reservation: The Beijing Tribunal on Accountability for Women's Human Rights* (New Brunswick, NJ: Center for Women's Global Leadership, 1996), 5–6.

53. Wilson, "Lesbian Visibility and Sexual Rights," 217.

54. Balakrishnan, interview with author, June 18, 2015; Nayar, interview with author, August 10, 2015; Friedman, "Gendering the Agenda," 320; Chen, "Engendering World Conferences"; Anand, *Beijing!*, 100–101; Jain, *Women, Development, and the UN*; Antrobus, *The Global Women's Movement*; Moghadam, *Globalizing Women*; Clark, Friedman, and Hochstetler, "The Sovereign Limits of Global Civil Society"; Jutta M. Joachim, *Agenda Setting, the*

UN, and NGOs: Gender Violence and Reproductive Rights (Washington, DC: Georgetown University Press, 2007), 33.

55. "What Came Out of the First Prepcom for Women 2000?" *Preview 2000* 2 (May 1999): 1; Barbara Crossette, "Women See Key Gains Since Talks in Beijing," *New York Times*, March 8, 1998; Sharon Kotuk, interview with author, July 16, 2014; Claudia Hinojosa and Susana T. Fried, *Bringing Women's Human Rights Home: Report of the 1996 Women's Global Leadership Institute* (New Brunswick, NJ: Center for Women's Global Leadership, 1996), 2–3; Adrienne Germain to author, September 3, 2019; Stanley Foundation, *Building on Beijing: United States NGOs Shape a Women's National Agenda* (Muscatine, IA: Stanley Foundation, 1996); Women's Environment and Development Organization, *Mapping Progress: Assessing Implementation of the Beijing Platform* (New York: WEDO, 1998); California Women's Agenda, *California Women's Agenda: Report of the Action Program to Bring the Beijing Platform to the Grassroots of California* (San Francisco: Women's Intercultural Network, 1997); Maria Riley, *Women Connecting Beyond Beijing: Facilitator's Guide, The Local Is Global, The Global Is Local* (Washington, DC: Center of Concern, 1996); Karen Garner, *Gender and Foreign Policy in the Clinton Administration* (Boulder: First Forum Press, 2013); Kathleen Hendrix, interview with author, June 2, 2014; Kathleen Hendrix to Lisa Levenstein, June 3, 2014; President's Interagency Council on Women, "U.S. Government Follow-up to the United Nations Fourth World Conference on Women, March 1997 Summary Update on Key Initiatives," www.feminist.com/resources/artspeech/wword/ww12.htm.

56. Rosalind Petchesky, interview with author, June 6, 2013.

57. Freidman, "Gendering the Agenda," 314.

58. Petchesky, interview with author, June 6, 2013; Bunch, interview with Morris and Ginsburg, June 10, 2011; Bunch interview with author, March 20, 2013; Victoria Tauli-Corpuz, interview with author, September 7, 2013; Antrobus, *The Global Women's Movement*, 114.

CHAPTER SEVEN: TACKLING WOMEN'S POVERTY FROM GLOBAL PERSPECTIVES

1. Accounts of the history of perceptions of Aid to Dependent Children include Linda Gordon, *Pitied but Not Entitled: Single Mothers and the History of Welfare, 1890–1935* (Cambridge, MA: Harvard University Press, 1994, 1995); Gwendolyn Mink, *The Wages of Motherhood: Inequality in the Welfare State, 1917–1942* (Ithaca, NY: Cornell University Press, 1995); Lisa Levenstein, "From 'Innocent Children' to Unwanted Migrants and Unwed Moms: Two Chapters in the Discourse on Welfare in the United States, 1960–1961," *Journal of Women's History* 11, no. 4 (Winter 2000): 10–33.

2. Levenstein, "From 'Innocent Children' to Unwanted Migrants and Unwed Moms"; Daniel Geary, *Beyond Civil Rights: The Moynihan Report and Its Legacy* (Philadelphia: University of Pennsylvania Press, 2015); Rachel Black and Aleta Sprague, "The Rise and Reign of the Welfare Queen,"

New America Weekly, September 22, 2016, www.newamerica.org/weekly /edition-135/rise-and-reign-welfare-queen/.

3. Gwendolyn Mink, "Feminists, Welfare Reform, and Justice," *Social Justice* 25, no. 1 (Spring 1998): 150; Marisa Chappell, *The War on Welfare: Family, Poverty, and Politics in Modern America* (Philadelphia: University of Pennsylvania Press, 2010). On the politics of welfare reform, see Felicia Kornbluh and Gwendolyn Mink, *Ensuring Poverty: Welfare Reform in Feminist Perspective* (Philadelphia: University of Pennsylvania Press, 2018).

4. Ryan Cooper, "Somewhere in Between: The Rise and Fall of Clintonism," *The Nation*, February 14, 2018, www.thenation.com/article/the -rise-and-fall-of-clintonism/; Kornbluh and Mink, *Ensuring Poverty*, 55.

5. Black and Sprague, "The Rise and Reign of the Welfare Queen," www.newamerica.org/weekly/edition-135/rise-and-reign-welfare-queen; Russell L. Riley, "Bill Clinton: Campaigns and Elections," n.d., Miller Center University of Virginia, https://millercenter.org/president/clinton /campaigns-and-elections.

6. Premilla Nadasen, *Welfare Warriors: The Welfare Rights Movement in the United States* (New York: Routledge, 2004); Felicia Kornbluh, *The Battle for Welfare Rights: Politics and Poverty in Modern America* (Philadelphia: University of Pennsylvania Press, 2007).

7. Mimi Abramovitz, *Under Attack, Fighting Back: Women and Welfare in the United States* (New York: Monthly Review Press, 2000), 139–139; Allen Harris, "National Welfare Rights Union Convention Draws up Plans to Fight Anti-Poor Budget Cuts," *People's Tribune* (Online Edition), September 18, 1995; Marian Kramer, interview with Loretta Ross, February 1–2, 2014, VOF.

8. Pamela Sparr to author, August 17, 2019.

9. NOW LDEF, *1995 Annual Report*, 1, box 1, folder 1, Records of Legal Momentum, 1978–2011, Schlesinger Library; Gwendolyn Mink, ed., *Whose Welfare?* (Ithaca, NY: Cornell University Press, 1999), 174; Mimi Abramovitz, *Under Attack, Fighting Back*, 141.

10. Felicia Kornbluh, "Feminists and the Welfare Debate: Too Little? Too Late?" *Dollars & Sense*, November–December 1996, 24–25.

11. Some continued to fight by documenting what happened to women who lost their benefits and arguing that the denial of welfare was a violation of human rights. For examples, see Unitarian Universalist Service Committee, *Is It Reform: The 1998 Report of the Welfare and Human Rights Monitoring Project* (Cambridge, MA: Unitarian Universalist Service Committee, 1998); Abramovitz, *Under Attack, Fighting Back*, 148–149; Linda Burnham, "Welfare Reform, Family Hardship, and Women of Color," in *Lost Ground: Welfare Reform, Poverty, and Beyond*, ed. Randy Albelda and Ann Withorn (Cambridge, MA: South End Press, 2002), 43–56; Linda Burnham, "Racism in US Welfare Policy: A Human Rights Issue" (Working Paper Series, No. 2, Women of Color Resource Center, 2002); Mary Bricker-Jenkins, Carrie Young, and Cheri Honkala, "Using Economic Human Rights in the Movement to End Poverty," in *Challenges in Human Rights: A Social Work*

Perspective, ed. Elisabeth Reichert (New York: Columbia University Press, 2007), 122–137.

12. Joyce Kelly, "Lending Agency Helps Unemployed Start Businesses," *Chicago Tribune*, July 18, 1993, http://articles.chicagotribune.com/1993-07 -18/features/9307180114_1_business-connie-evans-traditional-employers; Connie Evans, interview with author, July 16, 2014.

13. Helen Scheuer Cohen, "How Far Can Credit Travel? A Comparative Study of the Grameen Bank in Bangladesh and the Women's Self-Employment Project in Chicago" (Master's thesis, Massachusetts Institute of Technology, 1989), 18–20. By the end of the 1980s, the Grameen Bank had branches in over nine thousand villages, with more than 430,000 borrowers.

14. Alex Counts, *Small Loans, Big Dreams: How Nobel Prize Winner Muhammad Yunus and Microfinance Are Changing the World* (Hoboken, NJ: John Wiley & Sons, 2008), 18–19; Evans, interview with author, July 16, 2014.

15. Evans, interview with author, July 16, 2014; Cohen, "How Far Can Credit Travel?" 51–52. It is notable that neither program followed the example of the Self-Employed Women's Association (SEWA), a trade union of poor, self-employed women workers in India, which had established a Cooperative Bank in 1974. The women in SEWA coupled their banking practices with collective organizing and fought for resources such as housing and health care. See Ela R. Bhatt, *We Are Poor but So Many: The Story of Self-Employed Women in India* (New York: Oxford University Press, 2006).

16. Evans, interview with author, July 16, 2014.

17. Elaine Edgcomb, Joyce Klein, and Peggy Clark, *The Practice of Microenterprise in the U.S.* (Washington, DC: Aspen Institute, 1996), 1, 15–16. Eighty-six percent of Evans's Women's Self-Employment Project clients were minorities.

18. Evans, interview with author, July 16, 2014; Sara K. Gould, interview with Kelly Anderson, November 16, 2007, VOF; Elaine Edgcomb, Tamra Thetford, and Ilgar Alisultanov, *A Final Report on the Fourth Round of the Ms. Foundation for Women's Collaborative Fund for Women's Economic Development* (Washington, DC: Aspen Institute, June 2009), https://assets .aspeninstitute.org/content/uploads/2017/06/MsRpt09.pdf; Martha Shirk and Anna S. Wadia, *Kitchen Table Entrepreneurs: How Eleven Women Escaped Poverty and Became Their Own Bosses* (Boulder, CO: Westview Press, 2004), xxxi.

19. Gould, interview with Anderson, November 16, 2007; Evans, interview with author, July 16, 2014; Yma Gordon-Reid, phone conversation with author, August 6, 2018.

20. Jann S. Wenner, Hunter S. Thompson, William Greider, and P. J. O'Rourke, "Bill Clinton: The Rolling Stone Interview," *Rolling Stone*, September 17, 1992, www.rollingstone.com/politics/politics-news/bill-clinton-the -rolling-stone-interview-34047/; Muhammed Yunus to author, April 5, 2015; The White House, Office of the Press Secretary, First Lady Hillary Rodham Clinton, Remarks to the United Nations Development Fund for Women

"Women's Economic Empowerment Zone" Panel, Beijing, China, September 6, 1995, https://clintonwhitehouse4.archives.gov/WH/EOP/First_Lady/html/generalspeeches/1995/devfund.html.

21. Nancy C. Jurik, *Bootstrap Dreams: U.S. Microenterprise Development in an Era of Welfare Reform* (Ithaca, NY: ILR Press, 2005), 3; Seon M. King, "Evaluations of Women-Centered U.S. Microenterprise Development Programs," *Affilia: Journal of Women and Social Work* 27, no. 1 (2012): 72–73.

22. First Lady Hillary Rodham Clinton Presents Awards for Excellence in Microenterprise Development, The White House Presidential Hall, January 16, 2001, 2011-0415-S-Flotus Press Releases 9–99 Current Binder, January 2001, Clinton Archives; The White House, Office of the Press Secretary, Remarks by the First Lady and Secretary of the Treasury Robert Rubin at Microenterprise Awards Ceremony, January 30, 1997, box 1, folder Microenterprise Awards '98, WHORM Alpha File, 2006-1301-F, Clinton Archives.

23. S. Raheim and Jason J. Friedman, "Microenterprise Development in the Heartland: Self-Employment as a Self-Sufficiency Strategy for TANF Recipients in Iowa 1993–1998," *Journal of Microfinance* 1, no. 1 (1999): 67; Emily Huemann and Jean Wiley, *The Challenge of Microenterprise: The CWED Story*, ed. Jan Breidenbach and Mari Riddle (Oakland, CA: National Economic Development & Law Center and the Coalition for Women's Economic Development, 1998), I. For other statistics see, Jurik, *Bootstrap Dreams*, 70–71; PBS Online, To Our Credit, "Women," n.d., www.pbs.org/toourcredit/women_one.htm.

24. Yma Gordon, "Women and Microenterprise" (typescript), 2006, in author's possession; Sara K. Gould, "Women and Microenterprise—Learning from the New Nobel Prize Winner," November 8, 2006, Women's Media Center, www.womensmediacenter.com/news-features/women-and-microenterpriselearning-from-the-new-nobel-prize-winner.

25. Huemann and Wiley, *Challenge of Microenterprise*, I; Gordon-Reid, phone conversation with author, August 6, 2018; Jurik, *Bootstrap Dreams*, 78–117, 204–205, 213, 217.

26. Pamela Sparr, interview with author, August 27, 2014.

27. Sparr, interview with author, August 27, 2014; Pamela Sparr to author, August 17, 2019.

28. Sparr, interview with author, August 27, 2014; Sparr to author, August 17, 2019. On virginity tests, see Alan Travis, "Virginity Tests for Immigrants 'Reflected Dark Age Prejudices' of 1970s Britain," *The Guardian*, May 8, 2011, www.theguardian.com/uk/2011/may/08/virginity-tests-immigrants-prejudices-britain.

29. Sparr, interview with author, August 27, 2014; Sparr to author, August 17, 2019.

30. Sparr, interview with author, August 27, 2014; Sparr, interview with author, October 17, 2014; Sparr to author, August 17, 2019; Alt-WID, *Reaganomics and Women: Structural Adjustment U.S. Style, 1980–1992* (Washington, DC: Alt-WID, 1992).

31. Sparr, interview with author, October 17, 2014; Sparr to author, June 28, 2019; Catherine Wessinger, ed., *Religious Institutions and Women's Leadership: New Roles Inside the Mainstream* (Columbia: University of South Carolina Press, 1996); Sara M. Evans, *Journeys That Opened Up the World: Women, Student Christian Movements, and Social Justice, 1955–1975* (New Brunswick, NJ: Rutgers University Press, 2003).

32. Sparr to author, June 28, 2019.

33. Sparr, interview with author, October 17, 2014; Sparr to author, June 28, 2019.

34. Sparr to author, June 28, 2019.

35. Sparr, interview with author, August 27, 2014; Sparr, interview with author, October 17, 2014; Joanne Meyerowitz, "The Political Economies of the 1970s Women in Development Movement" (paper presented at the International Federation of Research on Women Conference, Vancouver, British Columbia, 2018); Arvonne S. Fraser and Irene Tinker, eds., *Developing Power: How Women Transformed International Development* (New York: Feminist Press at CUNY, 2004).

36. Pamela Sparr, Remarks on Panel on Women and the Global Social Economy, American Political Science Association Meeting, 1997, in author's possession; Sparr, interview with author, August 27, 2014.

37. Alt-WID, *Reaganomics and Women*; Carol Barton and elmira Nazombe, interview with author, March 17, 2015.

38. A search for "globalization" in the Google Books Ngram viewer confirms this point: https://books.google.com/ngrams/graph?content=globalization &year_start=1960&year_end=2015&corpus=15&smoothing=3&share=& direct_url=t1%3B%2Cglobalization%3B%2Cc0.

39. Dorothy Sue Cobble, "International Women's Trade Unionism and Education," *International Labor and Working-Class History* 90 (Fall 2016): 153–163; Mary Frederickson, "Citizens for Democracy: The Industrial Programs of the YWCA," in *Sisterhood and Solidarity: Workers' Education for Women, 1914–1984*, ed. Joyce L. Kornbluh and Mary Frederickson (Philadelphia: Temple University Press, 1984), 75–106; Paulo Freire, *Pedagogy of the Oppressed* (New York: Seabury Press, 1968); Sparr, interview with author, August 27, 2014; Pamela Sparr, *United Methodist Study Guide on Global Economics—Seeking a Christian Ethic* (prepared for the Women's Division by the Mission Education and Cultivation Program Department, General Board of Global Ministries, the United Methodist Church, 1993); Sparr, "How We Got into This Mess and Ways to Get Out," *Ms.*, March/April 1992, 29–36.

40. Sparr, interview with author, August 27, 2014; Barton and Nazombe, interview with author, March 17, 2015; elmira Nazombe, interview with author, April 30, 2015.

41. Linda Burnham, interview with author, July 11, 2013; Miriam Ching Louie with Linda Burnham, *WEdGE: Women's Education in the Global Economy* (Berkeley, CA: Women of Color Resource Center, 2000).

42. Sparr, interview with author, August 27, 2014; Sparr, *United Methodist Study Guide on Global Economics*; Sparr, "How We Got into This Mess and Ways to Get Out"; Nazombe, interview with author, April 30, 2015; Barton and Nazombe, interview with author, March 17, 2015; Marlene Kim, interview with author, May 27, 2016.

43. Kim, interview with author, May 27, 2016.

44. Margaret Prescod, interview with author, October 14, 2014; Prescod, interview with author, January 18, 2018; Kathleen Hendrix, "Waging the War Over Wages: Fight for Homemaker Pay Has Seen Ups, Downs," *Los Angeles Times*, May 7, 1987, http://articles.latimes.com/1987-05-07/news/vw -4294_1_unremunerated-work; Kathleen Hendrix, "Campaign Catches On: L.A. Pair Seek Wages for Women's Unpaid Work," *Los Angeles Times*, July 28, 1985, http://articles.latimes.com/1985-07-28/news/vw-5698_1_unpaid -work; Kathleen Hendrix, "Passionate Pursuer's Crusade Against the South Side Slayer: Margaret Prescod Trying to Raise Community Awareness on the Streets of South-Central L.A. . . . and Beverly Hills," *Los Angeles Times*, October 16, 1986, http://articles.latimes.com/1986-10-16/news /vw-5852_1_south-side.

45. Prescod, interview with author, October 14, 2014; Prescod, interview with author, January 18, 2018; Hendrix, "Waging the War Over Wages"; Hendrix, "Campaign Catches On."

46. Prescod, interview with author, October 14, 2014; Prescod, interview with author, January 18, 2018; Phoebe Jones Schellenberg, "Valuing Women's Unwaged Work," feminist.com, www.feminist.com/resources/artspeech /work/value.htm.

47. Prescod, interview with author, October 14, 2014; Prescod, interview with author, January 18, 2018; Schellenberg, "Valuing Women's Unwaged Work," www.feminist.com/resources/artspeech/work/value.htm.

48. Prescod, interview with author, October 14, 2014.

49. Phoebe Jones Schellenberg, "The Beijing Decisions to Measure and Value Unwaged Work—a Progress Report" (paper presented at International Association of Time Use Research Meeting, Montreal, Canada, 1998).

50. "Women's Beijing Conference Plans Brought Back Home," *New York Amsterdam News*, November 18, 1995, 22.

51. Lydia Williams, "Women's Eyes on the World Bank," *Agenda* 13, no. 34 (1997): 103–107; Sparr, interview with author, August 27, 2014. See also Lydia Williams, "Gender Equity and the World Bank Group: A Post-Beijing Assessment," *Women's International Network News* 24, no. 1 (Winter 1998): 7; Christopher H. Chamberlain, *A Citizens' Guide to Gender and the World Bank* (Washington, DC: Bank Information Center, 1996), 10.

52. Williams, "Women's Eyes on the World Bank," 103–107, esp. 106–107; Sparr, interview with author, August 27, 2014. See also Williams, "Gender Equity and the World Bank Group"; Chamberlain, *A Citizens' Guide to Gender and the World Bank*, 10.

53. Williams, "Gender Equity and the World Bank Group"; Emad Mekay, "Development: World Bank Pressed on Gender Equality" (wire feed), Global Information Network, January 22, 2004.

54. Edith Kuiper and Drucilla K. Barker, *Feminist Economics and the World Bank: History, Theory, and Policy* (London: Routledge, 2005).

55. Sparr, interview with author, August 27, 2014; Kim, interview with author, May 27, 2016.

CHAPTER EIGHT: ENVIRONMENTAL JUSTICE AND LABOR ACTIVISM

1. Pamela Chiang, interview with author, October 9, 2018; Chiang, interview with author, December 3, 2014.

2. Elizabeth Martínez, *De Colores Means All of Us: Latina Views for a Multi-Colored Century* (Cambridge, MA: South End Press, 1998), 169.

3. Chiang, interview with author, December 3, 2014; Chiang, interview with author, October 9, 2018.

4. Chiang, interview with author, December 3, 2014; Monika Z. Moore, "Hazards of Inequality: Comparing Two Neighborhoods in San Francisco in the 1989 Loma Prieta Earthquake" (Master's thesis, Oregon State University, 2007).

5. Chiang, interview with author, December 3, 2014; Chiang, interview with author, October 9, 2018. On the different paths of environmental activism, see Robert Gottlieb, *Forcing the Spring: The Transformation of the American Environmental Movement*, rev. ed. (Washington, DC: Island Press, 2005).

6. Teresa Córdova, "Grassroots Mobilizations in the Southwest for Environmental and Economic Justice," *International Journal of Public Administration*, 25, nos. 2–3 (2002): 334–335; Patrick Novotny, *Where We Live, Work and Play: The Environmental Justice Movement and the Struggle for a New Environmentalism* (Westport, CT: Praeger, 2000), 27–39; Southwest Organizing Project, *Intel Inside New Mexico: A Case Study of Environmental and Economic Injustice* (Albuquerque, NM: Southwest Organizing Project, 1995); Southwest Organizing Project, *Report on the Interfaith Hearings on Toxic Poisoning in Communities of Color* (Albuquerque, NM: Southwest Organizing Project, 1993).

7. Chiang, interview with author, October 9, 2018; Chiang, interview with author, December 3, 2014.

8. Martínez, *De Colores Means All of Us*, 101; Novotny, *Where We Live, Work and Play*, xv–xvii; Commission for Racial Justice, United Church of Christ, *Toxic Wastes and Race in the United States: A National Report of the Racial and Socio-Economic Characteristics of Communities with Hazardous Waste Sites* (New York: United Church of Christ Commission for Racial Justice, 1987).

9. Chiang, interview with author, October 9, 2018; Chiang, interview with author, December 3, 2014; Matt Reimann, "This Poor, Hispanic Town in California Has Been Fighting a Local Toxic Waste Dump for 35

Years," Timeline, April 29, 2017, https://timeline.com/this-poor-hispanic -town-in-california-has-been-fighting-a-local-toxic-waste-dump-for-35 -years-8f6f20f89f9d; Jesse McKinley, "In a California Town, Birth Defects, Deaths and Questions," *New York Times*, February 6, 2010, www.nytimes .com/2010/02/07/us/07kettleman.html.

10. Chiang, interview with author, October 9, 2018; Chiang, interview with author, December 3, 2014; Scott Sherman, "Environmental Justice Case Study: West County Toxics Coalition and the Chevron Refinery," www .umich.edu/~snre492/sherman.html.

11. People of Color Regional Activist Dialogue on Environment Justice, "Statement of Solidarity," 1990, box 6, folder SNEEJ/SWOP Founding Docs 1990, Miriam Ching Louie Papers, 1970–2012, Sophia Smith Collection, Smith College, Northampton, Massachusetts [hereafter cited as Louie Papers]; Marcia Cole, "When Movements Coalesce," *National Law Journal*, September 21, 1992, S10.

12. Chiang, interview with author, October 9, 2018.

13. Martínez, *De Colores Means All of Us*, 109–110; Córdova, "Grassroots Mobilizations in the Southwest for Environmental and Economic Justice," 335; Marianne Lavell, "Transition Meets with Minorities," *National Law Journal*, December 14, 1992, 3, 42; "Environmental Justice" (timeline), Avoice: African American Voices in Congress, www.avoiceonline.org /environmental/timeline.html; Environmental Protection Agency, "Summary of Executive Order 12898," www.epa.gov/laws-regulations/summary -executive-order-12898-federal-actions-address-environmental-justice; Chiang, interview with author, October 9, 2018; Chiang, interview with author, December 3, 2014.

14. Martínez, *De Colores Means All of Us*, 105–106; Marty Durlin, "The Shot Heard Round the West," *High Country News*, July 8, 2010, www.ejnet .org/ej/swopresponsearticle.pdf; Córdova, "Grassroots Mobilizations in the Southwest for Environmental and Economic Justice," 345; "Principles of Environmental Justice," www.ejnet.org/ej/principles.html; Southwest Organizing Project, "Major National Organizations and Problems of the 'Environmental Movement,'" 1990, box 6, folder SNEEJ/SWOP Founding Docs 1990, Louie Papers.

15. Chiang, interview with author, October 9, 2018; Chiang, interview with author, December 3, 2014.

16. Chiang, interview with author, October 9, 2018; Chiang, interview with author, December 3, 2014.

17. Jennifer Gordon, *Suburban Sweatshops: The Fight for Immigrant Rights* (Cambridge, MA: Belknap Press of Harvard University Press, 2005), 12–16; Miriam Ching Yoon Louie, *Sweatshop Warriors: Immigrant Women Workers Take on the Global Factory* (Cambridge, MA: South End Press, 2001), 4–7. Throughout the twentieth century, occupations such as domestic work and farm work that employed large numbers of low-income African Americans and immigrants remained riddled with abuse. But the working conditions in

many other jobs improved because of the reforms instituted. For an exploration of campaigns against sweatshops, see Eileen Boris, "Consumers of the World Unite! Campaigns Against Sweating, Past and Present," in *Sweatshop USA: The American Sweatshop in Historical and Global Perspective*, ed. Daniel E. Bender and Richard A. Greenwald (New York: Routledge, 2003), 203–224.

18. Louie, *Sweatshop Warriors*, 4.

19. Louie, *Sweatshop Warriors*, 34–37; Gordon, *Suburban Sweatshops*, 13–14. For examples of campaigns, see Dorothy Sue Cobble, ed., *The Sex of Class: Women Transforming American Labor* (Ithaca, NY: Cornell University Press, 2007); Eileen Boris and Jennifer Klein, *Caring for America: Home Health Workers in the Shadow of the Welfare State* (New York: Oxford University Press, 2012).

20. Dorothy Sue Cobble, "Introduction," in *The Sex of Class*, 3; Louie, *Sweatshop Warriors*, 34–37.

21. Karen Zugman, "Political Consciousness and New Social Movement Theory: The Case of Fuerza Unida," *Social Justice* 30, no. 1 (Spring 2003): 153–176; Martínez, *De Colores Means All of Us*, 92–93, 206–209.

22. By 2005, women were 43 percent of all union members. See Cobble, "Introduction," in *The Sex of Class*, 5. Other explorations of women in unions include essays in Cobble, *The Sex of Class*; Dorothy Sue Cobble, *The Other Women's Movement: Workplace Justice and Social Rights in Modern America* (Princeton, NJ: Princeton University Press, 2011).

23. Cobble, "Introduction," in *The Sex of Class*, 5–7; E. Tammy Kim, "Organizing the Unorganizable," *Dissent*, Spring 2015, 59–64; Vanessa Tait, *Poor Workers' Unions: Rebuilding Labor from Below* (Cambridge, MA: South End Press, 2005), 187–215; Eileen Boris and Jennifer Klein, "'We Were the Invisible Workforce: Unionizing Home Care," in *The Sex of Class*, 177–193; Boris and Klein, *Caring for America*, 183–210; Gordon, *Suburban Sweatshops*, 61–65; Richard Sullivan and Kimi Lee, "Lessons from the Los Angeles Garment Worker Center," *Signs* 33, no. 3 (Spring 2008): 527–532; Louie, *Sweatshop Warriors*, 200; Don Gonyea, "How the Labor Movement Did a 180 on Immigration," National Public Radio, February 5, 2013, www .npr.org/2013/02/05/171175054/how-the-labor-movement-did-a-180-on -immigration. On unionization among Chinese women garment workers in New York City, see Xiaolan Bao, *Holding Up More than Half the Sky: Chinese Garment Workers in New York City, 1948–92* (Urbana: University of Illinois Press, 2001).

24. Tait, *Poor Workers' Unions*.

25. *Fuerza Unida: 10th Anniversary, 1990–2000*, box 5, folder Fuerza Unida, Louie Papers; Martínez, *De Colores Means All of Us*, 83.

26. Chiang, interview with author, December 3, 2014; Chiang, interview with author, October 9, 2018; Louie, *Sweatshop Warriors*, 215–216; Lora Jo Foo, interview with author, January 8, 2014.

27. Chiang, interview with author, October 9, 2018.

28. Chiang, interview with author, October 9, 2018.

29. Zugman, "Political Consciousness and New Social Movement Theory," 170–171.

30. Louie, *Sweatshop Warriors*, 7, 3; Janet Fine, "Worker Centers and Immigrant Women," in *The Sex of Class*, 215–216; Janice Fine, *Worker Centers: Organizing Communities at the Edge of the Dream* (Ithaca, NY: Cornell University Press, 2006), 217–233.

31. Chiang, interview with author, December 3, 2014; Chiang to author, August 25, 2019; Martínez, *De Colores Means All of Us*, 83; "CSWA, Fuerza Unida & AIWA Swap Stories," *AIWA News*, June 1993, 2, box 4, folder AIWA-Newsletters—GWJC 1991–1996, Louie Papers.

32. Louie, *Sweatshop Warriors*, 227–228, 1–2, 41–43, 48–51. The terms of the settlement were confidential. McClintock did not accept legal responsibility for its contractors' wages and working conditions. On campus activism, see Julie Elkins and Shareen Hertel, "Sweatshirts and Sweatshops: Labor Rights, Student Activism, and the Challenges of Collegiate Apparel Manufacturing," in *Human Rights in Our Own Backyard: Injustice and Resistance in the United States*, ed. William T. Armaline, Davita Silfen Gasberg, and Bandana Purkayastha (Philadelphia: University of Pennsylvania Press, 2011), 9–21.

33. Chiang, interview with author, December 3, 2014; "Workplace Literacy Classes New Semester Begins," *AIWA News*, February 1994, 3, box 4, folder AIWA-Newsletters—GWJC 1991–1996, Louie Papers; "Workplace Literacy Students Ponder Proposition 187," 3, box 4, folder AIWA-Newsletters—GWJC 1991–1996, Louie Papers; "Leadership Training Wraps Up," 3, box 4, folder AIWA-Newsletters—GWJC 1991–1996, Louie Papers; "Workplace Literacy Classes Begin," *AIWA News*, Fall 1994, 3, box 4, folder AIWA-Newsletters—GWJC 1991–1996, Louie Papers; Jane Chen, "Workplace Literacy Spring Session Wraps Up," *AIWA News*, 1996, box 4, folder AIWA-Newsletters—GWJC 1991–1996, Louie Papers; Chuan Chen, "Immigrant Women Centered Education in Oakland," *AIWA News*, March 1997, 4, box 4, folder AIWA-Newsletters—GWJC 1991–1996, Louie Papers; Louie, *Sweatshop Warriors*, 104; elmira Nazombe, interview with author, April 30, 2015.

34. Eileen Boris and Premilla Nadasen, "Domestic Workers Organize!" *Working USA: The Journal of Labor and Society* 11 (December 2008): 413–424; Tera Hunter, *To 'Joy My Freedom: Southern Black Women's Lives and Labors After the Civil War* (Cambridge, MA: Harvard University Press, 1997); Premilla Nadasen, *Household Workers Unite: The Untold History of African American Women Who Built a Movement* (Boston: Beacon Press, 2015).

35. Ai-Jen Poo, interview with author, October 11, 2016.

36. Poo, interview with author, October 11, 2016.

37. Poo, interview with author, October 11, 2016.

38. Poo, interview with author, October 11, 2016.

39. Poo interview with author, October 11, 2016; Fine, "Worker Centers and Immigrant Women," 219–225; Boris and Nadasen, "Domestic Workers Organize!" 425–428; Nadasen, *Household Workers Unite*, 173–178;

Ai-Jen Poo, "A Twenty-First Century Organizing Model: Lessons from the New York Domestic Workers Bill of Rights Campaign," *New Labor Forum*, January 2011, http://newlaborforum.cuny.edu/2011/01/03/a-twenty-first -century-organizing-model-lessons-from-the-new-york-domestic-workers -bill-of-rights-campaign/.

40. Poo, interview with author, October 11, 2016. In 2011, the International Labor Organization passed the Convention Concerning Decent Work for Domestic Workers (Domestic Workers Convention, No. 189), which established the first global standards for domestic workers. Explorations of immigrant domestic workers include Pierrette Hondagneu-Sotelo, *Doméstica: Immigrant Workers Cleaning and Caring in the Shadows of Affluence*, 2nd ed. (Berkeley: University of California Press, 2007); Barbara Ehrenreich and Arlie Russell Hochschild, *Global Woman: Nannies, Maids, and Sex Workers in the New Economy* (New York: Metropolitan Books, 2003); Valerie Francisco-Menchavez, *The Labor of Care: Filipina Migrants and Transnational Families in the Digital Age* (Urbana: University of Illinois Press, 2018).

41. On struggles against NAFTA, see, for example, Paul Adler, "Fighting SHAFTA, GATTzilla, and More: The Rise of the Fair Globalization Coalition in the 1990s" (unpublished paper in author's possession, 2017); Debra J. Liebowitz, "Constructing Cooperation: Feminist Activism and NAFTA," in *Feminist Locations: Global and Local, Theory and Practice*, ed. Marianne DeKoven (New Brunswick, NJ: Rutgers University Press, 2001), 168–190.

42. Lisa Richwine, "Hispanics Ask Clinton to Renegotiate NAFTA," March 21, 1993, States News Service, accessed via LexisNexis; Dan Blackburn, "Clinton Meets Mexican President to Discuss NAFTA," CNN News, January 9, 1993, accessed via LexisNexis.

43. Mercedes López, "Discussing Economics on the Border," *Corresponencia*, Winter/Spring 1991/1992, 15–17; Debra J. Liebowitz, "Gendering (Trans)National Advocacy," *International Feminist Journal of Politics* 4, no. 2 (2002): 177–178.

44. Carol Barton, interview with author, March 24, 2015; Debra J. Liebowitz, "Constructing Cooperation: Feminist Activism and Nafta," in *Feminist Locations: Global and Local, Theory and Practice*, ed. Marianne DeKoven (New Brunswick, NJ: Rutgers University Press, 2001), 176–184.

45. Richwine, "Hispanics Ask Clinton to Renegotiate NAFTA"; Blackburn, "Clinton Meets Mexican President"; "NAFTA: No Good for Immigrant Women Workers," *AIWA News*, November 1993, 1–2, box 4, folder AIWA-Newsletters—GWJC 1991–1996, Louie Papers; Martínez, *De Colores Means All of Us*, 85; López, "Discussing Economics on the Border," 15–17; Liebowitz, "Gendering (Trans)National Advocacy," 177–178.

46. Richwine, "Hispanics Ask Clinton to Renegotiate NAFTA"; Blackburn, "Clinton Meets Mexican President"; "NAFTA: No Good for Immigrant Women Workers," 1–2; Martínez, *De Colores Means All of Us*, 85; López, "Discussing Economics on the Border," 15–17; Liebowitz, "Gendering (Trans)National Advocacy," 177–78; "Post-NAFTA Networking," *AIWA*

News, February 1994, 2, box 4, folder AIWA-Newsletters—GWJC 1991–1996, Louie Papers.

47. Debra Liebowitz, "Gender and Identity in an Era of Globalization: Transnational Political Organizing in North America" (PhD diss., Rutgers University, 2000), 205–212.

48. Sparr, interview with author, October 17, 2014; Sparr, interview with author, August 27, 2014; Peggy Antrobus, *The Global Women's Movement: Origins, Issues and Strategies* (London: Zed Books, 2004), 89–91. Antrobus lays out two different feminist positions on free trade that resembled their competing positions on development (those who sought to integrate women into development compared to Alt-WID's position).

49. "NAFTA: No Good for Immigrant Women Workers," 1–2.

50. Special Economic and Racial Justice Alert from the Women's Division, "Unemployed Levi's Workers Ask for Justice," n.d., box 5, folder UMC Women's Division—Fuerza Unida, Louie Papers; Pamela Sparr to Petra Mata, April 25, 1998, box 5, folder UMC Women's Division—Fuerza Unida, Louie Papers; Sara Shingler to Robert Haas, March 2, 1998, box 5, folder UMC Women's Division—Fuerza Unida, Louie Papers; Sparr, interview with author, August 27, 2014; Debra J. Liebowitz, "Governing Globalization: Feminist Engagements with International Trade Policy," in *Global Governance: Feminist Perspectives*, ed. Shirin Rai and Georgina Waylen (Basingstoke, England: Palgrave Macmillan, 2008), 213.

51. "UN World Conference of Women & Forum in Beijing," *AIWA News*, Winter 1995, 2, box 4, folder AIWA-Newsletters—GWJC 1991–1996, Louie Papers; Cai Fen, "AIWA Testified at UN Social Summit," *AIWA News*, June 1995, 2, box 4, folder AIWA-Newsletters—GWJC 1991–1996, Louie Papers; Poo, interview with author, October 11, 2016; Chiang, interview with author, December 3, 2014; Chiang, interview with author, October 9, 2018; Pamela Sparr to author, July 1, 2019. A popular education manual published by Linda Burnham's Women of Color Resource Center had blurbs from a staff member from Charlotte Bunch's Center for Women's Global Leadership (CWGL); a member of Just Economics, the group Marlene Kim worked with; Jeanne Guana, one of Chiang's role models who had cofounded the environmental justice movement; and a member of Alt-WID, the feminist research network Sparr helped found. See Miriam Ching Louie with Linda Burnham, *WEdGE: Women's Education in the Global Economy* (Berkeley, CA: Women of Color Resource Center, 2000).

52. "Getting Ready for Beijing," *AIWA News*, June 1995, 2, box 4, folder AIWA-Newsletters—GWJC 1991–1996, Louie Papers; "Bringing Beijing Home," *AIWA News*, November 1995, 2, box 4, folder AIWA-Newsletters—GWJC 1991–1996, Louie Papers; Poo, interview with author, October 11, 2016.

53. "What Is the World Trade Organization," World Trade Organization, www.wto.org/english/thewto_e/whatis_e/tif_e/fact1_e.htm; "Settling Disputes," www.wto.org/english/thewto_e/whatis_e/tif_e/utw_chap3_e.pdf. By 2016, there were 164 member countries.

54. Kit Oldman, "WTO Meetings and Protests in Seattle (1999)—Part 1," HistoryLink.org, October 13, 2009, www.historylink.org/File/9183.

55. WTO mobilization timeline, WTO History Project, https://depts .washington.edu/wtohist/timeline.htm; Kelsey Walker (PhD diss. in progress, University of North Carolina Greensboro).

56. Sparr, interview with author, August 27, 2014; "Women, Democracy/ Sovereignty, Development" (pamphlet), n.d., in author's possession; WTO mobilization timeline, https://depts.washington.edu/wtohist/timeline.htm.

57. "NGO's Sign-On Letter," WTO History Project, 1999, https://depts .washington.edu/wtohist/letter.htm. The representation of people of color in Seattle has been debated, inspired by Elizabeth Betita Martínez's critique: "Where Was the Color in Seattle? Looking for Reasons Why the Great Battle Was So White," *Colorlines*, March 12, 2000, www.colorlines.com/articles /where-was-color-seattlelooking-reasons-why-great-battle-was-so-white.

58. Sparr, interview with author, August 27, 2014. Examples of US feminist analyses include Pamela Sparr, "Sex, Seattle and Stock Markets: Engendering the Debate around International Trade and Investment Policies," n.d., circa 2000 in author's possession; "Free Trade's Impact on Women," in *Breaking Boundaries: Women, Free Trade and Economic Integration* (Washington, DC: Alt-WID, 1993). After the protests, Sparr helped form the International Gender and Trade Network, a team of researchers led by members of DAWN and other women from the Global South. The network received funding from the Ford Foundation and was run out of the Center of Concern. Their research explored how the liberalization of trade affected food security as well as women's employment and access to social services. See Women and Gender Institute, Development Alternatives with Women for a New Era, International Gender and Trade Network, "Trade Intensification in Asian Economies: What It Means to Women's Work," n.d., in author's possession; Mariama Williams, "A Perspective on Feminist International Organizing from the Ground Up," in *Feminist Strategies in International Governance*, ed. Gülay Caglar, Elisabeth Prügl, and Susanne Zwingel (New York: Routledge, 2012), 92–108.

59. Poo, interview with author, October 11, 2016.

CHAPTER NINE: HEART COMMUNITIES: SISTERSONG, SONG, AND INCITE!

1. Beth Richie, interview with author, January 29, 2018; Beth Richie to author, May 21, 2018.

2. Richie, interview with author, January 29, 2018; Beth Richie, *Arrested Justice: Black Women, Violence, and America's Prison Nation* (New York: New York University Press, 2012), 1.

3. Richie, interview with author, January 29, 2018; Richie, *Arrested Justice*, 1–2, 67, 148–150. Explorations of the battered women's movement include Susan Schechter, *Women and Male Violence: The Vision and Struggles of the Battered Women's Movement* (Cambridge, MA: South End Press, 1982);

Finn Enke, "Taking Over Domestic Space: The Battered Women's Movement and Public Protest," in *The World the Sixties Made: Politics and Culture in Recent America*, ed. Van Gosse and Richard Moser (Philadelphia: Temple University Press, 2003), 162–190; Clara A. Van Eck, "Changing the Message: Battered Women's Advocates and Their Fight Against Domestic Violence at the Local, State, and Federal Level, 1970s–1990s" (Master's thesis, Old Dominion University, 2017).

4. Richie, interview with author, January 29, 2018; Richie, *Arrested Justice*, 1–2, 67, 148–150. Historical studies of women of color's antiviolence organizing include Emily L. Thuma, *All Our Trials: Prisons, Policing, and the Feminist Fight to End Violence* (Urbana: University of Illinois Press, 2019).

5. Richie, *Arrested Justice*, 2; Richie, interview with author, January 29, 2018; Gloria T. Hull, Patricia Bell Scott, and Barbara Smith, eds., *All the Women Are White, All the Blacks Are Men, But Some of Us Are Brave: Black Women's Studies* (New York: Feminist Press at CUNY, 1993).

6. bell hooks, *Feminist Theory: From Margin to Center* (Boston: South End Press, 1984), ix–x.

7. Roberta Spalter-Roth and Ronnee Schreiber, "Outsider Issues and Insider Tactics: Strategic Tensions in the Women's Policy Network during the 1980s," in *Feminist Organization: Harvest of the New Women's Movement*, ed. Myra Marx Ferree and Patricia Yancey Martin (Philadelphia: Temple University Press, 1995), 122–123; Helen Neuborne, interview with author, August 28, 2014.

8. Richie, interview with author, January 29, 2018.

9. The feminists who supported the passage of the Violence Against Women Act allied with conservatives who were seeking to prosecute crime more aggressively. They distanced themselves from the progressive groups fighting for the inclusion of the Racial Justice Act in the crime bill, which would have allowed people on death row to appeal their sentences if they believed they were victims of racism. Richie, *Arrested Justice*, 86; Marie Gottschalk, *The Prison and the Gallows: The Politics of Mass Incarceration in America* (New York: Cambridge University Press, 2006), 150–153; Hannah L. F. Cooper, "War on Drugs Policing and Police Brutality," *Substance Use & Misuse* 50, nos. 8–9 (2015): 1188–1194. For a positive analysis of the act's accomplishments, see Van Eck, "Changing the Message," 118–127.

10. Andrea Smith, interview with author, January 15, 2017; Schechter, *Women and Male Violence*, 4. On the transformation of the antiviolence movement, see Richie, *Arrested Justice*, 65–98. On the antiviolence movement and the growth of the prison system, see also Gottschalk, *The Prison and the Gallows*, 139–164. Explorations of the postwar antecedents of women of color's antirape activism include Thuma, *All Our Trials*; Danielle L. McGuire, *At the Dark End of the Street: Black Women, Rape, and Resistance: A New History of the Civil Rights Movement from Rosa Parks to the Rise of Black Power* (New York: Alfred A. Knopf, 2010).

11. Smith, interview with author, January 15, 2017; Richie, interview with author, January 29, 2018; Thuma, *All Our Trials*, 144–150.

12. Pat Hussain, interview with author, April 19, 2017; Wesley C. Hogan, *On the Freedom Side: How Five Decades of Youth Activism Have Remixed American History* (Chapel Hill: University of North Carolina Press, 2019), 40–41.

13. Hussain, interview with author, April 19, 2017.

14. Hussain, interview with author, April 19, 2017.

15. Hussain, interview with author, April 19, 2017.

16. Mab Segrest, interview with author, March 9, 2018.

17. Segrest, interview with author, March 9, 2018; Mab Segrest, *Memoir of a Race Traitor* (Boston: South End Press, 1994), 229–246; Hogan, *On the Freedom Side*, 42.

18. Hussain, interview with author, April 19, 2017; Segrest, interview with author, March 9, 2018; Mandy Carter, interview with author, September 9, 2016; Suzanne Pharr, interview with author, January 17, 2017; Pam McMichael, interview with Rose Norman, April 3, 2013, Sinister Wisdom '93/ Southern Lesbian-Feminist Oral History Supplement; Mab Segrest to author, January 24, 2019.

19. Carter, interview with author, September 9, 2016; Hussain, interview with author, April 19, 2017; Pharr, interview with author, January 17, 2017; Segrest, interview with author, March 9, 2018; McMichael, interview with Norman, April 3, 2013; Segrest to author, January 24, 2019. Another Kentuckian, Carla Wallace, participated in the planning, but as the vision of the organization began to fall into place she volunteered to take a back seat so that the group would have the same number of Black and white founders. The group accepted her offer, believing that an antiracist feminist organization needed to have at least an equal representation of white people and people of color in its leadership

20. Hussain, interview with author, April 19, 2017; Carter, interview with author, September 9, 2016; Pharr, interview with author, January 17, 2017; Segrest, interview with author, March 9, 2018; McMichael, interview with Norman, April 3, 2013; Segrest to author, January 24, 2019; Hogan, *On the Freedom Side*, 44–45. For an account of regional identity and the Southern struggle, see Jacquelyn Dowd Hall, *Sisters and Rebels: A Struggle for the Soul of America* (New York: W. W. Norton & Company, 2019).

21. Loretta Ross, Lynn Roberts, Erika Derkas, Whitney Peoples, and Pamela Bridgewater Toure, eds., *Radical Reproductive Justice: Foundation, Theory, Practice, Critique* (New York: Feminist Press at CUNY, 2017), Kindle locations 893–902; Loretta J. Ross, "The Color of Choice: White Supremacy and Reproductive Justice," in *Color of Violence: The INCITE! Anthology*, ed. INCITE! (Durham, NC: Duke University Press, 2016), 63.

22. Ross et al., *Radical Reproductive Justice*, Kindle location 875; Loretta Ross, interview with author, April 20, 2013; Ross, "The Color of Choice." Explorations of earlier reproductive rights activism include Jennifer Nelson, *Women of Color and the Reproductive Rights Movement* (New York: New York University Press, 2003). For an important published work that contributed

significantly to framing the struggle, see Dorothy Roberts, *Killing the Black Body: Race, Reproduction, and the Meaning of Liberty* (New York: Pantheon, 1997).

23. Luz Alvarez Martinez, interview with author, January 7, 2014; Luz Alvarez Martinez, interview with Loretta Ross, December 6–7, 2004 VOF.

24. Martinez, interview with author, January 7, 2014; Martinez, interview with Ross, December 6–7, 2004; Jael Silliman, Marlene Gerber Fried, Loretta Ross, and Elena Gutiérrez, *Undivided Rights: Women of Color Organize for Reproductive Justice* (Cambridge, MA: South End Press, 2004), 241–245. Explorations of earlier Latina health activism include Elena R. Gutiérrez, *Fertile Matters: The Politics of Mexican-Origin Women's Reproduction* (Austin: University of Texas Press, 2008), 94–108.

25. Martinez, interview with author, January 7, 2014; Martinez, interview with Ross, December 6–7, 2004; Peggy Saika, interview with Loretta Ross, February 20, 2006, VOF. On earlier interactions between white and women of color reproductive rights activists, see Nelson, *Women of Color and the Reproductive Rights Movement*. On the Berkeley clinic, see Sandra Morgen, *Into Our Own Hands: The Women's Health Movement in the United States, 1969–1990* (New Brunswick, NJ: Rutgers University Press, 2002), 79–80.

26. Martinez, interview with Ross, December 6–7, 2004; Elizabeth Martinez, "Caramba, Our Anglo Sisters Just Didn't Get It," *Network News* 17, no. 6 (November–December 1992): 1, 4–5.

27. Martinez, interview with Loretta Ross, December 6–7, 2004; Luz Rodriguez, interview with Joyce Follet, June 16–17, 2006, VOF.

28. Rodriguez, interview with Follet, June 16–17, 2006.

29. Julia Chinyere Oparah, interview with author, February 3, 2017; Smith, interview with author, January 15, 2017.

30. Oparah, interview with author, February 3, 2017; Smith, interview with author, January 15, 2017. For an account of the roots of some of this organizing, see Thuma, *All Our Trials*.

31. Hussain, interview with author, April 19, 2017; Pharr, interview with author, January 17, 2017; Segrest, interview with author, March 9, 2018.

32. "Interlocking" in Combahee River Collective, "Combahee River Collective Statement," *Home Girls: A Black Feminist Anthology*, ed. Barbara Smith (New York: Kitchen Table Press, 1983; reprint, New Brunswick, NJ: Rutgers University Press, 2000), 264–274; "whole selves" in Hussain, interview with author, April 19, 2017.

33. Pharr, interview with author, January 17, 2017; Carter, interview with author, September 9, 2016; Segrest, interview with author, March 9, 2018; Hussain, interview with author, April 19, 2017. Their own Mandy Carter had laid some of the groundwork in her organizing on behalf of the Black Democrat Harvey Gantt, who launched an unsuccessful bid to defeat the Republican Jesse Helms in his reelection campaign for the US Senate. Carter's work for North Carolina Senate Vote 1990 had helped build an unprecedented coalition of gay people, feminists, teachers, environmentalists, and

civil rights activists, who registered close to ten thousand voters. See Ramya Ramaswamy, "Mandy Carter: Activism During the 1990 and 1996 Helms-Gantt Campaigns," *OutHistory,* http://outhistory.org/exhibits/show/nc-lgbt /party-politics/mandy-carter. On the Helms-Gantt race, see William A. Link, *Righteous Warrior: Jesse Helms and the Rise of Modern Conservatism* (New York: St. Martin's Press, 2008), 365–381.

34. Sujatha Jesudason, interview with author, October 11, 2017; Asian Communities for Reproductive Justice, *A New Vision for Advancing Our Movement for Reproductive Rights and Reproductive Justice* (Oakland, CA: Asian Communities for Reproductive Justice, 2005); Loretta Ross, interview with Joyce Follett, November 3–5, 2004, December 1–3, 2004, February 4, 2005, VOF.

35. Rachael Strickler and Monica Simpson, "A Brief History of Sister-Song" (typescript, in author's possession, 2017); Ross, interview with author, August 9, 2017.

36. Nadine Naber, interview with author, October 5, 2016; Jesudason, interview with author, October 11, 2017.

37. Pharr, interview with author, January 17, 2017. Historical explorations of Southern gay life include John Howard, *Men Like That: A Southern Queer History* (Chicago: University of Chicago Press, 2000); John Howard, ed., *Carryin' On in the Lesbian and Gay South* (New York: New York University Press, 1997); Brock Thompson, *The Un-natural State: Arkansas and the Queer South* (Fayetteville: University of Arkansas Press, 2010).

38. Hussain, interview with author, April 19, 2017.

39. Pat Hussain, interview with Lorraine Fontana, May 6, 2013, Sinister Wisdom '93/Southern Lesbian-Feminist Oral History Supplement; Hussain, interview with author, April 19, 2017.

40. Hussain, interview with author, April 19, 2017; "Retreat Participants," 1998, box 31, folder Schedule, Mandy Carter Papers, 1970–2013, David M. Rubenstein Rare Book and Manuscript Library, Duke University, Durham, North Carolina [hereafter cited as Carter Papers]; "Retreat Schedule," 1998, box 31, folder Schedule, Carter Papers; "Evaluation," box 31, folder Post-Retreat Work, Carter Papers; "Final Report from Mandy Carter," box 31, folder Post-Retreat Work, Carter Papers; Hogan, *On the Freedom Side,* 52–63. The responses to the LGBT people of color retreat were so positive that SONG turned it into a yearly event called the Bayard Rustin Project.

41. Quoted in Hogan, *On the Freedom Side,* 59.

42. "Retreat Participants," 1998, box 31, folder Schedule, Carter Papers; "Retreat Schedule," 1998, box 31, folder Schedule, Carter Papers; "Evaluation," box 31, folder Post-Retreat Work, Carter Papers; "Final Report from Mandy Carter," box 31, folder Post-Retreat Work, Carter Papers; Hogan, *On the Freedom Side,* 52–63.

43. "Workshops," box 6, folder SONG 2001, Southerners on New Ground Records, 1993–2003, David M. Rubenstein Rare Book and Manuscript Library, Duke University, Durham, North Carolina [hereafter cited

as SONG Records]; "SONG—Economics Training—Teresa Amott—March 6, 1996," box 31, folder training documents, Carter Papers; "Broadening the We: Building a Multi Issue Movement," Trainer's Agenda, 1999, box 1, folder Broadening the We, SONG Records; Hogan, *On the Freedom Side*, 52–63.

44. Mandy Carter, interview with Rose Norman, March 26, 2013, Sinister Wisdom '93/Southern Lesbian-Feminist Oral History Supplement; Segrest and Carter to author, May 3 and 7, 2018; Hogan, *On the Freedom Side*, 55. On freedom rides, see Vanessa Tait, *Poor Workers' Unions: Rebuilding Labor from Below* (Cambridge, MA: South End Press, 2005), 217–218. On the Mount Olive Pickle boycott, see Steven Greenhouse, "Growers' Group Signs the First Union Contract for Guest Workers," *New York Times*, September 17, 2004; Maria L. Ontiveros, "Female Immigrant Workers and the Law: Limits and Opportunities," in *The Sex of Class: Women Transforming American Labor*, ed. Dorothy Sue Cobble (Ithaca, NY: Cornell University Press, 2007), 251–252.

45. Smith, interview with author, January 15, 2017; Ann Russo, "The Feminist Majority Foundation's Campaign to Stop Gender Apartheid," *International Feminist Journal of Politics* 8, no. 4 (2006): 557–580.

46. Smith, interview with author, January 15, 2017; "Anti-War Stickers and Flyers," https://incite-national.org/anti-war-stickers-flyers/.

47. Max Sussman, "Incite! Women of Color Against Violence: Interview with Nadine Naber and Andrea Smith," *Critical Moment* 22 (2007); Smith, interview with author, January 15, 2017.

48. Sussman, "Incite! Women of Color Against Violence."

49. Critical Resistance, "History," http://criticalresistance.org/about/history/; Richie, interview with author, January 29, 2018; *The Critical Resistance–INCITE! Statement on Gender Violence and the Prison-Industrial Complex: Reflections, 2008*, https://trueleappress.files.wordpress.com/2017/11/cr-incite-statement-on-gender-violence-and-the-prison-industrial-complex.pdf; *The Critical Resistance INCITE! Statement on Gender Violence and the Prison Industrial Complex*, www.incite-national.org/sites/default/files/incite files/resource docs/5848 incite-cr-statement.pdf. Also on Critical Resistance, see Zoe Hammer, "Critical Resistance and the Prison Abolitionist Movement," in *Human Rights in Our Own Backyard: Injustice and Resistance in the United States*, ed. William T. Armaline, Davita Silfen Glasberg, and Bandana Purkayastha (Philadelphia: University of Pennsylvania Press, 2011), 244–250; Guest Editors, "The History of Critical Resistance," *Social Justice* 27, no. 3 (2000): 6–10.

50. Richie, interview with author, January 29, 2018; Smith, interview with author, January 15, 2017; *The Critical Resistance–INCITE! Statement on Gender Violence and the Prison-Industrial Complex: Reflections, 2008*; *The Critical Resistance INCITE! Statement on Gender Violence and the Prison Industrial Complex*.

51. Andrea Smith, interview with Maria Cotera, June 24, 2003, Global Feminisms: Comparative Case Studies of Women's Activism and Scholarship, University of Michigan.

52. Richie, interview with author, January 29, 2018; Beth Richie, remarks, Prison Abolition, Mass Incarceration and Black Feminism: What's the Connection? 20th Anniversary of Critical Resistance Panel, National Women's Studies Association Conference, Baltimore, Maryland, 2017.

53. Ross, interview with Follet, November 3–5, 2004, December 1–3, 2004, February 4, 2005; Ross to author, January 20, 2019; Loretta Ross, "Women's Rights Are Human Rights and the Women's March on Washington," *Rewire.News*, January 19, 2017, https://rewire.news/article/2017/01/19/womens-rights-human-rights-womens-march-washington/; Ross et al., *Radical Reproductive Justice*, Kindle locations 954–965; Jennifer Nelson, *More than Medicine: A History of the Feminist Women's Health Movement* (New York: New York University Press, 2015), Kindle locations 4227–4283; "Flashback: Over One Million March for Women's Lives," April 25, 2014, https://now.org/blog/over-one-million-march-for-womens-lives/; Jo Freeman, "The March for Women's Lives, April 25, 2004," www.jofreeman.com/photos/MFWL.html.

54. Ross, *Radical Reproductive Justice*, Kindle locations 954–965, 9045; "Flashback: Over One Million March for Women's Lives," https://now.org/blog/over-one-million-march-for-womens-lives.

55. Loretta J. Ross and Rickie Solinger, *Reproductive Justice: An Introduction* (Oakland: University of California Press, 2017), Kindle location 1654.

EPILOGUE

1. Mandy Carter, interview with author, September 9, 2016; Mab Segrest, interview with author, March 9, 2018; Beth Richie, interview with author, January 29, 2018; Monica Simpson, interview with author, August 9, 2017; Loretta Ross, interview with author, August 9, 2017.

2. Barbara Ransby, *Making All Black Lives Matter: Reimagining Freedom in the Twenty-First Century* (Oakland: University of California Press, 2018); Simpson, interview with author, August 9, 2017; "Free Marissa Now," www.freemarissanow.org/; Lizette Alvarez, "Florida Sit-In Against Stand Your Ground," *New York Times*, August 11, 2013; Christine Hauser, "Florida Woman Whose 'Stand Your Ground' Defense Was Rejected Is Released," *New York Times*, February 7, 2017; "Reproductive Justice and Marissa Alexander," www.freemarissanow.org/fact-sheet-on-reproductive-justice--marissa-alexander.html; Caitlin Breedlove, "Gay Marriage to Ferguson," *Huffington Post*, October 20, 2014, www.huffingtonpost.com/caitlin-breedlove/gay-marriage-to-ferguson_b_6009118.html; Jess Fournier, "Black Mama's Day Bailout Frees Black Mothers—and Fights Racist Bail System," Feministing.com, May 14, 2018, http://feministing.com/2018/05/14/black-mamas-day-bailout-frees-black-mothers-and-fights-racist-bail-system/; Sherri Williams, "'Mama's Bail Out Day' Brings Black Moms Home from Jail for Mother's Day," NBC News, May 14, 2017, www.nbcnews.com/news/nbcblk/mama-s-bail-out-day-brings-black-moms-home-jail-n759061.

3. Ransby, *Making All Black Lives Matter*, Kindle location 231.

4. Simpson, interview with author, August 9, 2017; "Free Marissa Now," www.freemarissanow.org/; Alvarez, "Florida Sit-In Against Stand Your Ground"; Hauser, "Florida Woman Whose 'Stand Your Ground' Defense Was Rejected Is Released"; "Reproductive Justice and Marissa Alexander"; Danielle Young, "Beautiful News: Activists Ban Together for 'Standing Our Ground' Week for Marissa Alexander," July 15, 2014, https://hellobeautiful.com/2733673/stand-our-ground-week-for-marissa-alexander/; "Standing Our Ground Week of Action," www.freemarissanow.org/standing-our-ground-week.html; Feminist Newswire, "Hundreds March for Marissa Alexander in Jacksonville," July 29, 2014, https://feminist.org/blog/index.php/2014/07/29/hundreds-march-for-marissa-alexander-in-jacksonville/.

5. "A Labor of Love: Black Mama's Bailout Action + Reflection," Southerners on New Ground, May 16, 2017, https://southernersonnewground.org/a-labor-of-love/; Williams, "'Mama's Bail Out Day' Brings Black Moms Home from Jail for Mother's Day." Examples of SONG's support of Black Lives Matter more generally include "Black Lives Matter Everywhere," October 24, 2014, https://southernersonnewground.org/black-lives-matter-everywhere/.

6. "A Labor of Love: Black Mama's Bailout Action + Reflection"; Williams, "'Mama's Bail Out Day.'"

7. Williams, "'Mama's Bail Out Day'"; Vera Institute of Justice, "Overlooked: Women and Jails in an Era of Reform," Report Summary, August 2016, https://storage.googleapis.com/vera-web-assets/downloads/Publications/overlooked-women-and-jails-report/legacy_downloads/overlooked-women-and-jails-fact-sheet.pdf.

8. Williams, "'Mama's Bail Out Day.'"

9. "A Labor of Love: Black Mama's Bailout Action + Reflection." On the second year of the bailout, see Fournier, "Black Mama's Day Bailout Frees Black Mothers." Explorations of LGBT people and the criminal justice system include Joey L. Mogul, Andrea J. Richie, and Kay Whitlock, *Queer (In) Justice: The Criminalization of LGBT People in the United States* (Boston: Beacon Press, 2011); Nat Smith and Eric Stanley, *Captive Genders: Trans Embodiment and the Prison Industrial Complex* (Oakland, CA: AK Press, 2011); Regina Kunzel, *Criminal Intimacy: Prison and the Uneven History of Modern American Sexuality* (Chicago: University of Chicago Press, 2010). Ransby, *Making All Black Lives Matter*, Kindle location 231.

10. Quoted in Rachel Seidman, *Speaking of Feminism: Today's Activists on the Past, Present, and Future of the U.S. Women's Movement* (Chapel Hill: University of North Carolina Press, 2019), 90.

11. Quoted in Seidman, *Speaking of Feminism*, 152.

12. For an example of a recent public flareup, see Monica Simpson, "Reproductive Justice and 'Choice': An Open Letter to Planned Parenthood,"

August 5, 2014, Rewire.News, https://rewire.news/article/2014/08/05/reproductive-justice-choice-open-letter-planned-parenthood/; Cecile Richards, "A Response to an Open Letter on Reproductive Justice and 'Choice,'" August 5, 2014, https://rewire.news/article/2014/08/05/response-open-letter-reproductive-justice-choice/; Dawn Laguens, "We're Fighting for Access, Not Choice," *Huffington Post*, September 29, 2014, www.huffpost.com/entry/were-fighting-for-access_b_5635999.

13. Premilla Nadasen, "Black Feminism Will Save Us All," *In These Times*, September 11, 2018, http://inthesetimes.com/article/21429/black-feminism-intersectional-donald-trump-class-race; Wesley C. Hogan, *On the Freedom Side: How Five Decades of Youth Activism Have Remixed American History* (Chapel Hill: University of North Carolina Press, 2019), 180–182; Sam Levin, "At Standing Rock, Women Lead Fight in Face of Mace, Arrests and Strip Searches," *The Guardian*, November 4, 2016, www.theguardian.com/us-news/2016/nov/04/dakota-access-pipeline-protest-standing-rock-women-police-abuse. On organizing among low-wage workers, see Annelise Orleck,*"We Are All Fast-Food Workers Now": The Global Uprising Against Poverty Wages* (Boston: Beacon Press, 2018).

14. Frederick Hewett, "A Model of Resistance: The Broad Coalition Against the Dakota Access Pipeline," WBUR, November 18, 2016, www.wbur.org/cognoscenti/2016/11/18/standing-rock-north-dakota-frederick-hewett.

15. "'No Climate Justice Without Gender Justice': Women at the Forefront of the People's Climate March," https://thefeministwire.com/2014/09/climate-justice-without-gender-justice-women-forefront-peoples-climate-march/. See also Mara Dolan, "The Invisible Young Women Driving Climate-Change Activism," Bitch Media, September 30, 2019, www.bitchmedia.org/article/young-women-climate-activists.

16. Veronica Arreola, interview with author, September 8, 2017.

17. "NARAL, MoveOn, Allies Hold Largest Single-Day Protest Against a Supreme Court Nominee in History with Events in Every State Today," August 26, 2018, www.prochoiceamerica.org/2018/08/26/naral-holds-largest-scotus-protest-in-history/.

18. Contemporary critiques of philanthropy include Anand Giridharadas, *Winners Take All: The Elite Charade of Changing the World* (New York: Alfred A. Knopf, 2018); Edgar Villanueva, *Decolonizing Wealth: Indigenous Wisdom to Heal Divides and Restore Balance* (Oakland, CA: Berrett-Koehler Publishers, 2018).

19. "Komen Learns Power of Social Media," Nation Now (blog), *Los Angeles Times*, February 3, 2012, https://latimesblogs.latimes.com/nationnow/2012/02/facebook-twitter-fueled-fury-against-in-susan-g-komen-for-the-cure-.html; "How Planned Parenthood Used Social Media to Crush Komen," Jill Stanek (blog), February 6, 2012, www.jillstanek.com/2012/02/how-planned-parenthood-used-social-media-to-crush-komen/; Seidman, *Speaking of Feminism*, 5, 216–217.

20. Courtney E. Martin and Vanessa Valenti, "#FemFuture: Online Revolution," *New Feminist Solutions* 8 (2013): 15.

21. Anita Sarkeesian, "Link Round Up: Feminist Critiques of Slut-Walk," Feminist Frequency, May 16, 2011, https://feministfrequency .com/2011/05/16/link-round-up-feminist-critiques-of-slutwalk/; Zeba Blay, "Reclaiming the Word 'Slut' Is an Entirely Different Beast for Black Women," *Huffington Post*, October 5, 2015, www.huffpost.com/entry /reclaiming-the-word-slut-is-an-entirely-different-beast-for-black-women _n_56128706e4b0af3706e14d49; Martin and Valenti, "#FemFuture," 17; Hanalei, "Critique of SlutWalk on Behalf of All Women of Color Communities," http://feministing.com/2011/09/26/critique-of-slutwalk-on-behalf -of-all-women-of-color-communities/.

22. Sandra E. Garcia, "The Woman Who Created #MeToo Long Before the Hashtags," *New York Times*, October 20, 2017, www.nytimes .com/2017/10/20/us/me-too-movement-tarana-burke.html; Zahara Hill, "A Black Woman Created the 'Me Too' Campaign against Sexual Assault 10 Years Ago," *Ebony*, October 18, 2017, www.ebony.com/news-views /black-woman-me-too-movement-tarana-burke-alyssa-milano#axzz53K gRevKC; Alex Langone, "#MeToo and Time's Up Founders Explain the Difference Between the Two Movements and How They're Alike," *Time*, March 22, 2018, http://time.com/5189945/whats-the-difference-between-the-metoo -and-times-up-movements/. On Black women and social media, see Feminista Jones, *Reclaiming Our Space: How Black Feminism Is Changing the World from the Tweets to the Streets* (Boston: Beacon Press, 2019).

23. Langone, "#MeToo and Time's Up Founders Explain the Difference."

24. Rinku Sen, "The Lefty Critique of #TimesUp Is Tired and Self-Defeating," *The Nation*, January 9, 2018, www.thenation.com/article/the -lefty-critique-of-timesup-is-tired-and-self-defeating/.

25. Sen, "The Lefty Critique of #TimesUp Is Tired and Self Defeating."

26. Sen, "The Lefty Critique of #TimesUp Is Tired and Self Defeating."

27. Sen, "The Lefty Critique of #TimesUp Is Tired and Self Defeating."

INDEX

Lisa Levenstein is the director of the Women's, Gender, and Sexuality Studies Program and an associate professor of history at the University of North Carolina Greensboro. Her first book, *A Movement Without Marches*, won the Kenneth Jackson Book Award. She lives in Chapel Hill, North Carolina.